**W9-DCI-784**

# Knowing
## Life
### and the
# Church

Witness Lee

***Living Stream Ministry***
Anaheim, CA • www.lsm.org

© 2005 Living Stream Ministry

All rights reserved. No part of this work may be reproduced or transmitted in any form or by any means—graphic, electronic, or mechanical, including photocopying, recording, or information storage and retrieval systems—without written permission from the publisher.

First Edition, December 2005.

ISBN 978-0-7363-2961-3

Published by

*Living Stream Ministry*
2431 W. La Palma Ave., Anaheim, CA 92801 U.S.A.
P. O. Box 2121, Anaheim, CA 92814 U.S.A.

*Printed in the United States of America*

17   18   19   20   21   22   /   9   8   7   6   5   4   3   2

# CONTENTS

# PREFACE

This book is composed of messages released by Witness Lee in August 1953 in service meetings in Taipei. The book consists of twenty-three chapters: Chapters 1 through 7 emphasize the matter of knowing life; chapters 8 through 14 emphasize knowing the church; chapters 15 through 20 emphasize basic knowledge of the service; and chapters 21 through 23 are words of leading in relation to work and service in all the churches. The messages have been translated from the original Chinese.

# CHAPTER ONE

# LIFE BEING THE GOAL
# OF GOD'S CREATION AND REDEMPTION

Scripture Reading: Gen. 1:26-29; John 1:1-4, 14; 14:6; 1 John 5:11-12; Col. 3:4; Rev. 22:1-2

## KNOWING LIFE AND THE CHURCH

Recently I have had a heavy burden: Even though the number of brothers and sisters is increasing, I wonder how much the measure of the stature of Christ is increasing in the church. Therefore, I have a strong feeling that we should help the brothers and sisters know life and the church.

Life and the church go together because there would be no church without life. Life produces the church. The church is the result of life, and life is the content of the church. According to God's Word, salvation is completely a matter of the life in us. Although man's natural mind cannot understand, from the beginning to the end of the Bible God cares only about the matter of life.

## THE GOAL OF GOD'S CREATION BEING LIFE

The Old Testament speaks of creation, and the New Testament speaks of redemption. Both in creation and redemption God's purpose and center is life. If we look at the first two chapters of Genesis under God's light, we can clearly see that life is the goal of His creation. Although God created many things of such diversity and variety, His purpose and final goal are simply life. If we read the first two chapters of Genesis and meditate quietly before God on His creation, we will see that God's creation involves life and produces life. Life is the center and goal of God's creation. In the beginning God created all things out of nothing.

In the orderly process of His creation, God first created inanimate objects, and then He created organic things. Furthermore, the creation of living beings started at the lowest level of life and advanced step by step to higher levels of life. Ultimately, the highest level of life created by God was man. Man is the highest life in God's creation, because the Bible says that God created man in His own image and according to His own likeness (Gen. 1:26-27). Man has God's image and likeness. Furthermore, God also gave man the authority to have dominion over all things (vv. 26, 28). Thus, among all created things, man is like God because he has God's image; he also represents God because he has God's authority. God saw everything that He had made, and it was very good (v. 31). In this vast universe, among all the myriads of created things, God obtained a man with His image and authority, who could express His glory and represent His authority. This satisfied God!

God rested on the seventh day after He finished His work of creation (2:2). Many people think that God was at rest and satisfied because everything was finished at this point. However, even at this point God had not reached the purpose of His creation. If we continue reading, we will see that there were still many considerations. After God created man, He put him in the garden of Eden (v. 8). In the center of the garden was the tree of life (v. 9). The tree of life is very special. The first time *life* is spoken of in the Bible is in relation to the tree of life. This shows that God was still not satisfied, because He had not yet reached His goal, even though He had created everything and even though man had been prepared to express and represent God. What is God's goal? God's goal is life. God brought the man that He created to the tree of life and put him in front of life.

We all need to be calm and consider the reasons God exerted so much effort to create everything, the reasons He created man with His likeness to represent Him, and the reasons He guided and directed man to the tree of life, hoping that man would contact the tree so that life could be imparted into him. God did these things in order to show that life is the goal and purpose of His creation. If man does not come to life and life does not come into man, God's creation of man would have no meaning, purpose, or result.

## SATAN DAMAGING
## BY TAKING MAN AWAY FROM LIFE

Since the goal of God's creation is life and God desires His creation to attain to life, Satan, His adversary, came to damage and hinder the matter of life. In the universe Satan, the evil one, opposes God, hinders God, and damages God's plan. Satan always tries to damage the most crucial matter and jeopardize the most important place. Therefore, when God put man in front of the tree of life, Satan came to lure man away from life and to turn him to another goal: the tree of the knowledge of good and evil. God's goal is life, but Satan caused man to pay attention to good and evil. Satan interrupted God's plan and took man away from God's goal. As a result, man fell into Satan's scheme and did not pay attention to God's goal. Instead, man paid attention to the goal upon which Satan's temptation was based. Consequently, man did not contact the tree of life but ate of the fruit of the tree of the knowledge of good and evil (3:1-7). God cares about life, but Satan's temptation leads man toward the goal of good and evil. Thereafter, man's goal before God changed. From that day forward, man lost his way before God.

God pays attention to life, but Satan focuses on good and evil. From the time that man was tempted and fell, he has paid attention only to the matter of good and evil. God was forced to give the law because man was concerned only with good and evil. God uses the law to test and prove man so that man will realize that he can do nothing. God gave the law to expose man (Rom. 7:7), and even though man earnestly desires to keep the law, he fails utterly. Although man knows that he should forsake evil and do good, he does not have the ability or the means to work out the good (vv. 18-19). He can only bow his head before the law and admit his inability to work out the good.

## LIFE BEING IN THE INCARNATED JESUS

Since man failed utterly with respect to the law, God became flesh and came into man (John 1:14). The One who came to mankind and became a man was the Lord Jesus. Life was in the Lord Jesus (v. 4). We need to pay special attention to John chapter 1 and Genesis chapter 2; we need to read these two chapters together. Without Genesis, we would think that it is quite strange for the first chapter of John, which outlines God's purpose, to begin by saying, "In Him was life" (v. 4). We surely would ask, "What is life? What does the phrase *in Him was life* mean?" Genesis helps by showing that after man was tempted and fell, he lost the top blessing of life; he lost a treasure, the center in the universe. After Genesis chapter 2, it is difficult to find the matter of life until we see in John 1:4 that life is in Him.

If we have the light, we will excitedly shout, "Now I see that the life in Genesis chapter 2 is actually in Him. The life that Adam lost because of sin is in Him. The life that God cares for is in Him. The center and purpose of the universe is in the Lord Jesus whom we know." One day He said to His disciples, "I am...the life" (John 14:6). He is the "I am" (8:24); whatever we need, He is. Life is in Him. He is the Word who was in the beginning. He is God Himself, and all things came into being through Him (1:1-3).

Since all things came into being through Him, we have been brought back to the purpose of creation in Genesis. In creation He is the Creator, and one day this Creator became flesh. The first chapter of John speaks of the beginning (v. 1), creation (v. 3), and becoming flesh (v. 14). *In the beginning* refers to eternity past before time even began. *All things came into being* refers to creation, and *became flesh* refers to incarnation. The incarnated Jesus is the God who was in the beginning and who is also the Creator. The life in the tree of life in Genesis chapter 2 refers to the life in Him. If we desire to touch this life, this life is in Him. If we desire to obtain this life, this life is in Him. He is the life. If we touch Him, we touch life; if we obtain Him, we obtain life. If we do not have Him, we do not have life (1 John 5:11-12).

## LIFE BEING THE GOAL
## OF CREATION AND REDEMPTION

The entire Bible shows the goal of life. Life is the goal of creation in the Old Testament, and also life is the goal of redemption in the New Testament. The purpose of God's creation is to bring man into life; likewise, the purpose of God's redemption is to bring man into life. As Christians, we have Christ as our life (Col 3:4). He is in us to save us and be our life. This life is Christ Himself, who is God Himself. This life will lead us into eternity, which means that even in eternity everything will be related to life.

Revelation shows that in eternity we will contact the river of water of life and the tree of life. The river of water of life proceeds out of the throne of God and of the Lamb, and on this side and on that side of the river is the tree of life (22:1-2). In eternity we will contact and see life. The river of water of life and the tree of life can be compared to an electrical wire. On one end of the wire is a powerhouse, God, and on the other end is a light bulb, man, and there is a current flowing between the two. A light bulb and powerhouse are one by means of an electrical current. All the believers are connected to God in life; thus, the believers and God are one in His life. In other words, just as life is in God, life is also in us.

## THE MEANING OF THE UNIVERSE
## BEING CONTAINED IN LIFE

The whole universe is a story of life, because our great universe originates from life. If living things were removed from the universe, the universe would become meaningless and lose its purpose. The beauty of the universe lies in life; without life, the universe is empty and ugly. In a family, a wife loves her husband because he has life and is a living person. When the life in him is gone and only an empty shell remains, even his wife will not like the shell. Life brings meaning to a family; without life, a family is empty and meaningless. The beauty of living things lies in life. The story of the entire universe depends on the presence of living beings, and the reality of living beings depends on the presence of life in them.

## THE HIGHEST LIFE BEING THE DIVINE LIFE

The highest life in the universe, however, is not the human life but the divine life. The story of the vast universe depends on the divine life. Plants come in many colors and shapes. Some have red flowers, and some have green leaves, but they are all produced by life. The different characteristics of each animal are an issue of life. A cat jumps and a rooster crows because of life. Even the characteristics of children, who become loud, angry, or happy whenever they desire, are matters of life. A child acts like a child, and an old man acts like an old man; these facts do not differ by nationality. All these characteristics are related to life.

All the stories throughout the vast universe are an issue of life. For example, each one of our homes is different. The furnishings in some homes, from the chairs to the coffee table, are yellow. This shows that the owner likes yellow. In other homes everything is white, and this shows that the owner likes white. Although we can design the furnishings in a home, we cannot design the universe. The universe is not produced from man's life; rather, the story of the universe comes out of God's life. God's life is higher than human life. We know that different kinds of trees produce different kinds of fruit according to their kind. In the same way, a higher life produces a higher life, a better life bears a better life, and a poorer life produces a poorer life. All the stories of the universe are matters of life, and this life is God's life.

## GOD BEING THE VAST LIFE IN US

The church is a corporate entity of life. The characteristics, marvelousness, and intrinsic mystery of the church depend on God's life. The church is the church because she has God's life. If life is taken away from the church, the church would become ugly, withered, and dead. All the beauty, power, brightness, and ability of the church come from the fact that the life of God is her inward content. This life is the life of Christ; Christ is God becoming flesh and coming into us through the Holy Spirit to be our life. God's life is in the Holy Spirit, and this life is the God who was in the beginning and the Creator who existed in the beginning. Through the Holy Spirit, the life in the incarnated God came into us. Thus, we have the life that created the universe and the life that is able to do great things in us. This life is the greatest, highest, and most vital life.

As believers, we have God's life in us, but we still need to ask about the condition of this life. Is it shallow and small? When a child is little, he may roll and crawl on the floor. He can cry or laugh whenever he wants to cry or laugh. However, an adult may not be allowed to do the same thing. This is because there are varying degrees of life. An adult cannot do as he pleases like a child, because the life in him is mature. In contrast, because the life in a child is immature, he often does as he pleases. This can be compared to an adult having five cubic meters of life and a child having only two cubic meters. Consequently, we need to frequently ask, "How much of the life of God is in us? Are there two cubic meters or five cubic meters?"

In terms of time, God's life spans from eternity past to eternity future. He is eternal, without beginning and end. In terms of space, the life of God includes the heavens, the earth, and the entire universe. He is omnipresent. This life is too great; it transcends time and space in the universe. Such a transcending, great life is in us. Being a Christian is not a matter of human cultivation but a matter of life. I can testify that often I am not angry, because the life in me is not angry, nor do I argue with others, because the life in me is not arguing. The life in me, which transcends time and space, is so great that it prevents me from losing my temper and arguing with others.

Many people lose their temper because they have only two cubic meters of life. They can remain angry for several months, and their anger cannot subside because they have only a small measure of life. The life in some sisters is only two cubic inches; they have no capacity other than to lose their temper when they encounter certain situations. They have no response other than to lose their temper, because they are short of the growth of life. This is the reason they also criticize others, saying that someone is not good or is wrong. The inward condition of their life is expressed outwardly in their environment. Because it is in the nature of a cat to jump, it will meow if it is forbidden to jump. Such a restriction is the same as taking away its life. What else can a sister with only two cubic inches worth of life do except lose her temper and criticize?

Such a person will not lose only her temper; she will also provoke others to anger, because this is her natural talent. When the measure of life increases in her from being like that of a small cat to that of an elephant, she will spontaneously stop being a "cat" who jumps and cries whenever she wants. As life grows, she will spontaneously stop losing her temper and will be able to be restricted. Thus, a certain kind of life produces a certain kind of result.

After we are saved, we have God's life within. This life needs to grow in us every day. But exactly how much life do we have? Do we have two cubic meters or five cubic meters? The God whom we know and serve has a great life. This life has a measure beyond that of the universe. Therefore, the life in us is a great matter. The church is the church because of life. The producing of the church depends upon God's salvation, and God's salvation depends upon life. After we are saved, we go to meetings, read the Bible, and pray in order to gain more life. If we do not know this life, we are not living as Christians. Our Christian living depends upon experiencing Christ as life.

What is the church? The church consists of Christ, who is the highest life. The content of Christ and the reality of the church depend on Christ as life; this life is God Himself. Now this life has entered into us to become our life. If we know this life, our measure will be enlarged and our view will be uplifted. If we know this life, our human life will have a wonderful, great change.

The great life that entered into us is not concerned with mere gain or loss. This life does not require us to be concerned with whether or not we can work out the good and improve ourselves. This life is both real and weighty in us. Just as God created the universe and everything in it, this life, which is Christ Himself, can do so much work in us. God clothes Himself with us to live and move in us; God created a small universe, a small world, in us, and He put Himself in the first place there. May God be merciful to us so that we would see this vision.

# CHAPTER TWO

# LIFE BEING GOD HIMSELF ENJOYED BY MAN

Scripture Reading: Psa. 36:7-9; John 1:4; 8:12; 10:10; 6:63; Rom. 8:2

We have already seen that God's goal in creation and redemption is life. God created man so that man would obtain life. Furthermore, the story of the entire universe is related to life in living creatures, with God's life being the highest life. The source of all life in the universe is God. Hence, the story of the universe comes from God's life. If we want to know and understand God's salvation, we must see that God's only goal is life; life is God's only purpose, and everything that happens in the universe is because of life and originates from life.

## AN OPENING WORD

Now we need to see two crucial points: what does the life that we speak of refer to, and how do we contact and touch this life? The Bible shows that the source of life is God; God is the origin of life. Psalm 36:9 says, "For with You is the fountain of life." In other words, life is in God. In verses 7 through 9, there are some related points that we must consider. Verse 7 speaks of God's lovingkindness and says that His precious lovingkindness enables the sons of men to take refuge in the shadow of His wings. Verse 8 speaks of the fatness of God's house and of the river of His pleasures for man's enjoyment. Verse 9 has two special points: "for with You is the fountain of life" and "in Your light we see light." Let us examine these four points: First, man can take refuge in God's lovingkindness; second, man enjoys God's fatness and the river of His pleasures when he takes refuge in God's lovingkindness;

third, man enjoys God's fatness and the river of His pleasures in God's life; and fourth, man can touch God's life in His light.

In the New Testament we can see more clearly that life is the incarnated Christ (John 1:1, 4, 14). In John 14:6 the Lord Jesus said, "I am the way and the reality and the life." He Himself said that He is life. God's being life means that life is not simply something that comes from God, but life is God Himself. John 1:4 says that life and light are one. John 8:12 connects life and light and speaks of the light of life. In 10:10 the Lord Jesus said, "I have come that they may have life and may have it abundantly." In 6:63 He said, "It is the Spirit who gives life…the words which I have spoken to you are spirit and are life." Verse 63 begins by saying that the Spirit gives life, and it ends by saying that the words the Lord spoke to us are spirit and life. Romans 8:2 refers to life, Spirit, and law when it speaks of "the law of the Spirit of life."

## LIFE BEING GOD HIMSELF FLOWING OUT
## TO BE ENJOYED BY MAN

In Psalm 36 God's lovingkindness, the fatness of His house, and the river of His pleasures all refer to God's riches; all the riches of God are in His life. When man touches God's life, he touches God's riches. We can enjoy, taste, and touch God's love, sweetness, and riches in His life. From this psalm, we can see that the riches in God's nature can be touched by us in His life. Life is God's nature, God's substance. All the fullness of the Godhead dwells in Christ bodily (Col. 2:9). Christ is life, that is, the divine life. He came to the earth so that man could obtain God and obtain His life (John 10:10). This proves that life is God Himself. Revelation 22:1-2 shows that the river of water of life and the tree of life proceed and grow out of God. Life originates with God because life is God. Therefore, when God flows out and is enjoyed by man, it is called life.

Steamed rice and raw rice are a good illustration. Steamed rice comes from raw rice; the two are essentially the same. If raw grains of rice are placed in front of us, they cannot be enjoyed or eaten by us, and they cannot satisfy our hunger. In order for raw grains of rice to be eaten and enjoyed by us and to satisfy our hunger, they need to be steamed. When God is alone in heaven, He has no relationship with us and cannot be enjoyed by us. In such a condition, He can only be called God. But when He dispenses Himself into us for us to eat and enjoy, then He can be called life. Life comes out of God, and life is God. If we understand these words, we will know why the Lord said to the Jews, "I am the living bread which came down out of heaven" (John 6:51). He is the bread of life. He is the God who existed from the beginning, and He stepped into time to be obtained and enjoyed by man on the earth and to fill up man's hunger for satisfaction.

### THE LORD BEING THE BREAD OF LIFE

The Lord is the bread of life, and He is life. When we eat steamed rice, we are not eating rice grains that have been taken directly from a rice bag or a rice bin. Steamed rice is rice grains that have been cooked, prepared, and placed on a table for us to eat. The One in heaven is actually the God in eternity. One day He stepped out of eternity, like rice grains being poured out from a rice bag. Then He entered into time and came to the earth to become "steamed rice" on a table to be enjoyed by man. At this point, He is called life, and He is the bread of life.

The Gospel of Matthew records that a Canaanite woman came to the Lord and cried out, "Have mercy on me, Lord, Son of David!" but the Lord did not say a word to answer her. She tried again and said, "Lord, help me!" The Lord answered, "It is not good to take the children's bread and throw it to the little dogs." Although this Canaanite woman was a Gentile, she was quite blessed and knew God, so she replied immediately, "Yes, Lord, for even the little dogs eat of the crumbs which fall from their masters' table" (15:22-27). The bread on the table is for the children, but even little dogs eat crumbs that fall from the table. This means that the Lord came down out of heaven as the bread of life for man to eat. The Jewish land can be compared to the dining table, and the Jews were God's children, but they wasted their bread and threw it under the table. They drove the Lord away from the land of the Jews toward the land of the Gentiles. The Canaanite woman's word indicates that even though she was a dog, the Lord Jesus was not on the table but under the table so that she could eat and enjoy Him as bread. She admitted that she was a dog, but a dog also has its portion. The bread under the table was her portion. Because of this, the Lord praised her: "O woman, great is your faith!" (v. 28). Our God is not only the God of heaven; He is also the bread of life. Furthermore, He is not only the bread of life; He is also the crumbs that fall from the Jewish land so that He can inwardly satisfy us, the Gentiles. Hence, life is God Himself.

If God does not have a relationship with man, He would remain high in the heavens where man could not touch Him or contact Him. God would be God, and man would be man. However, God came down from heaven and came to the door of man's heart. Now our God is the bread of life. When we open our heart to Him, He becomes our life as soon as He comes into us. This is the reason Paul says that Christ is our life (Col. 3:4). Life is God Himself.

## LIFE BEING GOD HIMSELF AND NOT HUMAN BEHAVIOR

We often hear people say that a certain brother or sister's life is truly wonderful and rich. If I heard such a word ten years ago, I would have believed it without a doubt. However, gradually God has opened my eyes to see that a certain brother's humbleness or a certain sister's gentleness may not be the issue of being rich in life. In 1948 when we were in Nanking, a sister came from Hopei, and the saints told me of her spirituality, suggesting that she was rich in life. I immediately asked them what their view was based upon. They could not answer. I told them that if outward appearances, such as the pace of her walking, the propriety of her speech, and the frequency of her smiles, were the basis for their consideration, then the statues of Mary in Catholic cathedrals should also be considered as being very spiritual because they are quiet, stationary, and never get angry. Whether or not a person is rich in life is not determined by outward appearances.

Life is God Himself, and life is Christ. There truly are such things as humility, gentleness, and quietness in life. However, the humility of many people is not life, and the gentleness of many people is not life. Instead, these characteristics are mere behavior. Genuine life is God Himself; behavior is man himself. Every time we speak of life, we are referring to the God whom we enjoy. He is the God who comes into us to deal with our problems and to solve our difficult situations. If we need satisfaction, He becomes our satisfaction; if we need gentleness, He becomes our gentleness. God is life, and life is God Himself. Behavior is man himself, and it is produced by man's working and doing.

## GOD BEING EXPRESSED IN OUR LIVING OUT OF LIFE

When we live out life, God comes out of us and is expressed in us. Sometimes when we contact a saint, we touch pride, and with another we touch humility. These are two different kinds of people. However, when we contact yet another saint, we cannot tell if he is proud or humble; instead, we sense that we are touching God, and it is as if we have come before God. We do not sense pride or humility; we sense only God and His presence. This is life.

Life is God Himself; life is God being lived out and expressed. When God is expressed, life is lived out. Many times man's humbleness is full of human flavor, not the divine flavor. On the contrary, sometimes we meet people who speak a frank and straightforward word to us. The frank and straightforward word may cause us to feel sad and hurt, but in the depth of our being, we sense that we have touched God and experienced His presence. This is life. Life is God Himself. When life is lived out, God is lived out.

This is not our theology or the result of our research; this is the revelation of the Bible. The Old Testament tells us that life is in God (Psa. 36:9). The New Testament speaks clearly about the Word who became the incarnated Christ. He is life, and He comes that man may have life and have it more abundantly (John 10:10). God wants man to gain Himself.

## ENJOYING THE RICHES OF GOD IN HIS LIFE

If we want to know God, we have to know life. If we want to obtain and touch everything of God, we need to touch God's life because all the riches of God's nature are in His life. This can be compared to beef containing a great amount of nutrients. If we want to receive the nutrients of the beef, we must eat it. Similarly, God is so rich and so sweet, and all of His riches and sweetness are in His life. Psalm 36:7-8 says, "How precious is Your lovingkindness, O God! / Thus the sons of men take refuge in the shadow of Your wings. / They are saturated with the fatness of Your house, / And You cause them to drink of the river of Your pleasures." The fatness and the river of life are to be enjoyed by man in the shadow of God, that is, in His house, in Himself.

At the end of the Bible, Revelation 21:22 says, "I saw no temple in it, for the Lord God the Almighty and the Lamb are its temple." In the New Jerusalem there is no temple, because the temple is God Himself. To enjoy the fatness of God's house is to enjoy God's riches in God Himself, for with Him is the fountain of life. We need to realize that God's fatness and riches are in His life. Unbelievers do not know life and cannot touch life. If they do not have life, they do not have the fatness because everything of God is in His life. All the riches of the rice grains are in the cooked rice, so if we want to receive the benefit of the grains, we have to eat and receive the cooked rice. Because God's riches are in His life, if we want to receive God's riches, we must touch life because God Himself is life.

### GOD BEING IN CHRIST, CHRIST BEING THE SPIRIT, AND THE SPIRIT BEING LIFE

Since life is God Himself, how can man touch and obtain life so that this life can come into him? One of the disciples made a very interesting request of the Lord Jesus, saying, "Lord, show us the Father and it is sufficient for us" (John 14:8). This indicates that they knew of God the Father but had never seen or touched Him. Was He fat or thin? Was He tall or short? What exactly did He look like, and what was His content and disposition? The disciples had no clue and were puzzled. They had heard of the Father, but they had never seen Him. Thus, they asked the Lord to show them the Father, and they would be content.

The Lord answered, saying, "Have I been so long a time with you, and you have not known Me, Philip? He who has seen Me has seen the Father; how is it that you say, Show us the Father? Do you not believe that I am in the Father and the Father is in Me?" (vv. 9-10). This means that the Lord is the Father, and the Father is the Lord. This can be compared to a person asking someone to show him what rice grains look like, even though he eats rice every day; this is very odd.

So where is God? God is in Christ. The *Me* in *the Father is in Me* is the Christ who is the incarnated Word. Where is Christ? In John 14 the Lord Jesus said that the Father is in Him, and then He said that He would leave the disciples in a little while. Although the Father is in Him, He did not want the disciples to treasure this and hold on to Him. The Lord told the disciples that they should not let their heart be troubled or be afraid, because He would leave them in a little while but would come again (vv. 18-19, 27-28). He came as the Spirit, "even the Spirit of reality, whom the world cannot receive, because it does not behold Him or know Him" (v. 17). This shows that God is in Christ, and Christ is the Spirit.

Where is the Spirit? The Spirit has a very special name; He is called the Spirit of life (Rom. 8:2), which means that the Spirit gives life to people. John 6:63 says that the words that the Lord speaks are spirit and are life. The Spirit is life. Some of us may be confused and feel that I am speaking in circles. We started speaking concerning life, and now we are speaking about the Spirit; it seems that speaking of life, God, Christ, and the Spirit is just like going around in a circle. Actually, the Spirit is the Spirit of life. In other words, life is God, God is in Christ, Christ is the Spirit, and the Spirit is life.

## LIFE BEING IN THE LIGHT
## AND LIGHT BEING IN GOD'S WORD

Where is life? Life is in those who believe into Him. This is absolutely true, but how does life enter into man? We need to see that life is the light of man. Psalm 36:9 says, "For with You is the fountain of life; / In Your light we see light." Please remember, life is in the light, and this life is the light of man. Wherever the light shines, life comes in. Wherever life comes, the Spirit is also there. Wherever the Spirit is, Christ is there.

Wherever Christ is, God is there. Wherever God is, life is there. Life is in the light.

Where is the light? The light is in the word of God. The words that the Lord speaks to us are spirit and life (John 6:63). We minister God's word because we hope that God's word will enter into everyone. As soon as God's word enters into man, it becomes light. As soon as we receive light inwardly, we have life. When light is received by man, it becomes life. Moreover, life is the Spirit, the Spirit is Christ, and Christ is God. This is not a theory but a spiritual reality. Everyone who has experienced this will bow in worship and say Amen.

Whenever we touch the Lord's word, the word becomes light in us, and the word becomes life to satisfy our hunger. We feel that we are eating of the fatness and drinking of the river of His pleasures, and we are full of God's presence, full of Christ's supply, and filled with the Triune God inwardly. Therefore, when God's word operates and starts to have an effect on us and if we willingly obey, we are immediately filled with light, life, the Spirit's presence, Christ, and God. In this way, people sense God, Christ, the Spirit, life, light, and God's word in us when they contact us. We should always remember that life is God, God is in Christ, Christ is the Spirit, the Spirit is life, life is light, and light comes from God's word.

## OBEYING GOD'S SPEAKING IN US

When we fellowship with the Lord in the morning, we may sometimes get a sense of receiving a word from God. Sometimes the word seems tangible, and it speaks clearly in us; sometimes the word seems more intangible, as if it is just a feeling. Regardless of its form, it is God's word. As soon as we receive such a word inwardly, we immediately have light. This light is the moving of the Spirit, and it issues in the filling of life. In this way, we inwardly sense God, Christ, and the Spirit, and we are inwardly filled with life and light. When people contact us, they have the sense that they are touching God, Christ, the Spirit, life, and light. Therefore, whether or not we can touch, contact, and obtain life all depends on how we handle God's word and how we contact God's word.

Often there is a word of God in us; it is the speaking through the moving of the Spirit in us, and its purpose is for us to contact and touch life. But how do we handle this word? Many people listen to messages, but they do not touch God's word. Many people read the Bible, but they do not hear God's word. Some people read spiritual books, but they never touch the Lord. This is because they disobey, ignore, and even reason and argue with the Lord. This is the reason that their light is lost and the reason that life and Christ disappear.

This is true not only in our daily living; we frequently have this kind of experience in the bread-breaking meeting. If the Spirit in us gives us a word or a feeling to open our mouth and praise the Lord, we should receive this word and open our mouth to praise the Lord. Thus, we will have light within, and this light is life, the Spirit, Christ, and God. When we respond to this feeling and offer a prayer of praise to the Lord, we sense the satisfaction of life, the sweetness of Christ, the presence of God, and the moving of the Spirit. Even after we go home, we will still sense God's sweet presence inwardly.

Regrettably, many people have a feeling, a word without form, but they are not willing to obey. Instead, they reason inwardly, thinking, "The Lord wants me to get up to praise and pray, but if my prayer is not good, I will lose face and become a laughingstock." As they begin to reason, the light in them disappears, and life, Christ, and God also disappear. As a result, they inwardly feel empty and unsatisfied in the bread-breaking meeting. When they go home, they are still empty within and cannot touch God, and they go to sleep with this empty feeling. When they get up the next morning, they feel that God is far away from them. Their inward fellowship will not be restored until they confess before God: "O Lord, forgive me. On that day You gave me a word in the bread-breaking meeting, but I did not obey You."

Thus, if we want to touch life, we need the word, the feeling given to us by the Spirit. Such a feeling is the living word of God. Although it is silent, it is indeed a living word. We should accept and obey it. If we do this, the word in us will become light. This light is life, Christ, God, and the Spirit. If we would all practice in this way, we could touch God every day. This is the way for us to touch God, and whoever touches God in this way is blessed. To be blessed is to have God's life as a spiritual reality.

# CHAPTER THREE

# THE OBSTACLES GOD'S LIFE ENCOUNTERS IN MAN

Scripture Reading: Phil. 3:6-8

## GOD'S LIFE ENCOUNTERING OBSTACLES IN MAN

We need to see the obstacles that God's life encounters in us. I believe that many brothers and sisters know and have seen a little about life. The brothers and sisters also have some understanding concerning the way to obtain life and the issue of obtaining life. However, from our experience, we know that God's life also faces obstacles and difficulties in us. Every part of our entire being, both inwardly and outwardly, presents some obstacles to life. Although we know that God's life has come into us to be our life and to be lived out of us, in reality, this life encounters obstacles in us. Thus, it is very difficult for life to be lived out from us.

Our whole being is a hindrance to God's life. God's life encounters many obstacles in us. It is difficult to find one Christian in a thousand who allows God's life to have a free way in him. It is difficult to find a tenth of one percent, much less one percent, who give God a free way. The most difficult problems and severe restrictions that God's life encounters in the universe are related to these obstacles in man. This is a very serious matter, and it is worthwhile to study this matter in a thorough way.

It is a fact that we have been saved and that God's life has come into us. We know about God's life, and we also know how to touch and contact His life. Nevertheless, God's life still does not have a way in us, and it is unable to get through in us because it faces obstacles in us every day. In our daily living, we do not give God's life the way, and we do not allow God's life to have the ground in us. Everything of our natural man is a restriction to God's life. Even our exhortation of others can be a problem for God's life. Everything we have, whether good or bad, approved or disapproved, can be an obstacle for God's life.

We should never think that the lukewarmness and backsliding of some brothers and sisters are a hindrance to God's life but that the zealous pursuit of the Lord by other saints is not a hindrance to God's life. This concept is false. Often, our zeal and pursuit are the greatest obstacles to God's life. Similarly, we should not think that the ungodliness and worldliness of some saints are a hindrance to God's life but that godly saints, who do not love the world and who forsake sin, do not present any obstacles to God's life. This is not necessarily true. God may encounter significantly greater and even stronger obstacles in these saints rather than in those who are ungodly and unrighteous.

Therefore, we need to spend much time to see the obstacles that God's life encounters in us. Although these are negative matters, the danger is quite serious; consequently, we must study them. We have met many people who love and pursue the Lord zealously and who are very pious, but we rarely meet people who allow God's life to have a free way in them. We rarely see God's life flowing freely out of anyone without encountering some difficulties. Among today's Christians, we can hardly find anyone who gives God the free way. If we could find such a person, it would be the greatest blessing and miracle in the universe. This means that it is very rare and noteworthy for us to find someone who does not place restrictions and obstacles before God. May the Lord have mercy on us so that we would not only know life and the way of life but also discover the things that hinder and restrict life.

## Not Knowing the Way of Life and
## Not Taking Christ as Life

The first problem that God's life encounters in man is the problem of ignorance. After any person is saved and becomes a Christian, he still has his thoughts and concepts. After a person is saved, he even has concepts and thoughts concerning what it means to be a proper Christian. A person may believe in the Lord on the first day, be baptized on the second day, and consider what kind of a Christian he should be on the third day. Everyone has human concepts. However, all human concepts are in darkness. It does not matter whether we are wise or foolish, whether we are highly educated or uneducated, all our human concepts are in darkness, and they prevent us from knowing life and Christ. No matter how good, lovely, and precious, all our concepts are in darkness, and they keep us from knowing Christ as life in us.

After some people are saved and become Christians, they have a concept that they need to be zealous and preach the gospel. They do not realize that even this concept can be in darkness and prevent them from knowing life. Other people have a different concept. They think that being a real Christian involves forsaking the world, fame, and wealth. They look down on everything that is physical and worldly, and they even attempt to forsake everything that is worldly. In their view, this is what it means to be a model Christian. Nevertheless, we must remember that these concepts are in darkness, and they prevent us from knowing life. People have such concepts because they do not know life.

Therefore, the first problem that God's life encounters in us is that we do not realize the darkness of our human concepts. We do not realize that our concepts, even though they seem proper and upright, are actually full of darkness and without life. Most Christians think that they should be zealous and forsake the world once they become Christians. From man's view, this sounds very logical. But without God's life, this is not practical.

Being a Christian is not a matter of zeal, nor a matter of spreading the gospel, nor a matter of forsaking the world, nor even a matter of not caring for material enjoyment. Being a Christian does not depend upon doing anything; it does not depend upon anything under the sun. Being a Christian depends upon how we take care of the Christ in us. The day we were saved, we received a living Christ, who became our life in us. From that day forward, our being a Christian has not depended on anything other than taking care of the living Christ in us. The only thing that matters is how we take care of the living Christ in us.

After we are saved, the concept of trying to be good is within all of us. We think that being a Christian means to forsake the world, to be zealous, and to preach the gospel fervently. This is a natural, human concept. This is our thought, not God's thought. As soon as we are baptized, we typically think that we should be zealous and preach the gospel. However, when we pray and fellowship with God in the morning, the living Christ in us may touch us in a different way according to His constant operation and move in us. Then things truly begin to happen in us. For example, as He operates in us, we will see that some things we may have done in the past are inappropriate, such as beating our wives, blaming our husbands, and complaining about others. We will even have a sense that we should apologize. Therefore, we need to lose our face and go to those whom we have offended and say, "I am truly sorry about how I treated you in the past. I also offended God. Now I ask you to please forgive me." This is what Christ is doing in us. When we pray, the living Christ will move in us and touch us to apologize to those whom we have offended.

However, after experiencing this kind of moving within, a brother may not apologize but instead begins to reason, "I am a man, a real man. I will lose my face if I apologize to my wife. I will go and preach the gospel, and that will be enough." So he asks the Lord, "Grant me the power to preach the gospel." If we are this kind of Christian, we are wrong because preaching the gospel and zealousness have become our goal, rather than following the living Christ in us. I have been in the church life for many years, and I have seen some people who are very zealous and tireless in preaching the gospel, but when we go to their homes, their wives say, "Others believe in Jesus, but I will not believe. Others may preach the gospel, but I do not believe what my husband preaches." This often is our situation.

We may preach the gospel and be zealous, but this does not mean that the living Christ is living Himself out of us. We can be zealous and active in preaching the gospel but totally ignore the sense of the living Christ in us. The living Christ wants to conquer and break us, but we are not willing. From the day we were saved, we have not allowed Christ to break us even once. We accept what fits our taste, such as zealousness and preaching the gospel, but we completely ignore anything that does not fit our taste, such as apologizing to our wife. This is our true situation. While we are spending much effort in considering what to do before we go to preach the gospel, our wife or husband may be thinking, "You are going to preach the gospel! You have no Christ and no reality." This shows that our zeal and preaching of the gospel are merely religious activities. The living Christ is not moving or being lived out of us.

If we genuinely know the Lord, when we pray to Him in the morning, He will move in us and give us a sense of our need to apologize to our wife. After praying, we should humble ourselves and apologize for our past wrong doings to our wife. After apologizing, we need to say to the Lord, "O Lord, thank You. I have obeyed Your moving in me. I have no choice; I do not want to have my own concept. You are my only choice and my only concept." If we would all do this, the living Christ would have more ground and opportunity to speak to us and to give us even more feelings. The result of this continual operation would spread to our dealings with others, or it may touch our wrong actions toward others. At such moments, we need to care only for Christ, not for our face or self-esteem. We need to go to people and apologize for our past wrong doings. In this way, Christ will surely have more ground in us.

I believe that those who have experienced this can testify that after such an experience, they truly feel that they are filled with Christ's presence. Even though we are on the earth, we feel as if we are in the heavens. We cannot describe the sweet, happy, peaceful, and clear feeling in us. At this point, we may ask the Lord, "O Lord, how will You lead me? I care for Your feeling." Then the Lord will direct us to do something else, and without relying on our own concepts and opinions, we can simply follow Him. This is what it means to be a

Christian, and this is the Christian's pathway of life. Our old concepts involve us only in religious activity; they cannot cause us to become normal Christians.

It is difficult to change our concepts, but we will not have a way to go on unless we put aside our own concepts and opinions. Being a Christian means not taking anything other than Christ as our aim. Many people have difficulty in their spiritual life after they are saved because they do not know the pathway of life, and they do not take Christ as their life.

## Hypocrisy

The second problem that life encounters in us is hypocrisy. There was a sister in the church in Nanking who spoke slowly and walked softly; everything she did was soft and gentle. Consequently, all the responsible brothers in the church in Nanking thought that she was very spiritual. However, strictly speaking, this was a false spirituality. We need to see that being slow is not necessarily of life and being quick is not necessarily of life. Whether or not something is of life is not determined by whether it is quick or slow. These have nothing to do with life.

Many people think that to be slow is of life and to be quick is not life. For example, if a certain brother does things quickly or does too many things when he serves, some saints think that he has a quick temper and is not spiritual, and that he needs to be dealt with and broken. On the other hand, if another brother wipes chairs and sweeps the floor slowly when he cleans the meeting hall, many saints think that he is very spiritual and that his life has been dealt with and broken. This is not correct. Just as being quick is not life, being slow is not life also. Whether or not a person's actions are of life does not depend upon whether he is quick or slow; rather, it all depends upon how he takes care of Christ.

Furthermore, a certain brother may be born with a disposition like a sharp stone. It seems as if he had eight horns when he was born, and it is very difficult for others to get along with him. Both at home and at work, his horns easily touch other people. Even after being saved, his horns continually touch people in the church. People cannot speak a few sentences to him before he starts an argument with them; he can pound the table and glare at people. Because of this, people quickly say that he is fleshly and needs to be broken. On the other hand, another brother may be born with a smooth personality like Jacob. A smooth stone does not have any sharp edges or protrusions. Some people are born this way; they never offend their siblings and parents at home, and they never offend their co-workers and superiors at work. Regardless of how people treat them, they are always smooth and even. When such a person is saved, he becomes a smooth Christian in the church. Three to five years may pass, and he never offends anyone. Many brothers and sisters praise him, saying, "This person is truly spiritual. He never argues at home or causes trouble outside. We see him doing many things, but he never gives his opinion. He is truly spiritual and full of life." This kind of speaking shows a lack of knowledge about life. We need to realize that this is actually hypocrisy. If his behavior were truly spiritual, then it would mean that he was spiritual even before he was saved. This is not possible. A person's spirituality is not determined by outward appearance but by how he takes care of Christ.

Not only do other people think that such a brother is spiritual, but even the brother himself thinks that he is spiritual. He not only deceives others; he even deceives himself. Although he does not criticize others outwardly, he is full of criticism inwardly. For example, when he sees a certain brother lose his temper, he questions why this brother has such a bad temper. He inwardly criticizes the brother for not being like himself, because he has never lost his temper or fought with others since being in the church life. Although he may not say anything outwardly, he feels this way inwardly. He thinks that others are in their flesh and need to be broken but that he does not need any breaking. Moreover, he can even pray to the Lord, saying, "O Lord, have mercy on my brother. Although I do not dare to say too much, may You have mercy on him and break his flesh." He never prays for himself because he thinks that his smoothness is spiritual. He does not realize that his spirituality is false and that it is actually a great hindrance to life.

Some people may be naturally gentle, modest, unconten-
tious, caring, willing to shed tears for others, sympathetic,
and self-sacrificing. They have many good points and virtues.
After they become Christians, they bring these natural virtues into the church. They think that these virtues are of life
and that Christians should have them, but they do not realize .
that their inner eyes have not been opened. They are blind
and do not realize that these virtues are false. From the point
of view of morality, people should have these virtues, but from
the point of view of life, these virtues are false. Life is God
Himself, life is Christ, and life is the Holy Spirit. Anything
that is not of God, Christ, or the Holy Spirit is not life. Hence,
regardless of how much a person can meet—and even go
beyond—the standard of morality, this is still not necessarily
life.

Life involves only the expression of Christ Himself out of
us. Suppose a person treats his wife in very harsh way, including hard looks and beatings. After being saved, the Lord will
begin to operate in him and give him a strong feeling to stop
his habit of oppressing his wife, to apologize to her, and even
to ask her for forgiveness. This is not something natural and
inborn; this is Christ being expressed from him. Such an operation breaks and defeats him so that Christ can be expressed
out of him. When he apologizes to his wife and asks her to forgive him, life and Christ are being expressed in him.

There are actually some people who never lose their temper.
However, there is a greater possibility of these people becoming truly spiritual if they would lose their temper once or
twice. This is because they often truly know the self and
Christ only after losing their temper. We should never think
that it is easy for people to lose their temper. Some people are
born with a disposition that does not lose its temper even
when others try hard to make them lose their temper. It is difficult for some people not to lose their temper, but for others,
it is difficult for them to lose their temper. This is due to their
disposition, and their disposition cannot be changed easily.
Nonetheless, when Christ operates and moves in them, urging
them to speak some frank, strong words, life will be expressed
if they go against their disposition and obey the inner feeling

to speak a frank word. This is very difficult for them, and it requires that they pay a great price.

Thus, the expression of life involves the rejection of our natural disposition and preference, and simply allowing Christ to operate in us and break us. Then our actions through the inner operation of Christ will be of life. If we always do things according to our disposition and natural being, the outcome will always be hypocrisy. We must see this matter clearly.

## Rebellion

The third problem that life encounters in us is rebellion. Christ operates and moves in us in order to make us clear about His will and requirements for us and about His leading and dealing with us. However, if we do not obey but go against the feeling within, not accepting His leading or paying the price, this unwillingness and opposition are rebellion. In this case, we may have our freedom and choice, but we will not have the way of life.

Many times, we think that we are obeying the Lord, but actually we are rebelling against the Lord. For example, we may want to preach the gospel, but the Lord's operation in us is to pray. Since we do not like to stay at home and pray, but instead prefer to speak to gospel friends and fellowship with the brothers and sisters, we may simply act according to our desires. This is to act in rebellion. Nevertheless, we may think that we are following God by visiting people for the gospel and fellowshipping with the saints.

We may truly have an inward feeling that Christ wants us to pray and quiet ourselves in fellowship with Him, to draw near to Him, and to muse upon His Word. But instead we may visit with a brother, a sister, or even a gospel friend because we do not like to stay at home and fellowship with the Lord. We do not have the thought that our preaching of the gospel without prayer is rebellion. Actually, we are fully in rebellion. If we visit people in this way, they will certainly not be able to sense God's presence with us, because we have disobeyed the living Christ in us. At such a time we should realize that our outward work of preaching the gospel is merely a religious activity.

Visiting gospel friends and fellowshipping with the brothers and sisters are very pleasant things to do. However, we may be very active and zealous in doing those things but still may imprison the living Christ within us by ignoring Him. Thus, we are actually disobeying the living Christ in us. He wants us to do things in a certain way, but we refuse to follow His way. Our unwillingness to do things according to His will is clearly rebellion. Many of us commit this sin every day. The sin that we commit the most frequently and most severely is not an outward and visible sin; rather, it is the sin of disobeying the sense of Christ in us. Christ is living in us, and He is constantly giving us an inward sense of life. We should obey Him, but we often disobey Him. We often do not do what He wants us to do, and we often do what He does not want us to do. We often rebel against Him. Rebellion continually creates obstacles for His life in us.

## Natural Capability

The fourth problem that life encounters in us is our natural capability. Our natural being, disposition, and self are all problems that prevent God's life from coming out of us. However, the problem of our natural capability and ability is even more serious, and it is a strong obstacle that prevents God's life from flowing out of us. Many brothers and sisters truly love the Lord, are zealous for the Lord, and are very godly. Nevertheless, their greatest problem is the strength and greatness of their capabilities and abilities. Consequently, Christ has no ground or way in them.

We all know that some people have a problem with sin, others have a problem with the world, and still others have a problem with their disposition. However, it is not easy for us to be aware of the problem of our natural capability. For example, a group of brothers and sisters, who are very strong in their natural capability and ability, may truly love and pursue the Lord. But when a person touches them, he only senses their capability and ability because they have never been broken in their capability and ability. When he contacts them, he can only say that they seek and pursue the Lord but that their natural capability has not been broken. This is because the Lord is unable to get through in them when He encounters their capability.

There are many brothers and sisters like this among us. They are capable and talented, but they do not consider these things as sin or filthiness. They even think that these are good and useful things to the church. They think that they need such capabilities and talent in order to serve God. They do not despise their natural capabilities; instead, they treasure them. If these capabilities remain unbroken in them, they will become a problem to Christ's life.

### THE SOLUTION TO THE PROBLEM

May the Lord have mercy on us so that we would be enlightened to see how many obstacles there are in us and how much these obstacles restrict God's life. Actually, the obstacles in us are not limited only to these things. Nevertheless, there is one solution to all these obstacles in us—we must pass through the cross and let the cross break us. If we want Christ's life to be unhindered in us, we must experience the breaking of the cross and allow these obstacles to be dealt with and removed. This will allow Christ's life to be lived out from us.

# Chapter Four

# THE SUBJECTIVE OBSTACLES ENCOUNTERED BY GOD'S LIFE IN US

Scripture Reading: Rom. 12:2; Phil. 2:5, 13; 2 Thes. 3:5

## FOUR DIFFERENT KINDS OF OBSTACLES

In the previous message we saw four different obstacles that God's life encounters in us. Although these four problems are in us, relatively speaking, they are objective rather than subjective. Now we need to see four additional obstacles that God's life encounters in us. These four obstacles are not only in us, but they are also very subjective in our experience. They are not like the four previous obstacles which are mainly outside of us. For example, some people have difficulty with some aspect of their behavior and actions, but these problems are mainly outward and objective. However, there are some obstacles that God's life encounters in us that are more subjective and intrinsic.

## THE LIFE OF GOD BEING MINGLED WITH MAN

We need to understand that God's life does not come into us to be our life in an outward way. Furthermore, God's life does not nullify our person in order to be our life. Rather, God's life comes into us to mingle with us and be our life. Therefore, He still needs our person, and our person continues to exist. God does not become our life by putting us aside and eliminating our person. This is not what God is doing. Although God's life becomes our life, God still wants our person to exist because He needs our person. God's purpose is to mingle with our person; His desire is to be mingled with us as one.

For example, tea begins as water inside a cup. When the element of tea is added to the water, it becomes tea. This does not mean, however, that there are only tea leaves and no water in the tea; the tea leaves are mingled with the water, and the water becomes tea. The water and the tea become one. Even though we were originally only human, God's life has come into us to become our life. This does not mean that our person has ceased to exist and that only God's life is in us. Some people correctly think that before they were saved, they did not have God's life but then incorrectly assume that God's life replaced their human life after their salvation. In their understanding, these are two successive events, but this is not true. After we are saved and regenerated, God's life is mingled with our human life.

In the first stage of our human life, we have only the human life, not God's life. After we are saved, God's life comes into us. On the one hand, God's life wants to be our life; on the other hand, our personal life still exists. God's life has not replaced our life but has mingled with us. Now, we are not merely a man but a God-man. This can be compared to a cup of tea, which is no longer merely water but rather both tea and water. When the element of tea is added into water, it becomes tea-water. As saved ones, we are no longer simply human; we are humans mingled with God. If we said to an unbelieving friend, "You are not merely human," this would sound like an insult to him, and he would feel uncomfortable. However, this is a very practical word to Christians because it is exceedingly precious and sweet when God's life comes into us.

## THE COOPERATION BETWEEN THE INNER MAN AND THE OUTER MAN

After God's life comes into us, we are no longer merely human; we also have God's life and God's element. We can say that we are God-men. We are no longer merely men, but we are men mingled with God; we are God-men. However, even though God is mingled with us, are we willing to cooperate with Him? There is a popular game in elementary school called a three-legged race. Those who participate in the game form a team of two students, and one leg of each student is tied together so that the two must walk on three legs. Both of the students have to walk together in one accord to a destination. In the end, the ones who run the best are the teams that have the best mutual understanding and the ability to coordinate together. In fact, it often does not matter if they run slowly, because winning in a three-legged race does not depend on speed as much as it does on not tripping and falling. Of course, if a team can run faster, that is even better. But it is dreadful when a fast student and a slow student cannot coordinate together and soon fall. Once they fall, the race is lost. Thus, the team that typically wins the final victory is made up of two people with similar disposition, pace, view, and understanding. Since they run as one person, they are able to win.

Before we were saved, we were only one person. After we were saved, God came into us, and now He wants to live with us as if we were in a three-legged race. He wants us to cooperate with Him and move with Him. It is at this point that problems begin to arise, because we lived entirely by ourselves before we were saved. We did whatever we wanted to do, loved whatever we wanted to love, and chose whatever we wanted to choose. Everything was our own personal matter, and we made decisions entirely by ourselves. Even though we outwardly seem to be the same as we were before our salvation, many of us can testify that now there are two persons in us. For example, when we decide to do something, another person in us disagrees. I believe that we have all had this kind of experience. It often seems that Someone in us wants us to do a certain thing, but our outer man disagrees. In such a situation, we clearly sense that there are two persons in us—one inside and one outside.

This can be compared to a Chinese two-man comic show. [Ed. note: In this type of show, one person acts according to what a person hiding behind him is speaking or singing]. During the performance, if I am the person hiding behind the person in the front, I may say, "Bend at the waist," and he will bend at the waist. If I say, "Move your head," he will move his head. To perform a two-man comic show well, the person hiding in the back and the person in front must act in unison. If they do not perform in unison, the audience will easily see that they are not performing together. The living of a genuine Christian can be compared to a two-man comic show. There is a person in a Christian who causes him to cry or laugh. Nevertheless, there are times when the One in us is sad, but we are laughing on the outside, or we may be sad, but He is happy. He may want to do a certain thing, but we want to do something else. Then we clearly sense that there is one person on the outside and another person on the inside.

Every genuine Christian can testify that he is not a normal Christian when his living within and without are in contradiction. God may want him to go east, but he wants to go west. If so, his outer person is not one with his inner person, and he is not a proper Christian. In other words, he may be a genuine Christian, but his living is abnormal. Under normal circumstances, he should be one person, both within and without. When God is happy in him, he is happy; when God is sad in him, he is sad; and when God gives a command, he immediately follows. His entire person corresponds with God completely.

This kind of Christian is not only a genuine Christian but also a normal Christian. This kind of Christian is consistent within and without. Consequently, he will be joyful and peaceful within. When he prays, he is filled with God's presence. He can act in perfect unison with God as if he were in a two-man comic show. Whenever God moves, he moves; whenever God urges him to speak, he speaks with one voice, and the words that God speaks within, he speaks outside. Whatever God shines in him, he shines forth the same light on the outside; whatever leading God gives him within, he follows this leading on the outside. He is in perfect harmony with God, and he can cooperate with God. This is the normal Christian living of a normal Christian.

## SUBJECTIVE PROBLEMS IN US

Regrettably, there are very few normal Christians. It is as if we are all bad actors in a two-man comic show, who cannot act in unison and who are not "professional." God's life may move in us, but we do not move according to Him; we are not one with Him. We do not cooperate with Him and obey Him. Thus, God's life encounters obstacles in us. These problems can be divided into three categories, but there may also be a fourth category that needs some final consideration.

Our spirit is the deepest part of our being, and God's life is in His Spirit. When the Spirit comes into us, He comes into our spirit. The spirit in us can be compared to a filament in a light bulb. The filament is the innermost part of a lamp, and it allows the electrical current to flow. When electricity flows into a light bulb, it flows into the filament of the light bulb. If there is no filament in a light bulb, electricity cannot flow into it and the bulb cannot shine forth any light. The filament can be compared to the spirit in us with the Holy Spirit coming into our spirit with God's life. Our mingled spirit can also be compared to the hidden actor in a two-man comic show: The Spirit, hidden in our spirit, prompts us with orders and feelings in our spirit.

Our innermost part is our spirit, but surrounding our spirit is our person, our self, which is also the soul spoken of in the Bible. Our soul surrounds our spirit. The three parts of our soul are the mind, which is the organ through which we think; the will, which is the organ through which we choose and make decisions; and the emotion, which is the organ through which we express feelings. The mind, emotion, and will equal our self, which is also our person, our soul. The Holy Spirit dwells in our spirit, which is in the deepest part of our being. Surrounding our spirit is our mind, emotion, and will. Therefore, in order to be consistent within and without, our mind, emotion, and will in our soul must cooperate with our spirit. The mind, emotion, and will equal our person, which is the outer man spoken of in the Bible; the Holy Spirit in our spirit is the inner man (2 Cor. 4:16). Our soul can be compared to the actor at the front of the stage, and our spirit can be compared to the person hiding at the back of the stage. There is one person inside and another person outside.

A proper Christian is one whose mind, emotion, and will cooperate with his spirit. An abnormal Christian is one whose mind, emotion, and will cannot cooperate and even contradict his spirit. Thus, he lives under a veil. If our mind, emotion, and will cannot adequately cooperate with our spirit, we will have problems.

## The Problem of Our Mind

A certain brother may be very zealous after he is saved, and he may have the concept that he should preach the gospel for the Lord and save sinners. This concept comes from his mind. He thinks that once he becomes a Christian, he should be zealous for the Lord and preach the gospel because this is what a proper Christian is supposed to do. However, he does not realize that this is only a natural opinion, which comes from his mind and thoughts. The Lord Jesus lives in his spirit, and when he prays in the morning, the Lord may give him a feeling to apologize to his wife. This feeling does not come from his mind and thoughts; instead, it comes from his spirit, which is where the Lord's Spirit dwells. Such a thought is unrelated to his natural mind or natural thoughts. He has absolutely no concept of apologizing to his wife.

While he desires to zealously preach the gospel for the Lord, the Spirit of the Lord is moving in his spirit and urging him to apologize to his wife. This shows that the thought in his mind of going to preach the gospel is different from the feeling in his spirit that he should apologize to his wife. The thought in his mind and the feeling in his spirit do not match. Inwardly, there is a sense that he should apologize, but outwardly, his thoughts are focused only on preaching the gospel. The two are not one. This is a problem because his thoughts do not match the sense in his spirit. His only consideration is to preach the gospel zealously; he has no thought to apologize to his wife, even though he has a sense in his spirit. There are thousands of stories like this. This shows the problem of our mind.

The year after China won the Sino-Japanese War, I went to Nanking and met a brother whom I had known for ten years. He was prominent in the textile industry. One day, he invited us to eat with him, and he purposely sat beside me. He said, "Brother Lee, I genuinely feel that I should do more things; that is, I should do more things for the Lord." When I heard this, I did not agree with him, and I did not feel very comfortable within. I looked at him, and he continued to tell me that he wanted to care for orphans and that he wanted to do this and that. He spoke of many things, and the more he spoke, the more excited he became. At the end of our time, he asked, "Brother Lee, what do you think?" I could not say anything. I could only think inwardly, "Do these things come from the moving of Christ within?"

I was very disappointed that day. This brother had been saved for a long time, and he had passed through many things, but it seemed as if he had not learned any lessons or made any advance. I actually wanted to ask him, "Is this something that the Lord wants you to do, or does it come from your own thoughts and opinions?" I also wanted to ask, "Brother, have you dealt with the matter of consecration over these past few years? Have you dealt with sin thoroughly? Has the Lord gained the ground in you? If the things you want to do originate from your thoughts, then they will be nothing more than religious activities even if they are successful. They will not help people see and gain Christ, because they are merely religious activities that originate from your thoughts; they are not a testimony of Christ being lived out from your spirit."

Christ is the Spirit, and the Spirit dwells in our spirit. When the Spirit comes out of us, it is life. Nevertheless, we are often like an unwilling participant in a two-man comic show with God. When the Spirit moves in us, we ignore, suppress, and put Him aside; instead, we exercise our mind to think and our eyes to watch. We use our mind to think about what others would do, and we use our eyes to watch what others are doing rather than following the living Christ in us. Consequently, even if we accomplish some religious enterprise, we are not living out Christ's life. His life will be blocked and unable to get through in us. Although we have the life of Christ within, we do not cooperate with Christ's life in our thoughts and in our actions, and so this life cannot be lived out from us. This is the problem of our mind.

## The Problem of Our Will

There is also the problem of our will. Even though our mind often understands the intention in our spirit and we know the will of God, we are unwilling to submit and obey. For example, consider the brother who decides to preach the gospel according to the concept in his mind. When he prays and the Lord gives him a feeling in his spirit to apologize to his wife, his mind has no difficulty in understanding this feeling, but his will is stubborn and unwilling to submit. This shows the problem of the will. Such a brother is not able to submit even to the Lord, much less to his wife. Thus, our will is another great obstacle. We may understand, know, apprehend, and deeply sense that the Lord wants us to do a certain thing, but our will refuses to submit and surrender. Our will is stubborn and hard, and we refuse to be softened, to let God break us, and to submit to Him. Although this brother clearly knows that the Holy Spirit wants him to apologize to his wife, his will is too strong, and he refuses to obey. Thus, God's Spirit and life encounter an enemy and an obstacle.

We should not think that only brothers have a stubborn will. It often is much more difficult to subdue a sister's will than a brother's. There was a sister who once prayed, "O Lord, I know clearly that I should apologize to a sister, but I cannot submit. If she were a stranger on the street, I would apologize, but she is a sister who serves in the church, so I cannot submit." This sister was bold in speaking such a word to the Lord. She even had excuses for not submitting.

A sister can argue and quarrel with her husband at home but sit with him before the Lord's table in the bread-breaking meeting. She may even pray, "O Lord, allow me to pay my debt to You, and I will apologize to my husband later at home." By doing this, she seemingly has a peaceful conscience. However, after coming home, she will refuse to submit, inwardly thinking, "I am willing to apologize to any brother in the church whom I offend, but I cannot give in to my husband. If I apologize to him, I will be admitting that I am wrong and that I have lost. How can I let this happen?" She can even have morning watch the next day, and her conscience can bother her in regard to her cheating of the Lord, but her mind will also tell her that it is not reasonable to apologize to her husband. This kind of struggle can drag on for weeks, even half a year. Because of her refusal to apologize, she can lose the

Lord's presence for half a year. Thus, the Lord encounters a strong obstacle in her stubborn and unyielding will. Our will is truly a great hindrance to God.

Some people are very weak in their will; their will is so weak that they cannot be strong. Their will is as soft as a well-cooked noodle, and others do not know how to deal with them. Even though a brother knows that he should submit to the Lord, he can be incapable of moving because he is not strong in his will. He may clearly know the Lord's will but be unable to carry it out. No matter how much he is exhorted, he is like a soft, wet noodle that cannot be propped up with a pair of chopsticks. It is possible for a person to be clear about what the Lord wills when he is praying in his room but be unable to do anything once he steps outside of the room. Both a strong will and a weak will are hindrances to God's life.

A will that has been dealt with is both strong and pliable. Being pliable is not the same as being soft. Being pliable means that one is not insistent or stubborn. However, when a need arises, one can be strong and bold; such a one is not afraid to give up his own life. Only a person with such a will can carry out the Lord's command and act according to the Lord's leading. A person with this kind of will allows the Lord's Spirit to come out of him as life. Having a will that can cooperate with God is a great matter.

## The Problem of Our Emotion

Furthermore, our emotion is also a big problem to God. The New Testament does not speak only of Christ being our life and of God coming into us so that we can live out Christ through the Spirit. The Bible speaks also of the need for our mind to be renewed so that we have the mind of Christ and so that God can operate in our decisions (Eph. 4:23; Rom. 12:2; 1 Cor. 2:16; Phil. 2:5, 13); the apostles who wrote the New Testament knew the intention of the Holy Spirit. They realized that without the renewing of our mind and the dealing with our will, God's life could not be expressed through us. This is the reason the New Testament speaks so much about our mind, emotion, and will.

Second Thessalonians 3:5 says, "The Lord direct your hearts into the love of God." This means that our emotion needs to have God's emotion and that we need to fully enter into God's emotion. We should love whatever God loves, like whatever God likes, and hate whatever God hates. Our feelings of love, anger, sorrow, and joy should be God's feelings of love, anger, sorrow, and joy. Our likes and dislikes should be God's likes and dislikes. Everything of God is ours because His nature has been wrought into us. Our emotion and His emotion have become one emotion.

We often have the Lord's presence and feeling within, but our emotion has some preference other than the Lord's. Our likes and dislikes are different from the Lord's feeling and moving. Thus, even though we truly have the Lord's feeling and moving within, we disobey this feeling and ignore His moving because they do not match our likes and tastes. Therefore, we move according to our own likes and emotions and do not cooperate with the moving of the Lord's life. Hence, the Lord's life encounters an obstacle in our emotion.

Although the saints should fellowship with one another— brothers with the brothers and sisters with the sisters—we often fellowship beyond a limit and are influenced by our emotion. A problem develops when our fellowship with one another turns into friendship with one another. Sisters, especially, develop friendships with other sisters through their fellowship. This is a problem related to emotions. Although the Lord may give a sister a clear sense to deal with a friendship, she is often unwilling. Such a friendship takes her away, and in the end, she follows her outward friendship while disobeying her inward feeling. This is an example of the Lord's life encountering the obstacle of our emotion.

We need to see a great principle: In order for God's life to have a way in us, we need to turn from our emotion, have a strong and pliable will, and be renewed in our mind. We need to drop our concepts and views, and we need to read the Bible and allow the Lord's Word to renew our mind and thoughts so that we will think and see things according to God's view in the Bible. In this way, our mind can cooperate with God's life. At the same time, we need to learn to surrender our will to the Lord so that our will would be pliable. Then when we need to be strong, we will be able to stand up for the Lord. Thus, our will can be both strong and pliable, and we will be able to cooperate with the Lord.

Furthermore, our emotions and tastes need to match the Lord's. We need to let God lead us so that our disposition is one with His disposition in order that we would have His emotions and tastes. Each and every part of our soul—our mind, emotion, and will—must cooperate with the Holy Spirit's operation in us and with the Lord's feeling. Then God Himself will be lived out of us. This is the best cooperation that we can give to God so that His life will have a way to live out of us. If we do not cooperate, our mind, emotion, and will will remain as obstacles to the divine life.

## The Problem of Our Person

When we consider the problems related to our mind, emotion, and will together, we can see that our person is the problem; our person is truly an obstacle for the living out of God's life. If we analyze this matter, we see that some problems are related to the mind, others are related to the will, and still others are related to the emotion. Speaking as a whole, however, all of our problems are due to our person, which has never been broken by God. We may have been saved by grace, but our person remains unbroken; we have never been broken by God, and we remain intact. Our self, which is our person, is a problem for God's life. God's life cannot come out of us because our person is an obstacle; our person hinders God's life. In order for God's life to come out of us, we need to exercise to have our person broken and shattered. The more severely we are broken, the more God's life will be able to come out of us.

# CHAPTER FIVE

# THE PATHWAY OF LIFE

Scripture Reading: John 12:24; 2 Cor. 4:10-11

Philippians 3:10 says, "To know...the fellowship of His sufferings, being conformed to His death." According to the original Greek, these two phrases are two of the hardest phrases to translate because there is no such expression in Chinese. The meaning of the original Greek is "to realize, or to know." Having fellowship in the Lord's sufferings is to have fellowship with the Lord in His sufferings and through His sufferings. To be conformed to His death means that His death is like a mold and that we are in this mold to be conformed to His death.

## THE DEATH OF THE CROSS

In the previous chapters we saw the obstacles that the life of God encounters in us. Now we need to see how God deals with these problems and how He opens a clear pathway for His life in us. This pathway is called the pathway of life. Although the life of God is in us, His life often cannot come out of us because there are strong hindrances, obstacles, and restrictions in us. Thus, the life of God has a difficult way to get through in us; it is rebuffed at every point and resisted in every matter. A part of God's work in His salvation is to pave a clear way for His life in us. This work is accomplished through the death of the cross.

In God's salvation, there is life and there is death, and His salvation involves several matters of faith that are not the subject of other "faiths." For example, no other "faith" speaks of the blood or redemption by the blood. In God's salvation, however, the blood is an important matter because without the shedding of blood, there is no forgiveness of sins (Heb. 9:22). This point is not stressed by other "faiths." Furthermore, life is also a very special matter in God's salvation. However, only in God's salvation is the matter of life considered and emphasized. From beginning to end, the Bible is focused on life. The goal of God's center and purpose is life. In religion there is not much speaking concerning life; instead, self-cultivation, character improvement, and charitable and pious deeds are emphasized. However, in God's salvation there is blood and life.

Most people do not like to hear about death. The Chinese like to display words in their homes like *blessing, wealth, longevity,* and *happiness,* but no one likes the word *death.* Nevertheless, in God's salvation, there is the matter of death, and it is a great matter. Those who know God's salvation not only appreciate the preciousness of the blood and the importance of life but also realize the importance of death. In the provisions of God's salvation, He has prepared blood, life, and death for us. In regard to God's salvation, we often say that we have received the life of God, a life that is eternal, holy, full, and shining. However, we may not realize that there is also something else that is precious in God's salvation, which people do not like to hear—the matter of death.

Paul, who knew both God and His salvation, not only pursued His life but also His death. He said, "To know Him and the power of His resurrection and the fellowship of His sufferings, being conformed to His death" (Phil. 3:10). The fellowship he desired to know was not in Christ's life but in His sufferings. Knowing this fellowship meant that Paul participated in this fellowship, which caused him to be conformed to Christ's death. Paul desired, pursued, and also treasured Christ's death. Even though many people do not like death, Paul treasured it. Just as the blood is precious and life is important in God's salvation, so is death. Whoever desires to know God's salvation must know these three precious things: the blood, life, and death.

We all know the preciousness of the Lord's blood and how the blood enables our sins to be forgiven. When we fall short before the Lord and cannot come to Him because of condemnation in our conscience, we can look to the blood, trust in the blood, and come to the Lord. Through the blood our sins are forgiven, and through the cleansing of our conscience our fellowship with God is restored (Heb. 10:19; 9:14). In this way, we experience the preciousness of the blood.

Many saved ones emphasize life and the experience of the Lord's life. Nevertheless, very few of us realize that God has prepared another wonderful thing for us in His salvation—the *death* of Christ. We may have been Christians for many years, but have we ever realized that God has prepared *death* for us in His salvation? In our Christian experience, how much do we genuinely experience death in the Lord's salvation? We have ignored this great matter of death in God's salvation.

In the Bible we can see that God's salvation and life have been concealed in death. John 12:24 says, "Unless the grain of wheat falls into the ground and dies, it abides alone; but if it dies, it bears much fruit." This means that there is life in a grain of wheat, but unless the grain falls into the ground and dies, the life within the grain will not be released. If, however, the grain dies, the life will be released. This shows that death is the way for life to be released. Since death is an outlet for life, life must pass through death. Regardless of whether it is a grain of wheat or another kind of seed, a seed must pass through death in order to release the life that is in it.

If we love a seed and put it in a very beautiful place or even in a precious box, the life within the seed, that is, all the content and splendor concealed within the seed, will not be expressed. However, if we bury the seed in the earth, the seed will have an opportunity to enter into death so that all of the seed's content will come out. The life within the seed is released through death. After a short time, we will see a green seedling growing up. After more time, we will see a leaf sprouting on the seedling, and after still more time, the leaf will be full grown and a flower will blossom. Eventually, the seedling will blossom, bear fruit, and be full grown.

This shows that it is only through death that the life in a seed can be released. This is a natural law in the universe, and this law signifies the pathway to release the life of God in us. Both plant and animal life are released through death.

For example, the life of a chicken is in an egg, but if the egg-shell is not broken, life cannot come out. Those who raise chickens know that in order for the life in an egg to be born, the eggshell must be broken. The breaking of an eggshell is a process of death. Regardless of whether it is plant or animal life, life must pass through the process of death in order to be born. This is a natural law, and it is also a principle. This law signifies that in order for the life of God to come out of us, it must pass through death.

Similarly, in order for the life of God to come out of the Lord Jesus, He had to pass through death. He said that without death there would be no life (John 12:24). Without death as the pathway, life cannot be released. The way of life is the way of death; wherever there is death, there is a way for life to come out. If there is no death in us, God's life will not be able to find a way to be released from us. Paul said, "Always bearing about in the body the putting to death of Jesus that the life of Jesus also may be manifested in our body" (2 Cor. 4:10). The expression of the Lord's life in us is contingent upon one thing: death. The extent to which death has worked in us is the extent to which the Lord's life has a way to come out of us. For this reason, even Paul, who was full of experience and was mature in life, pursued to know Christ's death; he wanted to be conformed to Christ's death. He pursued this death because he knew that the extent to which death worked in him would be the extent to which the Lord's life could be released from him.

### THE CHRISTIAN LIFE NOT BEING A MATTER OF CULTIVATION OR IMPROVEMENT BUT A MATTER OF DEATH

Some people may ask, "How can we apply this principle?" First, we need to realize that we have a mistaken concept. When we consider the matter of religion, for example, we spontaneously associate it with self-cultivation. If a person believes in Buddhism and is a devout Buddhist, he surely tries to cultivate and improve himself. If a person believes in Catholicism and is a devout Catholic, he also tries to cultivate himself. Regardless of whether a person is a Muslim or a Christian, as long as he is sincere and not careless, he will have a concept related to cultivation and self-improvement. This is particularly true of those who are saved in a strong way. As soon as they are saved, such ones desire to become good Christians and serve God, and they immediately begin to act according to their concept of cultivation and improvement.

For example, before he is saved, a person may have a bad temper and often lose his temper with his wife. Once he becomes a Christian, however, he feels it is improper to lose his temper with his wife. Consequently, he spontaneously has a thought of correcting and cultivating himself. Truly speaking, among all those who are saved, no one can escape from this concept of cultivation. For example, we may have good fellowship with the Lord in the morning and touch His presence. However, once we come out of our room, someone can provoke us to the point that we speak some impetuous words. As soon as these impetuous words come out of our mouth, we immediately do not feel peaceful. Then we pray and ask the Lord to forgive us, but after asking for forgiveness, we also make up our mind to correct ourselves so that we do not lose our temper again. This comes from our concept of self-cultivation and improvement.

Many saints live a life of spiritual cultivation. Nevertheless, we cannot find the word *cultivation* in the Bible; spiritual cultivation is not the central thought in the Bible. Christianity has deviated from the course and is short of light and grace; it uplifts self-cultivation according to man's concept and encourages people to cultivate themselves spiritually. This is a religious concept according to man's religious view, but it is not the revelation of the Bible or the revelation of God's light. If someone asks what word in the New Testament should replace *cultivation,* we would answer *death.* Death is the real way to change a person's temper. A brother who loses his temper does not need cultivation but death. Death does not sound good, but in order for a man of the old creation to be transformed, death, rather than cultivation, is required.

Therefore, whether a person is in life does not depend on whether he is fast or slow. Being fast does not necessarily mean that a person is not acting according to life, and being slow does not necessarily mean that a person is acting according to life. Whether we have life and are in life does not depend on whether we are fast or slow but on whether God has been released from us. We may even change from being fast to slow or change our temper from bad to good, but it will not be according to life if God is not manifested from us. At the most, we will express our cultivation. Life is related to God, not cultivation, and when the New Testament speaks of life, it also speaks of death. Life is not a matter of cultivation but of death.

In the entire Bible, no apostle was ever inspired by the Holy Spirit to teach people to cultivate their conduct; on the contrary, the apostle Paul said, "I am crucified with Christ; and it is no longer I who live, but it is Christ who lives in me" (Gal. 2:20). By this he meant that as a person with God's life and as a person with Christ living in him, he had been crucified with Christ on the cross. He was dead. The cross accomplished a work of death in him so that God's life would have a way. The New Testament does not teach us to cultivate ourselves; rather, it teaches us to walk in the way of death. When we pass through death and move in death, the life of God will gain an open way in us. We need to know the way of life through death. We need to see that cultivation is not God's will, because God does not intend that we would improve ourselves. God wants us to see that the cross of His Son comes to us through the Holy Spirit. The cross does a work of death in us so that we may pass through death in order for His life to have an open way in us.

## THE WAY FOR GOD TO LIVE OUT OF US

### Knowing the Life of God in Us

How can the life of God live out of us? First, we need to realize that we have the life of God in us. From the day that we were saved, God's life came into us to be our life. However, this life is surrounded by our person. The life of God wants to come out of us, but our person hinders and restricts Him. Therefore, it is difficult for Him to come out of us.

Many saints become behavior-improving Christians and

take the way of self-improvement because they do not know the life of God that dwells in them or the way of life. They think that they will arrive at the standard of a Christian by improving their temper a little and doing good rather than bad things. The way they take is unrelated to life; it is merely the way of religion and self-improvement. They are Christians in name, but they are not Christians in their actual living. The actual living of a Christian is the living out of God. Our problem depends on the divine life opening up a way in us so that God can live out of us. This is what we need to seek and discover.

## Seeing That Our Natural Man Is a Hindrance to the Life of God

Second, we need God to open our eyes to see that we are a hindrance to the life of God. We may be naturally irritable or meek, or we may be naturally quick or slow, but in any case, we are a problem to the life of God. As long as we have a heart for God, sooner or later He will show us that we are a problem to His life. In other words, if we want to let the life of God come out of us and if we want to walk the way of life and live the Christian life, we need to look to God to open our eyes and show us that our very person is a problem to the life of God.

## Seeing That We Have Been Crucified on the Cross

Third, if God has opened our eyes, we will hate our self. When we are enlightened, we will truly hate the way we are. About twenty years ago, I was shown mercy and was enlightened to see my actual condition, and I truly hated and abhorred myself. I said, "O God, the problem that You encounter in me is my very self. I truly should be cursed. O God, I hate myself. No matter how I think, how I view things, how I make decisions, how I form opinions, or how I honor my parents, it all is a problem to You. O God, I hate myself. I abhor myself." When we abhor and hate our self, the Holy Spirit will show us that our self, which restricts and opposes God, has been crucified on the cross (Rom. 6:6).

At such a moment, we will see a vision, a revelation, that

we are already on the cross. This can be compared to being saved and enlightened by the Holy Spirit to see our sins. At the moment of our grief, sorrow, and repentance for our sins, the Holy Spirit showed us that the Lord Jesus was crucified for us on the cross. When we repented of our sins, the Holy Spirit showed us that the Lord Jesus had borne them on the cross for us. When we saw this, we praised Him immediately, saying, "O Lord, my sins are on the cross. Thank You. The sins that were mine are now on the cross. Lord, Your cross has dealt with my sins." We were saved at that time, and we clearly knew that we were saved. In the same principle, the Holy Spirit will show us that our self, as an enemy of God, is the real hindrance and restriction to the life of God. We will loathe, hate, abhor, and condemn our self; however, at the same moment, the Holy Spirit will show us that the Lord Jesus bore our person on the cross with Him. We also were crucified on the cross. At such a moment, we will see a vision of the cross for the second time.

In our experience we first saw that our sins were crucified on the cross. Now we need to see that our person was crucified on the cross as well. Our self has been crucified on the cross. Everyone who sees this vision will praise, worship, and immediately say, "O Lord, my person has been crucified on the cross. I thank and praise You. Just as my sins have been dealt with on the cross, I also have been dealt with on the cross." This is our true experience, and this is also the beginning of being on the pathway of life. Christian living starts from this point.

### THE APPLICATION OF THE WAY OF GOD'S LIFE DEPENDING UPON OUR SEEING

Thus, we need to realize several things. First, we need to realize that we have the life of God in us. Second, we need to realize that we ourselves are a hindrance to the life of God. Regardless of whether we think we are good or bad, fast or slow, eventually the Holy Spirit will show us that the life of God is in us. At the same time, He will show us that our person is a problem to the life of God. Our mind is a problem, our will is a problem, and our emotion is also a problem to the life of God; it is our very person that is a problem to the life of God.

We know this because even though our thoughts are not wrong, our judgments are right, and our emotions are proper, God often is not expressed through our mind, emotion, and will. If God's life cannot be released from us, there is an obstacle to His life in us. This is the reason we say that the obstacle that the life of God encounters in us is our person. It means nothing to God if we are good or bad, fast or slow. Just as losing our temper is not necessarily related to the life of God, controlling our temper is not necessarily related to the life of God. Every good thing and every bad thing, when measured against the standard of the life of God, are hindrances and obstacles.

Third, we need to realize that we have been crucified on the cross. According to God's view, reckoning, and judgment, we are already on the cross. The preceding three points are the way of life and the revelation of life. Anyone who wants to take the way of life must see these three points. Such a vision and revelation are clearly shown to us when the Holy Spirit enters into us. In such a vision we see the living and immeasurable God with His eternal and mighty life in us, and in this revelation we see that our very person is a hindrance and restriction to life. However, He also shows us that we are crucified on the cross. This vision is the beginning of our walk on the way of life.

Everyone who is before the Lord and who wants to walk on the way of life must start from this point. We need God's mercy and the Holy Spirit's shining to show us that the life of God is in us, that we are a hindrance to the life of God, and that we have been crucified on the cross. Everyone who wants to take the way of God's life eventually must see this.

When the Holy Spirit opens our eyes to see that we have been crucified on the cross, the death of the cross will shine into us and become an inward vision. Then wherever we go, this vision will be deeply impressed into us. Once we have seen this vision, we will start on the way of life, and the life of God will begin to be expressed through us.

After we have seen this vision, we will realize that we

have died on the cross and have been terminated. Even if it later seems that we have forgotten everything and begin to act according to our old thoughts, decisions, and choices, the vision, as if it is a voice within, will remind us, asking, "Have you not been crucified? Have you not been terminated on the cross?" While we are thinking and deciding to act according to our own choices, a voice, a word, a light will question us within, "Are you not on the cross? Are you not crucified?" At such a time, we will practically experience the vision that we have seen. Even though we may try to think according to our way, we will be unable, and even though we try to decide and choose according to our way, we will be unable. We will be like a deflated ball that was once filled with air.

Before we see such a vision, we can be compared to a ball filled with air; however, after we see the vision that we are crucified with Christ, a hole will be punctured in us without our even knowing it. Thus, when we try to think by our self, we will be unable; when we try to decide by our self, we will be unable; and when we try to choose by our self, we will be unable. Once the vision of the cross enters into us, it works in us and "punctures" us. When we see the vision, we will be broken.

Someone may ask, "Is it true that a person who has seen the cross will not lose his temper, and that a person who has not seen the cross will lose his temper?" No. A person who has not seen the cross will lose his temper, and so will a person who has seen the cross, but there is a difference. When a person who has not seen the cross loses his temper, the more he loses his temper, the more he takes pleasure in doing so, and the more he becomes enlivened by it. On the other hand, a person who has seen the cross may still lose his temper, but the more he loses his temper, the more he loses his taste for it, and the more uneasy he feels. A person who has seen the cross does not need to be exhorted by others; after he murmurs for half a sentence, he cannot utter the rest of the sentence. If he quarrels with his wife, he feels deflated after only one sentence and realizes that something is not right. There is no need for others to exhort him. A person who has not seen the vision and who is unwilling to bear the cross will quarrel in the evening after quarreling in the morning. This shows the difference between the two. Those who have not seen the cross are energized by their quarrels, but those who have seen the cross are deflated by their quarrels. Experiencing the vision of the cross is not a matter of cultivation but a matter of being broken. God's salvation is not a matter of improvement but a matter of dying.

# Chapter Six

# THE WAY AND LIFE OF THE CROSS

Scripture Reading: Rom. 8:13-14; Gal. 5:16, 24

## SEEING THAT WE HAVE BEEN CRUCIFIED WITH CHRIST

At a certain point in our Christian life, the Holy Spirit will show us that we have been nailed to the cross, even though we restrict and hinder God as life. In other words, the Holy Spirit will show every pursuer and follower of the Lord a vision, a revelation, that his person has been put to death on the cross of Christ. This is a turning point that every lover and pursuer of the Lord must experience; it is unavoidable.

When we are saved or revived, we always have a certain amount of zeal, a love for the Lord, a desire to pursue Him, an eagerness to follow Him, and a fervency to express our love for Him. However, we soon discover that our very being hinders Him the most, even though we pursue and zealously follow the Lord. Regardless of whether we are good or bad, we are a hindrance to the Lord. At this moment, the Holy Spirit will show us that we have been crucified. With such a view, we pass through a gate. From this point forward, we will begin to touch the way of life in our Christian living. We also will realize that we were merely being zealous and excited in our pursuit and love of the Lord and that we have not actually entered the pathway of life. When we are shown this mercy by the Lord, we will realize that our very person hinders and troubles Him the most.

The Holy Spirit will show us that the one thing that hinders the Lord the most in the universe is our person. Then the Holy Spirit will open our eyes to fully show us that our person has been put to death on the cross. At this point we will experience death; we will pass through a gate, and we will enter onto the pathway of the spiritual life. This is the beginning of our taking the way of the spiritual life. From this point forward, the Holy Spirit will bring us into the way of the cross every day, and He will bring us into the life of the cross.

## SPIRITUAL MATTERS REQUIRING US TO FIRST ENTER THROUGH THE GATE AND THEN WALK ON THE WAY

When we speak of the cross, whether it involves the way or the living of the cross, we are not referring to suffering, which is a common thought. The cross actually refers to *death*. The final result of the cross in us is not suffering but death. For us to live a life of the cross and to walk on the way of the cross mean that we live a daily life of death and take the way of death. To unbelievers, this sounds strange, but to believers, who are pursuing the Lord, it is a sweet and real experience.

In other words, if we have really touched the way of life and if the Holy Spirit has brought us into the way of life, we will live under death and walk in death every day. Although we may love, pursue, and follow the Lord, the Holy Spirit still must open our eyes to show us that we are a hindrance to God. At such a moment, the Holy Spirit will also show us that we have been crucified and have died on the cross. Then we will pass through the gate.

However, passing through the gate does not mean that everything is complete and finished. Passing through the gate is only an entrance; after we pass through the gate, we still need to walk on the way. In spiritual matters we do not walk on the way and then enter through the gate; instead, we enter through the gate and then walk on the way. Matthew 7:13-14 speaks of this principle: We enter the narrow gate, and then we walk on the constricted way. In our Christian living, the Holy Spirit eventually will bring us through the gate of the cross, and then He will lead us to take the way of the cross. This means that the Holy Spirit will lead us to a point where we see that we have been crucified with Christ on the cross. Thereafter, we will know the cross and the death of the cross, and the Holy Spirit will bring our whole being into the way of the cross. We will enter through the gate and walk on the way of death. It is at this point that we will truly begin to take the way of the cross and live a life of the cross. In other words, we will enter into death, and the effect of death will be in us every day. Christ's death will target and deal with us, putting us to death and killing our thoughts, opinions, preferences, choices, and emotions; it will deal with all of our likes and dislikes. This death, which is carried out in and by the Holy Spirit, is like a sharp razor, a sharp knife, which continuously does a killing work in us. This is the cross.

In spiritual matters we need to go through the gate and then walk on the way. Consider the matter of prayer. Many people do not know how to pray when they first believe in the Lord, so they imitate others' prayers and even write down prayers before praying. After imitating others for a period of time, the Holy Spirit will bring them to the point of passing through the gate. Once they know the purpose of prayer and touch the secret of prayer, they will know how to pray. This, however, does not mean that they have graduated from prayer or no longer need to pray. On the contrary, touching the secret of prayer is the beginning of prayer; it is an initiation. Thereafter, they need to live a life of prayer, praying daily to advance in the way of prayer.

Our experience of faith is the same. Many saved ones hear the truth of the gospel and sing songs of faith, but they do not live by faith. One day, however, they are enlightened by the Holy Spirit and begin to know the reality of faith, fully believing into God, relying upon God, and touching God's faithfulness. This does not mean, however, that they have graduated from believing. On the contrary, they are just beginning to enter into a life of faith. It is at this point that they can begin to live a life of faith and walk on the pathway of faith. In spiritual matters we first pass through the gate and then walk on the way. Consequently, in our experience of Christ's death and of being put to death on the cross, we first pass through the gate and then walk on this way in life.

Many Christians have been saved for five, ten, or even twenty years without passing through the gate of the cross.

They are zealous. They love and pursue the Lord, and they preach the gospel. Few, however, have experienced the Lord by passing through the gate of the cross. We meet Christians everywhere who are zealous, love the Lord, pursue the Lord, preach the gospel, save souls, and help the saints. But it is very difficult to meet a saint who has passed through the gate of the cross and who knows the death of the cross.

Some people ask, "How can we tell whether someone has passed through the gate of the cross?" When we contact someone who has passed through the gate of the cross, we immediately sense the imprint of the cross, the dealing of the cross, and the breaking of the cross in him. There is a mark of the cross in him from the work of the cross. Even if he has only passed through the gate of the cross and its work is not very deep or very great in measure, it is still possible to sense that he has passed through the gate of the cross. Since he has passed through the gate, he knows something of the cross and of the meaning of being crucified with Christ. Thus, he spontaneously begins to take the way of the cross and live a life of the cross.

## EXPERIENCING THE PUTTING TO DEATH
## OF THE CROSS

The meaning of the cross is death, and the function of the cross is to put us to death. When the Lord Jesus was on the cross, He was not just suffering; He was dying. The ultimate significance of the Lord Jesus being on the cross relates to death. The death of the cross is applied to us through the power of the Holy Spirit, and its effect is to put us to death, to kill us. Every day the Holy Spirit operates to work the cross of Christ and the death of the cross into us so that every part of our being can be brought into death.

The truth concerning death is not an easy matter. No one's death is simple and easy. In our spiritual experience, when the Holy Spirit enlightens us to see that we have been crucified, we rejoice, we are happy, and we praise the Lord. Many saints have this experience. When we first see that we have been crucified with Christ, we praise and rejoice. About twenty years ago, when I saw this light, I was in my study, and I was so joyful and exultant that I was jumping, running, praising, and giving thanks. Even though I was corrupt, full of lawlessness, offensive to God, opposed God, and incurable, I still saw that I was crucified. Even a person such as myself had been dealt with on the cross. The Lord said, "You have died," and I also said, "I have died." I believed the Lord's word. On that day I died. This caused me to rejoice in exultation; I was happier than when I was saved. However, after a short time, I realized that I was still alive and had not died. I was the same as before and had not changed at all. Consequently, I became confused. I continued to fail, and my failures were greater, more serious, and more severe than before. Although I saw that I had been crucified with Christ, I realized that I was still alive.

Then the Lord's Spirit showed me that dying with Christ involved more than just passing through the gate of death. I still needed to be led by the Spirit to walk on the way of death and to live the life of death. From that day forward, the Spirit applied and worked death into me. Death began to operate and have an effect in me. This operation put me to death daily, killing every part of my being. The first day it killed some of my emotions; the next day it put some of my opinions to death; the day after it put some of my thoughts to death; on yet another day it dealt with some of my concepts. Elements of my person were being killed every day. The Holy Spirit used the death of the cross, which I had seen, to do a killing work and to put me to death. The killing of the Spirit gradually became deeper, stronger, and more intense. The Spirit worked in me continually. In terms of my living, I lived under the cross every day; in terms of my walk, I was on the way of the cross every day.

Some people may ask, "What does it mean to apply the death of the cross to kill the natural element in us? What does it mean for the cross to put us to death every day?" As an example, a brother may see the vision that he has died with the Lord and realize that he has been crucified with Christ. He will tell himself that he has seen the matter of his death and termination on the cross. This is the work of the Holy Spirit. However, when he wakes up the next morning, he will have a thought of doing this or that, and he will decide what he is going to do based on his own likes and dislikes. While he is thinking and choosing, however, he marvelously will sense the Holy Spirit working in him, as if the Holy Spirit is speaking and asking, "Is this your thought or Christ's? Is this your decision or the Lord's? Are these your likes and dislikes or the Lord's?" The Holy Spirit will operate in him in this way. If he thinks and chooses according to his own choices and preferences, the Holy Spirit will fight against them strongly, and the Spirit will stop, condemn, or rebuke him. As a consequence, the brother clearly will know his choices are not of the Lord.

As the Holy Spirit operates, shines, and rebukes in this way, and as the brother confesses his sins, a killing work is being carried out invisibly in him, putting a nail into his ideas and opinions. Even though the Holy Spirit condemns him, he still may have a strong will and hold on to his opinion. Nevertheless, even though he insists on his opinion, there is now a hole in his opinion, and his opinion has changed a little. The Holy Spirit has done a little work of killing and breaking in him. As he continues on this way, the Holy Spirit will work in him more intensely to the point that he will be conquered inwardly by the Spirit. Then he will bow and say, "O Lord, I thank and praise You. I am already on the cross, and I have been crucified." His ideas, opinions, and thoughts will be crucified, and his likes and dislikes also will be on the cross. The cross can penetrate him to a point that his preferences, will, mind, and whole being are affected. This is the Holy Spirit's operation and application of the death of the cross in him, which produces an effect of putting his thoughts, preferences, and self to death. After this experience, there will be a few more holes and cracks in this brother's being because he has been broken a little more.

Although he still lives and walks, he has seen some light of the cross and has some experience of the cross. However, most of his natural element still exists and is present in his living. His self unconsciously rises up and continues to give opinions, to make decisions, and to choose. However, the process of death also repeats itself in him. Based on his seeing of the cross, the Spirit will shine on him and the light will condemn and question: "Is this you or the Lord? Is this you or Christ?"

At a certain point, he will be conquered and subdued again, and once again he will bow and say, "O Lord, I thank and praise You. My person is already on the cross." Thus, his preferences, thoughts, and opinions will be put to death on the cross, and he will receive and experience the cross once again. As the Holy Spirit furthers His work in him, the mark and the breaking of the cross in him will be deepened. There will be a further breaking in him, and more of his own element will be put to death. Consequently, little by little, day after day, and event after event, he will experience the cross in the Holy Spirit.

### THE TWO-SIDED TRUTH OF THE CROSS

From his Epistles we can see that Paul speaks of the cross in two different ways. First, he speaks of our having been crucified with Christ; this was accomplished by Christ. When Christ was crucified, He took us with Him so that we died in Him. This is an accomplished fact, and we simply need to believe and receive it. Romans 6:6 says, "Knowing this, that our old man has been crucified with Him," and Galatians 2:20 says, "I am crucified with Christ." Both of these verses speak of Christ's accomplished fact. Paul speaks of the cross also in 5:24, which says, "They who are of Christ Jesus have crucified the flesh with its passions and its lusts." Romans 8:13 says, "By the Spirit you put to death the practices of the body."

Those who teach the truth concerning the cross make a mistake of speaking only about one side of this truth in the Bible. Some people speak only of the eternal accomplishment of Christ by His crucifixion on the cross. They say that we do not need to be crucified, because we need only to receive this accomplished fact. This is true, but this is only one side of the truth. It is not enough simply to have this side of the truth, because there is another side in Paul's Epistles. Romans 6:6 says, "Knowing this, that our old man has been crucified with Him," but Romans 8:13 says, "If by the Spirit you put to death the practices of the body, you will live." On the one hand, we have been crucified on the cross; on the other hand, we need also to put to death the practices of the body by the Spirit. To put to death the practices of the body by the Spirit involves cooperating with the Spirit to put our flesh to death, which is putting a part of our element to death. This involves putting ourselves to death and also the Spirit putting us to death.

Through the Holy Spirit we are enlightened concerning Christ's accomplished fact. This enables us to pass through the gate. Then the Spirit executes and works this fact into us inwardly so that we condemn what the Spirit condemns, we criticize what the Spirit criticizes, and we put to death what the Spirit puts to death. In this way, we experience the death of the cross.

## THE WAY AND LIFE OF THE CROSS

On the day I saw the light of the cross and the fact that I have died with Christ in Romans 6, I was full of joy, thanks, and praise. Nevertheless, I was only passing through the gate; it was one side of the truth. At that time, I did not see the other side of the truth, that I needed to take the way of the cross. I saw only that Christ's death had terminated and solved everything. Nevertheless, even before I went downstairs the next morning, I saw that I was still alive. I did not realize that I needed to walk on the way after passing through the gate. I was helped by the Holy Spirit to pass through the gate, but I still needed to be led by the Holy Spirit to walk on the way. However, since the Holy Spirit wanted to apply the cross and daily shined the light of the cross in me, the light of the cross questioned, condemned, rebuked, and showed me what was of myself whenever I had a preference or opinion. When I was willing to obey, cooperate, and work with Him, I would bow and say, "Amen, Lord, I will put this matter on the cross." I would condemn it and crucify it.

As I was daily put to death, enlightened, and led and as I was cooperating with the Holy Spirit's continuing work of killing and putting me to death, the death of the cross was constituted into me. Thus, the work of killing and of being put to death in the Spirit, according to the Spirit, by the Spirit, and through the Spirit, was accomplished in me every day. This was not about putting others to death but about killing and putting my own inward element to death. This is the way of the cross and the life of the cross; this is the leading of the Holy Spirit in us every day.

A brother who has seen the light of the cross may still quarrel with his wife at home because quarreling is according to his natural being. When he quarrels with his wife, however, the Holy Spirit will shine the light of the cross in him and question, "Is this Christ or you yourself?" When the Spirit shines and questions him in this way, he will be punctured by the cross and be unable to continue to quarrel with his wife. As long as he quarrels, the Holy Spirit will continue to ask, "Are you a crucified person? Are you hanging on the cross? Where is the light of the cross that you have seen?" As the Holy Spirit questions him, he will lose his ability to quarrel. Whenever this situation arises, the Holy Spirit will ask, "Is this from you or from Christ? Are you a crucified person? Is this what it means to see the light of the cross?" Thus, even if he is riding on a bus, he will be able to confess, and when he comes home from work, the Holy Spirit will ask, "Does a crucified person care about his face? Are you going to keep frustrating the Spirit and not apologize?" After such questioning, he will submit to the Lord and apologize to his wife. If a person wants to save his face, he does not have Christ; if he has Christ, he will be able to apologize. When we cooperate with the living Spirit, the Holy Spirit will kill our face and any effort to save our face. This is the experience and living of the cross.

## THE CROSS BRINGING IN RESURRECTION LIFE

All of these Christian experiences are precious and cause us to pass through death. The more we pass through death, the more life will be expressed from us. For example, the same brother who quarrels with his wife also endeavors to express the Lord and to allow the Lord's life to flow out. However, his natural strength is insufficient to express Christ and to allow His life to flow out. Once he is under the discipline of the Holy Spirit, however, the Spirit will enable him to cooperate with and submit to the Holy Spirit. Then his wife will sense a flavor of Christ coming from him, and she will see a little of

Christ's life in him because the death of the cross has been realized and is being carried out in him. The cross brings in both death and the expression of the resurrection life.

The Spirit will lead us into the death of the cross hour by hour and day by day. This is the leading of the Holy Spirit and the work of the Holy Spirit. The Holy Spirit in us wants to bring us into death every moment. The stronger the Holy Spirit's work in us is, the stronger our experience of the cross will be. Without the death of the cross, there is no work of the Holy Spirit; wherever the Holy Spirit works, there is a putting to death by the Spirit.

From morning until evening and from evening until morning, the Holy Spirit is working in us. He requires that we receive the cross, and He puts us into the death of the cross. When death operates in us, resurrection life can be manifested (2 Cor. 4:11-12). The way of life is death, and death is the way of life. When we walk on the way of life, we walk on the way of the death of the cross. The Christian life is a living of the cross and a living of death. Every day we experience death in the Holy Spirit, and we live and walk under death. Death deals with our person. As we are dealt with and broken, the life of God in us will have a free and smooth way. May the Lord be merciful to us!

# CHAPTER SEVEN

# KNOWING AND EXPERIENCING THE DISCIPLINE OF THE HOLY SPIRIT

Scripture Reading: Rom. 8:26-29

## THE OUTER MAN NEEDING TO BE BROKEN

The only goal of the Holy Spirit's work in us is to bring us into the experience of the death of the cross. The Holy Spirit desires to find a place and an opening for Christ in us; He is working Christ into us so that Christ can come out from within us. In order for Christ to come into us, we need to be broken and broadened, and in order for Christ to come out of us, our outer man needs to be torn down and many things in us need to be broken.

The result of the continual working of the Holy Spirit in us is to call us to receive the cross. The cross does the work of breaking and tearing down in us. God has put us on the cross in Christ so that our person, which troubles and limits God, can be dealt with through the cross.

After we have seen that the cross deals with our person, the Holy Spirit inwardly calls us to experience the cross day by day and moment by moment. In our daily living and in all things great and small, the Holy Spirit corrects and asks, "Are you living by yourself, or are you allowing Christ to live in you?" If we are willing to obey the voice of the Holy Spirit in everything, the Holy Spirit will ask, "Is your natural man the source of this matter, or is Christ the source of this matter? Is this being done by the natural man or by Christ?" These questions cause us to receive the breaking and tearing down work of the cross.

## SEEING MAN'S PROBLEM

When the Spirit does a killing work in us, we are brought into the death of the cross. However, it is not easy for us to receive the cross. Although we have seen the light concerning the cross, and the Spirit is inwardly calling us to come to the cross, we do not submit to Him easily. We do not receive the cross in a simple, unconditional, and straightforward way; we are not simple people. It is very difficult to deal with man, and it is very difficult to deal with our "I." We should not deny this before God. No matter how much light we receive, how much truth we hear, how often we read the Bible, how much we are touched by God, and how many lessons we learn, we still have places within us that we do not want to be broken by the cross. Hence, it is very difficult to deal with our person.

It was very easy for God to create the universe. He created everything out of nothing. However, it is very troublesome and difficult for God to deal with our person. In His creation of the universe, God spoke, and it was; He commanded, and it stood (Psa. 33:9). The universe was created in an instant. Nevertheless, when God deals with us, it may take Him twenty or thirty years, and He still may not complete His dealing with us. A carpenter who wants to modify a counter or a table will take only one or two days to finish the job, even if he spends much time and effort. But a few years or even a few decades can pass and God's dealing with man can still be unfinished. Dealing with man is truly a great problem.

Some people are not willing to receive the breaking of the cross even after much discipline; they pass through many difficulties but still cannot submit. They go through years of dealing and discipline from God and suffer many things to the point that it seems as if they have no strength to stand. However, when people contact them, they have not changed at all; they are intact in spite of the fact that they are full of wounds and scars. They have suffered much, but they are very shallow in their experience with very little learning and breaking and little or no experience of the cross. During their times of suffering, they encounter many hardships—their spouses pass away, their children become sick, their businesses fail, and their health deteriorates. Everything seems like a blow and affliction to them, but their person is not broken. We often think that those who pass through many afflictions and sufferings before the Lord have definitely learned some lessons, received some grace, and experienced the breaking of the cross. This is not necessarily true. Some can be full of wounds and scars yet remain intact and unbroken without learning any lessons. When we encounter such ones, it is a cause for worry, regret, and grief. It seems as if the more they are disciplined and afflicted, the more stubborn and hardened they become. Although they could be compared to a pile of cotton before their dealing, it is almost as if they have become a hard stone after their experiences of suffering. This is regrettable! Consequently, we must realize the difficulty of dealing with our person.

No one is easy to deal with; everyone is difficult. Sisters may feel that they are meeker than the brothers, but strictly speaking, the meeker one is, the harder it is to deal with her. Many people are stiff-necked and are subdued only with great difficulty. If we hit a piece of glass, it easily breaks; however, if we hit a piece of rubber, it will not break, no matter how hard we try. Brothers can be compared to glass, which breaks immediately, but sisters can be compared to rubber, which does not break no matter how hard it is hit. Since man is such a difficult case, God arranged for sufferings after man fell. For the male, He gave sufferings outside the body; for the female, He gave sufferings within the body. If we pay attention to grace, we will see that it is easier to deal with brothers and harder to deal with sisters. In the church life we do not need to be too concerned if we have to deal with brothers, but it takes much more effort to deal with sisters because they cannot be convinced with reasoning or common sense. If we cannot convince brothers with reasoning, we can convince them with common sense; however, when we deal with some sisters, we are utterly unable to convince them. They have their own reasonings and their own self. Sisters often think that their reasonings are right and that they even embody common sense itself; consequently, they feel that everyone should give in to them. It is very difficult to deal with sisters.

Thus, under God's arrangement, sufferings for sisters are often more difficult than those for brothers.

## GOD SOVEREIGNLY ARRANGING EVERYTHING IN OUR ENVIRONMENT TO BREAK OUR OUTER MAN

It is very hard to deal with man. We should not assume that because the Bible speaks of the shining and touching of the Holy Spirit and of the shining and calling of the cross that man will receive the cross and willingly accept the breaking of the cross. This is not the case. In fact, it is extremely rare to find such a person. Therefore, we need much grace, life, Spirit, truth, the word of the ministry, spiritual books, and the testimony of the church.

Furthermore, God also arranges the persons, things, and matters we encounter; He orders the environment and circumstances in our life so that He can break our person. He created the heavens and the earth, and He also prepared the air, water, and sunlight for our existence. He predestinated us before the foundation of the world (Eph. 1:4-5, 11), and He called us in time as His called ones (Gal. 1:15; 1 Cor. 1:1-2). After we are saved, God does a work of grace in us to cause us to love, desire, and pursue Him. Our neighbors may criticize us and think that we are superstitious. They may feel that our believing into Jesus is too much, but the more we love, pursue, and serve the Lord, the more joy we have within. All of these things are the result of the Lord's work of grace.

The Lord has predestined everything before the foundation of the world; He has ordered the family, spouse, and children we need for our transformation. He knows the kind of boss, co-workers, classmates, and neighbors that we need; therefore, He prepares and orders everything for us. We are God's chosen and predestined people, and we are those who find grace in God. God is doing a work of grace in us, and He has prepared everything in our environment and our circumstances in life for us.

The Holy Spirit also works in us through the messages spoken by His servants, the testimony of the saints, and the leading and fellowship of the church so that we may be touched to love the Lord Jesus, desire to pursue Him, and allow Him to live out of us. We even desire and pray to the Lord that we would be willing to be broken, subdued, and filled with Christ in order to live out Christ. While our desire and prayer come from the work of the Holy Spirit and are out of the Lord's grace, God knows that this alone is not sufficient to deal with our person. Consequently, He arranges everything in our environment, even the things that occurred before we were saved.

There was once a brother who suffered quite much from his parents before he was saved. He did not know the reason, but after he was saved, he realized that the suffering was prepared by the Lord to enable him to learn some spiritual lessons. After he was saved, he loved and pursued the Lord, and he prayed for a good wife. Because he had suffered much through his parents, he wanted a wife like Rebekah, who could comfort him (Gen. 24:67). The Lord accepted his prayers, and from that time forward, he began to consider whom to marry. Many older saints cared for him and introduced different sisters to him, but after he prayed and considered, he felt that these sisters were not the right one and did not fit his taste. In the end he met a sister with a peculiar disposition. As soon as they met each other, however, he felt she was very suitable. He eagerly hoped that she would be like Rebekah and comfort him; however, the dealing he received from this sister far surpassed the dealing he received from his parents. Nevertheless, he could not change his situation, because he could not divorce her and could not fight with her. Eventually, he realized that this arrangement was for him to learn more lessons.

We know of many similar examples. Many saints, after much consideration in choosing a spouse, eventually choose a "dear one" who deals with them. If we do not like an employee, we can fire him, and if a garment does not fit, we can tear it apart and use it as a rag; however, we cannot get rid of our spouse. Hence, we can only ask the Lord to make a way in us. Apart from being raptured or our spouse passing away, we have no options other than the way of the cross, the way of the discipline of the Holy Spirit. The discipline of the Holy Spirit is evident not only in small matters, but also in the big matters of our life. God often gives us a "dear" wife or "dear" husband, and at times we do not know whether we should laugh or cry. In reality, all we can do is turn to the Lord and pray to Him, because many years may pass, and we will not be raptured, and our spouse will be healthy and strong. Eventually, both husband and wife will live together for many years. This is a great discipline.

A great British evangelist named John Wesley lived in an environment where there was the freedom to choose whom to marry, and he chose a "dear" wife. One day Wesley was preaching, and many people were touched by his message; however, his wife came and yelled to everyone, urging them not to listen to his nonsense. Wesley's dear wife stayed the same and never changed; this was a great discipline to Wesley. Their married life was like a three-legged race involving much stumbling and even falling flat on their backs. These are clear indications of the discipline of the Holy Spirit.

There are great disciplinary arrangements in our human life that we cannot avoid or escape because we cannot be raptured nor die. These arrangements are severe. Before we were born, God chose and predestined us. He ordained everything for us. We make thousands of mistakes in our lives, and these mistakes are not our fault; everything has been set forth by God. In the matter of marriage, we may reject someone who lives near us, and we also may reject someone with whom we are familiar. If, in the end, we choose a peculiar person, we can only blame ourselves. Apparently it is our fault, but if God had not allowed it, He would only have needed to move His little finger, and the marriage would not have been possible. Two people must pass through many steps in order to marry. Thus, even if we do not have good discernment and make a wrong judgment, we still need to admit that it must have been allowed by God, because so many things need to occur in order for a marriage to take place. Without God's allowance, we could not have made a mistake even if we tried. I absolutely believe this.

Many times we purposefully want to do something that is wrong, but God does not allow it; thus, we cannot make a mistake no matter how hard we try. Sometimes, we are afraid of making mistakes, and we try to avoid and prevent mistakes, but after trying everything, we still make mistakes. Truly speaking, these matters are not in our hands; a man's heart devises his way, but Jehovah directs his steps (Prov. 16:9). We may choose a different path, but God Himself directs our steps. Nothing happens to us without God's permission, and nothing happens to us without being measured by God. Things do not happen to us randomly; everything that is measured to us by God is exactly right. God measures a certain person to be our spouse; this is arranged by God or, at the very least, permitted by God.

### THE DISCIPLINE OF THE HOLY SPIRIT

God's arrangement, ordination, permission, and move in our environment are the discipline of the Holy Spirit. The Holy Spirit rules over our environment, and He moves and arranges everything to break our person. Our spouse is God's helper in breaking us. Sometimes our spouse's cooperation with God is not sufficient, so He gives us children. If our spouse, as God's chief helper, is not sufficient to deal with us, He adds more little helpers to deal with us. If these helpers are not sufficient, He can add three, four, or even five more helpers. Sometimes it is not enough to have sons, so God also gives us daughters.

Every brother and sister is created and redeemed by God, and we are all under God's grace and care. We are all led, cultivated, and perfected by God. Since we admit that this is true, we should see that every important matter in our human life, such as our husband, wife, parents, or children, did not come to us by chance. Nothing comes to us without a purpose. Everything is arranged by God; some things were arranged by God before we were born, and some things come to us through our prayer. For example, because a sister may have only daughters, she prays for a son and receives a son. However, this son should actually be named Dealing because the more he grows up, the more he brings dealings to his mother. These things are all accomplished and arranged by God.

I hope all the brothers and sisters would have a deep impression that the tools God uses to grace us are the Bible, the Holy Spirit, the church, the saints, the light of the truth, and especially the environment. Strictly speaking, the environment and our circumstances are the discipline of the Holy Spirit. The discipline of the Holy Spirit is the greatest tool in God's ordination. Many people treasure the Bible and pay much attention to the Holy Spirit, but they do not pay attention to the environment; they do not pay attention to the people, things, and matters they encounter. A Christian who is spiritual and lives before God needs to "read" three things every day. First, he needs to read the Bible. Second, he needs to read his inward sense. Third, he needs to read his environment and circumstances, which are the people, things, and matters around him. Many people read the Bible well, and they also can read the sense in their spirit, but they are unable to read the people, things, and matters they encounter. Have we ever considered why God gave us our spouse? Why did God give us a certain kind of child? Have we ever studied them and tried to understand them? Many brothers and sisters memorize the Bible and are also keenly aware of the sense in their spirit, yet regrettably they have never studied and do not understand the environment around them. They neglect and ignore their circumstances and environment, and they miss the benefit that can be gained from them. This is a big mistake. Our circumstances and environment are a great means arranged by God for dealing with our person and subduing us.

## THE DISCIPLINE OF THE HOLY SPIRIT CONFORMING US TO THE IMAGE OF GOD'S SON AND MANIFESTING GOD'S GRACE AND POWER

Romans 8 speaks specifically about the Holy Spirit; the first half of chapter 8 speaks of the Holy Spirit, and the second half speaks of the environment, circumstances, and sufferings, including God causing all things to work together for good (v. 28). For our spiritual understanding, it is not enough only to know the Holy Spirit; we must also know the "all things" in our circumstances. The purpose of all things working together is to gain man's cooperation to conform him to the image of God's Son and to deal with man to the extent that he is exactly the same as God's Son. For this reason, the Holy Spirit raises up a yearning prayer in us, and He intercedes for us with groanings which cannot be uttered, causing us to desire God's grace within, to have Christ's image, and to be filled with Christ's life (v. 26). With this kind of desire and prayer of the Holy Spirit within us, these prayers and groanings pass through the Holy Spirit and reach God. When God hears such prayer, He prepares the environment around us to cause all things to work together to break and deal with us and, thereby, to transform us. When our desire to be filled with Christ and to bear the image of God's Son is matched with the Holy Spirit's intercession, God hears our prayer and raises up an environment to deal with us. This environment may be our spouse or children, but everything occurs in order to break and subdue us. This is a great discipline.

Even a person like Paul, who was greatly blessed and experienced grace in such a strong and deep way, spoke of a thorn that pierced and pricked him every day. When it reached a point where he could bear it no longer, he prayed that the Lord would remove the thorn. The Lord answered, "My grace is sufficient for you" (2 Cor. 12:9). The thorn in Paul enabled him to enjoy the grace of God and experience God's power being perfected in weakness. Some wives may be thorns to their husbands, some husbands may be thorns to their wives, and some children may be thorns to their parents, but all of these things are allowed by the Lord in order to deal with and break us. We may pray and hope that others will change, but the more we pray in this way, the clearer we are that nothing will change. Our thorn will continue to pierce us, trouble us, and bother us. This is the environment that God has created to cause us to know the Lord's grace and to experience the Lord's power.

In the eyes of unbelievers, a Christian's circumstances often seem very strange, and they lack an understanding of what they mean. God, however, knows that He is the One who arranges everything. There is not one proper Christian who does not have some troubles and pressure in his life; there is not one proper Christian whose living is smooth and care-free. Every proper Christian has some difficulty or burden and is under some kind of oppression or affliction in all kinds of circumstances. This is the discipline of the Holy Spirit. The purpose of the inward shining and calling of the Holy Spirit and of the outward pressure of the environment is simply to defeat our person. If we see this, we will bow and say, "O God, I worship You. What You arranged can never be wrong. This is what I need. Even if I make mistakes, You never make mistakes, and I still worship You." At such a moment, we will be blessed within, and the power of the Lord's life will bear us, support us, and enable us to endure the things that we cannot endure in ourselves. At such moments, we will have the Lord's inward presence and joy.

If we learn these lessons well, our spouse will produce the effect of the cross in us, and our self, preference, opinion, inclination, thought, and all that we are will be put to death. God often breaks us through our spouses. If we submit ourselves to the Lord and receive this, we will meet the Lord within, and we will be blessed by having life as the power that carries us through and enables us to endure what we could not endure.

## CONCLUSION

We need to see that real growth in life does not depend only on the outward shining of the Bible and our inward cooperation with the Holy Spirit; we also need our environment and circumstances, which are the discipline of the Holy Spirit. If we really live before the Lord, we will live in the Spirit and treasure the circumstances arranged by God. We will treasure the people, things, and matters around us. When truth is released, there will be a response in us, and through our prayer the Spirit will begin to work in us. At the same time, God's hand will also arrange things in our outward environment to reinforce the light of His truth and the work of the Spirit. The purpose of this inward and outward work is to break, subdue, and deal with our person. If the Lord is merciful and gracious to us, these messages will help us see how the Lord's life has become our life and how much His life wants to have the ground to live out of us.

God's life, the revelation and light that we have seen, and the discipline of the Holy Spirit in our circumstances carry out the work of the cross in us. The cross brings in the life of Christ, and the death of the cross brings in resurrection. Those who have the expression of the death of the cross also have the expression of life. This is the way of life.

# CHAPTER EIGHT

# KNOWING THE CHURCH AND
# THE BASIS FOR DISCERNING THE CHURCH

Scripture Reading: Matt. 16:15-18; Eph. 1:22-23; 5:29-32

Concerning the matter of life, I believe the Spirit of God has shown us some light in the preceding chapters to see the life in us and what it wants to produce in us. In this chapter we will look at the matter of the church. Today, regardless of who they are, everyone feels that the church is a great thing. Consequently, the matter of the church is a great subject.

## THE CHURCH BEING THE BODY OF CHRIST

We must know the church, which is the Body of Christ (Eph. 1:22-23). I believe that when many saints first read about the Body of Christ, they feel uncertain about the meaning of the church being the Body of Christ.

There are many different thoughts about the church. Some people say that a chapel where Christians meet is the church, some people say that any organization or group in Christianity is the church, and some people even think that an evangelical group or a missionary organization is the church. According to man's natural thought, the church refers to either a building, chapel, organization, group, or denomination. These interpretations come from man's concept, not from the Bible. The Bible never speaks of these things. The church is spiritual, high, and even mysterious (5:32; 1 Tim. 3:15-16); therefore, the church is not merely a building, a chapel, or a Christian organization, group, or denomination.

The Bible clearly speaks of the church as the Body of Christ (Eph. 1:22-23). This word may be difficult for us to understand, but if we apply it to a human body and consider it from the perspective of the human body, we will see something. For example, when we look at a brother, we see his body and his head, and by looking at him, we can understand a little more about the church as the Body of Christ.

## THE LIFE OF THE CHURCH BEING CHRIST

When we look at the brother, we see his body and his head. This reveals two significant things. First, the body is the brother's person; it is he himself. Second, his head and his body have the same life; the two are just one. No one would ever think that he has one life and that his body has a different life. Everyone can clearly see that the body and the person have one life. Truly speaking, his body is a part of him. He has two parts—the head and the body. These two parts together, that is, his head with his body, make him a complete person. Sometimes when we take pictures, we accidentally capture only the head or half of the body. Typically we do not like such photographs. In a normal condition, there is one complete life when the head and the body are joined together.

We are clear that a person has only one life. The life in the body is the life in the head, and also the life in the head is the life in the body. The two are one. This is also true of the mysterious relationship between Christ and the church; Christ is the Head of the church, and the church is the Body of Christ. The two are complete in one life. The life in the Head is also the life in the Body. The life in the Body is also the life in the Head; in fact, it is the life of the Head. Please remember that the church as the Body of Christ means that the life of Christ is the life of the church. Christ and the church have not only the same life but one life. The two lives are not only the same, but they are one as well. Christ's life is in the church, and the life of the church is Christ's life. The two have one life, which is Christ Himself.

## THE CHURCH AND CHRIST BEING JOINED TOGETHER AND THE CHURCH BEING CHRIST

The body and head of a person are joined together; nevertheless, they are not two but one. Similarly, the church as the Body of Christ means that the church and Christ are joined together; the two are one. Ephesians 5:31-32 speaks of a husband and wife becoming one flesh, signifying that Christ and the church are one body. The church is "bone of Christ's bones" and "flesh of Christ's flesh" (cf. Gen. 2:23); the church and Christ are one. We need to keep these references firmly in mind, because from them we know where the church comes from, what the church is, what the church should be called, and what the church should do.

Hence, we can boldly declare that the church is not only the Body of Christ but that the church is Christ (1 Cor. 12:12). When we see a brother and touch his body, we say, "This is Brother So-and-so"; we do not say, "This is Brother So-and-so's body." His body is not merely his body; the body is the brother himself because his body is a part of him. In the same way, the church as the Body of Christ means that the church is a part of Christ. The church is Christ because the church and Christ have one life; thus, the church is Christ.

## THE CHURCH BEING OUT OF CHRIST, UNTO CHRIST, AND ONE WITH CHRIST

The church comes from Christ; it is out of Christ. When Peter realized that Christ is the Son of God, the Lord Jesus immediately spoke of the building up of the church (Matt. 16:15-18). This means that as soon as we know Christ, the church is produced. Once we know the living Christ and have His life, the church is produced in us, and the element of the church is in us. This is possible because the church is Christ. When we believe into Christ, His life comes into us, and we have Christ within. When we have Christ, we have the church.

When God first created man, He formed Adam out of clay. God did not create two persons in the beginning; He created only one person. God did not create two persons, a male and a female, and then put them together. God created only one man. This man was perfect and lacked nothing. The man whom God created was called Adam. God opened Adam's side and took out a rib from which He built a woman, Eve. God brought Eve to Adam, and the two became one (Gen. 2:21-24). This is a type of Christ and the church in the Bible.

God took clay from the earth and molded it into a man,

and He called the man Adam, who was a complete person. Nevertheless, this man was only Adam, a male; there was no female. When God made the woman, He did not create her apart from Adam; instead, God took a rib out of Adam, and this rib became Eve. Then God brought Eve to Adam, and the two became one.

When God became flesh, He became a man. Adam typified Jesus the Nazarene (Rom. 5:14). When the Lord Jesus went to the cross, His side was opened, and blood and water flowed from His side (John 19:34). His redeeming blood and eternal life flowed from Him and entered into us and millions of others, making us the church. The church comes out of Christ and becomes one with Christ. God's life, which was in Jesus the Nazarene, passed through death and resurrection and entered into us. Those of us who are saved are called the church.

God's life came into Jesus, and He was called Christ; God's life also entered into everyone who is saved, and we are called the church. The content of the church and the content of Christ are the same; there is no difference. The life in Jesus the Nazarene is also the life in the church; these two are really one life. The church is out of Christ, produced from Christ, and unto Christ. The church and Christ are one. Hence, the church is out of Christ, unto Christ, and in Christ. The church and Christ are one.

## THE BASIS FOR DISCERNING THE CHURCH

Now we must consider how to discern the church, that is, what the church is and what it is not. This is a great question. When we meet some Christians or a Christian group, they may say that they are the church, but how do we discern whether or not they truly are the church? How can we judge this matter? If we want to discern whether a Christian group is the church, the strongest basis for discerning this is the fact that the church is the Body of Christ. The church as the Body of Christ comes out of Christ and is unto Christ. This is the strongest basis for discerning the church. If a person does not know this, he cannot know the church in an accurate way; his knowledge concerning the church will be outward rather than inward.

We need to realize that the church is out of Christ and produced by Christ. Since Christ produces the church, the church and Christ are one, and the church is Christ Himself. This word may sound very simple, but we must have a thorough understanding and a clear view in order to discern whether or not a Christian group is the church. Because there are many aspects in the interpretation of this matter, we need to spend some time to study it.

We cannot remain as children; rather, we need to become full grown. We all know that children like outward excitement. If we tell them stories and play with them, they are very interested and excited. However, if we talk to them about their grandfathers and genealogy, they quickly become bored. This is because they cannot receive serious matters; they can only receive exciting things. Often we are like little children, who can receive only exciting messages, not serious messages. If someone wants to tell us about our spiritual genealogy, we begin to fall asleep and are unable to listen. It seems as if these things do not matter to us. Consequently, few among God's children are able to receive these words.

Indeed, these words cannot be received by those who like outward excitement. This word can be received only by those who follow the Lord in a serious way, those who want to know their spiritual genealogy and history, those who desire to know who they are. These matters are of no consequence to an immature Christian; however, the more mature a Christian is, the more he wants to know these matters.

## THERE BEING ONLY ONE CHURCH IN THE UNIVERSE

No person has two bodies. If someone had two bodies, he would be a monster. Christ has only one Body, and this shows that in the whole universe there is only one church, not two. In the past I traveled quite frequently, and when people met me, they always asked, "Where do you live?" If I replied, "I live in Taipei," then they would ask, "How many churches are in Taipei?" I did not know how to answer them because this can be compared to asking, "How many bodies does a person have?" Regrettably, many Christians ask this kind of question. Similarly, if someone comes from Tainan, people ask, "How many churches are in Tainan?" This question has no basis in the truth; however, this kind of talk is very common in Christianity.

When people ask how many churches are in the place we live, we should be very clear that this is the same as asking someone from the United States how many moons are in New York or asking someone from England how many suns are in London. This would be a joke. Everyone knows that there is only one sun and one moon for us in the universe, but there are thousands and millions of stars. According to typology in the Bible, the sun typifies Christ (Mal. 4:2), the moon typifies the church (S. S. 6:10), and the stars typify the saints (Gen. 22:17). Just as there is only one sun, there is also only one moon; just as there is only one Christ, there is also only one church. The church as the Body of Christ cannot be two; she can only be one.

Some have asked, "Since there are several dozen local churches in Taiwan, how can there be only one church?" This is like saying that there must be many moons in Taiwan since there are different expressions of the moon in Taiwan. If we ask the brothers from England how many moons are in England, they would laugh and answer that there is only one moon. Only a little child, thinking there must be many moons because there is an expression of the moon in many places, would say, "I saw a moon in England, and I saw another moon in the United States." Even in two hundred and eighty different places, there will not be two hundred and eighty moons. We all know that there is only one moon.

## THE CHURCH BEING EXPRESSED IN EACH LOCALITY

There is only one church in the universe. However, the church is expressed in each locality. There is one expression in Taipei, one expression in Tainan, one expression in Taichung, and one expression in Kaohsiung. Wherever there is a group of Christians, there is an expression of the church in that place. We need to see that the church is one and that there is only one church in the universe. Nevertheless, the church is expressed in localities; every locality has an expression of the church. In a large locality, there may be a larger expression; in a small locality, there may be a smaller expression. But whether the locality is large or small, the nature of the expression is the same; the church is one. Regardless of how many expressions there are and regardless of whether these expressions are large or small, they are all one.

We have clearly seen that there is only one church in the universe. In principle, the church should have only one expression in the locality of Taipei. This is correct. Nevertheless, we need to ask about the present condition in Taipei. If we ask how many churches are in Taipei, we are speaking like those in Christianity. Instead, we should ask about the condition of the church in Taipei. Today there should be only one expression of the church in Taipei, but we actually see a different situation. Seemingly there are many different expressions, as if someone has cut the moon into pieces, hanging one piece in the southwest corner of the city and another piece in the southeast corner. It seems as if people are unable to see one moon in Taipei. Instead, they see individual pieces, perhaps as many as thirty-five scattered and broken pieces. This is not a normal situation.

We should see only one "moon" in Taipei. However, we do not see one "moon" in Taipei but rather many fragmented and individual pieces. Consider the neighborhood around Jen-Ai Road. There are at least three different signs: one says Baptist Church, another says Presbyterian Church, and a third says Christian Assembly Place. This is not normal; it is abnormal. This abnormality is caused by man's confusion. I do not need to say too much here, but I want to show the saints that the genuine condition of the church is one of confusion. Based on the revelation in the Bible, there is only one church in the universe, and there should be only one expression of the church in each locality. However, today this expression is fragmented, confused, and abnormal. We can see many different groups in one place, but they are not proper. The church should express a condition of being one, not one of being fragmented and scattered.

## DIVISIONS BEING CAUSED BY BRINGING THINGS OTHER THAN CHRIST INTO THE CHURCH

If we study the reason for the division and scattering of

the church, we find one thing: things other than Christ have been brought into the church. We all know that the church is Christ Himself, that Christ and the church are one, and that the church is joined to Christ. The church is divided and confused because of one reason only—something other than Christ has been brought into the church. As soon as something other than Christ is brought into the church, the church becomes divided and confused. All division and confusion are due to bringing something other than Christ into the church.

Today's Christianity has been divided into many sects and denominations because things other than Christ have been brought into the church. There is only one Christ, and Christ cannot be divided (1 Cor. 1:13); however, divisions and confusion occur when things and matters other than Christ are brought into the church, creating a human mixture. When things and matters other than Christ are brought into the church, the church is divided. If a brother brings his thoughts into the church, the church will have a problem, and if another brother brings his concepts into the church, the church will be in confusion. There are not many reasons for division and confusion in the church; there is one basic reason—things other than Christ are brought into the church.

## THINGS THAT THE CHURCH SHOULD NOT HAVE

Having nothing other than Christ is a principle by which we can measure all of Christianity. If we measure according to this principle, we will discover that there are three categories of things that the church should not have and which are outside of Christ. This does not mean that there are only three categories. There are many categories, but we will speak of only these three.

### Special Names

The first category is the matter of special names. Since the church is the Body of Christ, she should not have another name. We can speak of the church as the church of Christ or the church of God (cf. 1 Thes. 1:1; 1 Cor. 1:2), but we cannot add any other name. If we add any other name, we will bring things other than Christ into the church. However, in today's

Christianity many different names have been brought into the church. For example, the Lutheran Church brought in Luther, and the Wesleyan Church brought in Wesley. There are so many examples that we cannot enumerate them all. According to one survey, there are approximately 1,500 different names of groups in Christianity.

We should not overlook the matter of the name. If a woman is married to Brother Huang, according to the Chinese proverb, she is following Brother Huang. Prior to marrying Brother Huang, she was Miss Tsai because her maiden name was Tsai, but now she is Mrs. Huang. Since she is Mrs. Huang, she should not print name cards calling herself Mrs. Chang. This would be terrible! If Brother Huang learned of this, it would be a very serious matter. Hence, we need to see that we should not overlook the matter of a name. Since the church of Christ is the church of Christ, why should we call her the Lutheran Church or the Methodist Church? This can be compared to calling a sister Mrs. Chang when she is really Mrs. Huang. If she wants to be called Mrs. Chang, her husband's last name must be Chang. Even if a Christian group receives much help from Wesley, they are unconsciously bringing the things of man into the church when they call themselves the Wesleyan Church. When the things of man are brought into the church, the church becomes confused and divided.

## Special Beliefs

The second reason for the confusion and division of Christianity is that they have special beliefs and creeds. Many sects and factions are produced because of these differences. It seems that the Bible is not sufficient for many groups in Christianity, because in addition to the Bible they must have creeds. Every sect has a different creed. We need to realize that these creeds are not according to the Bible. Practices based on special beliefs and creeds result in separation and division from others. For example, the Presbyterian Church emphasizes the elders' management of the church, and the Baptist Church emphasizes a method of baptism. These things become ordinances or creeds that distinguish Christians from one another. Many of these things are apart from the Bible and cannot be found in the Bible. The Bible says, "He who believes and is baptized shall be saved" (Mark 16:16); the Bible does not regulate how a person should be baptized or what method to use. Insisting on certain methods results in that method becoming a special creed among a group. This separates them from others.

When we study this matter in a serious way, we can see that every sect and group has a special creed. Sometimes people ask, "Even though you say that you have no special name and that you are not a denomination, what are your beliefs?" We do not have any belief apart from the Bible. All our beliefs are in the Bible, and we do not have anything other than the Bible; we do not have special creeds or beliefs. Special creeds and special beliefs come from man's will and natural concept. When the things of man are brought into the church, the church becomes confused and divided. This is the second thing that the church should not have.

## Special Fellowships

The third thing that the church should not have is special fellowships. This also causes confusion and division. Among Christians, there are groups that insist on everyone having the same beliefs. For instance, if they believe there is one rapture before the great tribulation, they insist that everyone must believe that Christians will be raptured before the great tribulation. This fellowship is a special fellowship, not a common fellowship. In proper circumstances, as the children of God with the same Father, we can have fellowship with one another in the Father's life (1 John 1:3). However, some Christians will not fellowship with those who do not share their views, beliefs, and feelings. Their fellowship is a special fellowship which has been brought in by man; it is outside of Christ.

Having special names, special beliefs, and special fellowships are three main factors that cause division and confusion in the church. If a group has any of these, it loses both the nature and the ground of the church. If any Christian group has a special name, special belief, or special fellowship, it immediately loses the ground of the church because there is only one church in the universe, and there is also only one expression of the church in each locality.

## Man Being the Greatest Hindrance to the Church

In addition to the preceding three matters, being independent is another serious point concerning the church. Some Christian groups do not violate the three matters above; that is, they do not have special names, special beliefs, or special fellowships, but they are independent. Since they do not have special names, special beliefs, and special fellowships, their condition should be quite normal. However, they remain individualistic and independent; they do not have fellowship with the saints in other localities and even do not recognize such fellowship. This is another great problem brought in by the things of man.

If we know that the church is Christ and that the church and Christ are one, we will see the seriousness of this matter; the church is a strong test to us. Today the church has lost her nature and the proper ground because the things of man have been brought into the church.

The saints are lovable and love the Lord very much. Nevertheless, when we touch the matter of the church, a few say, "I think this matter should be done this way, and that matter should be done that way." It seems as if things should be done only according to their preferences. These are human words; they are the things of man which should not be brought into the church. There are so many divisions in today's Christianity because many people bring their own views and preferences into the church. When we speak of the matter of names, for example, some people say that having a name is good, and they even have a list of names that can be used. They speak in a very light and loose way, and sects are produced.

If we do not touch the matter of the church, everything is fine; however, once we touch the matter of the church, our whole being should be in awe because the church and Christ are one. Anything that is apart from Christ is not the church. Therefore, the church does not have anything that is of you, me, or any man. The only things that can be brought into the church must be of Christ and must be Christ (Col. 3:10-11).

Whenever we bring our own things, our own views, our own preferences, opinions, intents, desires, and ways into the church, the church is nullified. All of these cause the church to lose her nature and the local ground of oneness.

Thus, we need to see that the reason there is so much confusion and division in Christianity is because believers do not want to submit and prostrate themselves before the church. Man's views, intentions, inclinations, and preferences have come into the church, and these things result in different sects. When believers who love and seek the Lord are willing to prostrate themselves, putting aside the things of man, their eyes will be opened to see the ground of the church. Today the most difficult problem is for the things that are apart from Christ to be put aside; instead, believers continue to hold on to these things rather than to Christ. This is the greatest frustration to the church.

### THREE TESTS FOR EXAMINING THE CHURCH

When we touch the matter of the church, we should not simply look at the outward things. We also need to touch the church's inward essence. It is easy for us to bring our own opinions, preferences, ways, and practices into the church life. This is a big problem. Some may ask, "How can we be certain that what we bring into the church is not something of man?" There are three tests in this regard. The first test is the Bible. We must consider whether our actions, including our thoughts, views, activities, and practices, are according to the Bible. Whatever does not match the Bible is certainly something of man. If something does not match the Bible, we cannot allow it into the church. We need to filter everything with the Bible so that we can keep out everything that is not according to the Bible.

However, it is not sufficient simply to test everything by the Bible. We need another test, and that is to examine whether the things we are bringing into the church are of Christ or of ourselves. The church is Christ, and the content of the church is also Christ. Everything in the church should be Christ. We should examine ourselves to see whether the things we bring into the church are of Christ or of ourselves.

The third test is the Holy Spirit. We need to pass through the test of the Holy Spirit. We need to ask ourselves if what we are bringing into the church is under the ruling of the Spirit in us or if it is from our own decision. Is it from the operation of the Spirit in us, or is it from our own opinion? This is the root of every problem.

Today the churches in most localities can pass the first test; their condition is according to the Bible. Nevertheless, when we examine them according to the second test, we have to admit that many of their ways are not necessarily of Christ; probably, they are related to the things of man. If we examine them with the third test, we discover even more problems. The activities in some local churches are mainly the work of the flesh; we cannot see the authority of the Holy Spirit in these activities. Outwardly, they are according to the Bible, but in reality, the flesh is moving and reigning, and the Holy Spirit has no authority among them.

When we examine the church, we need to examine her from within and without, according to these things, to determine whether it has a special name, special belief, or special fellowship. Are they an independent unit or an independent group? Are their activities according to the Bible and of the Holy Spirit? If the results of these tests are positive, we can bow our heads and say, "O Lord, I have met the church here." But if the results are negative, we should be very cautious.

The church is the Body of Christ, and the church is Christ Himself; thus, in the church there is nothing other than Christ. Everything in the church should be out of Christ and out of the Spirit. Moreover, every local church should have fellowship with the churches in other localities. I hope we all would see how to have the reality of the church in our practice of the church.

CHAPTER NINE

# THE PROPER CHURCH—
# THE MINGLING OF GOD WITH MAN

## THE MYSTERY OF SALVATION—
## GOD MINGLING WITH MAN

The saints need to see the basic point that the church is Christ Himself, that is, Christ Himself in the saints. Even though this is a very basic matter, the church is a great subject. We must look to the Lord for His mercy to see that the church is nothing other than Christ. Anything that does not match Christ is not the church. This may cause some people to ask, "What is Christ?" Christ is God becoming flesh, and God becoming flesh means that God is mingled with man.

God established a special law in the universe when He created everything: each is "according to their kind" (Gen. 1:11-12, 21, 24-26). God does not mix two things of different kinds together; He wants everything to be according to its kind. However, God also has a great intention to mingle Himself with man; God wants to mingle divinity with humanity in order to make them one. The issue of such a mingling contains both the element of man and the element of God. Both God and man are included in this mingling.

In God's salvation the one goal that He wants to attain, the one matter that He wants to accomplish, and the one result that He wants to produce in the universe are to mingle the divine and human natures into one. Apart from this mingling, God does not allow different things to mingle and become one. The mystery of salvation hinges upon God and man becoming one. The center of salvation depends upon God working Himself into man and mingling man with Him. Regrettably, many saints do not see this matter, but if we take this matter away from God's salvation, there would be no more salvation. If we take away the joining of God and man, the mingling of God Himself with man, there would be no salvation. The mystery of God's salvation, the center of salvation, the mystery of life, and the mystery of union all hinge upon this: God entering into man and mingling Himself with man so that the two become one.

## THE NATURE OF THE CHURCH
## BEING THE MINGLING OF GOD AND MAN

The first step of the mingling of God with man was in one person, that is, in Jesus the Nazarene, and this One is Christ. Christ is God becoming flesh, the mingling of God with man. When Jesus the Nazarene was on the earth, it would have been correct to say that He was a man, but it would also have been correct to say that He was God (John 1:1, 14). He is God and man mingled together. After the death and resurrection of Christ, this principle in Christ was expanded through the enlargement of the mingling of God and man. All the saved ones are His expansion and enlargement.

Through the death and resurrection of Christ, God in the Holy Spirit has entered into thousands, even millions, of people and mingled with them. The result of this mingling is an enlarged Christ. This enlarged Christ is a mysterious Christ, a corporate Christ. When God was incarnated in Bethlehem, the result of the mingling of God with man was small and individual. But through the death and resurrection of Christ, God in the Holy Spirit has entered into millions of people and mingled with them. The result of this mingling is an enlarged Christ, a universal Christ, a mysterious Christ. This Christ is the church, which is also called the Body of Christ. The church is the enlarged Christ, and this enlarged Christ is the same as Christ.

After we receive this word, we must apply it. For example, a person studying mathematics may understand theories of mathematics, but he still needs to solve math problems and apply the theories practically. All the serving brothers in the church should pay attention to how much our service contains the element of man and how much it contains the element of God. When we serve in our locality, we are often required to lead the saints to serve together, and sometimes we also make arrangements for the brothers who function as deacons. We should make these arrangements according to the mingling of God and man in us. Making practical arrangements should not come out of the human element of a certain brother but out of the mingling of God and man.

If we can sense only our self when we are doing things, it is not the church. The church is an entity composed of the mingling of God with man, an organism made up of the mingling of God with man. If we are acting without God, it is not the church. The church is an entity composed of the mingling of God with man. The nature of the church is God mingled with man; she is the mingling of God with man.

Today the situation in Christianity is very chaotic. Everyone says that he is right, and it seems as if it is quite difficult to judge who is right and who is wrong. However, if we have spiritual insight and knowledge, we will know what the church is. Everything has a nature, and its nature determines what it is. If we paint two chairs using gold paint, some people may think that the chairs are made of gold because they look only at the outward color. However, the final determination depends upon the nature of the two chairs. Today if some people put up a sign that indicates they are the church, it does not necessarily mean that they are the church. If someone contacts them, he will know whether they are actually a sect, because a sect will have a special belief, special name, or special fellowship.

We should not judge based on outward appearances without considering the inward nature. Therefore, regardless of where we are, we need to ask ourselves whether the nature of our church is the mingling of God with man or merely the element of our self. If all we have is our self, it lacks the nature of the church, and it is not the church. A cup of tea is the mingling of tea and water. If a cup of water has only the color of tea without the taste of tea, it is not a cup of tea. The church is the mingling of God with man; the church is Christ, the Body of Christ, and the fullness of Christ. The portion overflowing out from Christ is the church; the church is Christ Himself.

Whenever we have some activities in the church, regardless of whether it involves a decision, an arrangement, or a suggestion, we should always remember that God must be mingled with us, that we must be mingled with God, and that we must submit to God. We may make an arrangement, but we should be able to say, "I am mingled with God, and I live in God." We need to pray first and ask, "O Lord, does this matter please You? Is this how You want to decide things? Is this how You want to arrange things? Is this what You want to do?" We need to continually touch the sense of the Lord's presence within, and we need to put all our views, opinions, plans, and ideas under His feet, under the Lord Himself, and submit to His light. We should not choose according to ourselves; instead, we should choose what God chooses, suggest what God suggests, and decide what God decides. Then we will be able to see brothers moving on the earth according to the mingling of God and man.

If God finds a person on the earth and mingles Himself with him, such a one is surely in God's move. Such a move becomes the move of the church. This is a very crucial and advanced point: the church is Christ—the mingling of God with man.

## SUBJECTION TO GOD BEING NECESSARY
## FOR THE MINGLING OF GOD AND MAN

The church is the mingling of God with man, but a great principle in this mingling is man's subjection to God. The mingling of God with man involves man's subjection to God, not God's subjection to man. Quite often people ask, "Why are men and women not equal in the church?" An older sister once questioned me, "Why does God want the sisters to be subject to the brothers?" So I asked her, "Why is your eye placed under your eyebrow?" She replied, "Forget it; you always win." The relationship between a husband and a wife is an exact description of the relationship between Christ and the church. A wife's subjection to her husband signifies the church's subjection to Christ.

Ephesians 5:31 says, "For this cause a man shall leave his father and mother and shall be joined to his wife, and the two shall be one flesh." Since the wife and the husband become one, who is the head? If there are two heads on the same body, this would be monstrous. In a wedding the bride generally covers her head with a veil. Why does the bridegroom not cover his head? When two people are married, one person's head should be covered because there can be only one head for the couple, each of whom previously had their own head. When a couple is married, they declare to the universe that the two have become one; that is, they have one head. Nevertheless, we must ask the married brothers who have some experience in their married life whether their marriage has two heads or one. In the saints' homes we often see many heads; consequently, there are many problems. Having more than one head makes our living a very complicated matter.

We need to ask ourselves whether there are two heads or one in our married life. I am afraid that some will say that they have at least one and a half heads in their married life, with one head being the brother's and the half head being the sister's. The sisters need to cover their "half head" so that they do not nullify the meaning of head covering.

The universe has laws. It is a marvelous thing that in every place and throughout all time, brides have covered their heads during a wedding. According to God's light, when two people are married, the two become one. There is only one head, not two. In order for there to be one head, the second head needs to be covered. This is a picture of Christ and the church becoming one. When two become one flesh, one head needs to be covered. The church is not the head; rather, Christ is the Head of the church. Christ is the Head of the church, and the church is His Body. Just as the church is subject to Christ, a wife should be subject to her husband. The two become one. Hence, in order for God and man to be mingled together as one, man needs to obey God and be subject to Him.

Some may ask, "If a wife is subject to her husband, does she become a person without any consciousness? Is she like a chair that has no feelings about where it is placed and how it is used?" This is not a reasonable thought, because sisters have a mind, emotion, and will. Being subject to her husband does not mean that a sister no longer uses her mind, emotion, and will; rather, it means that she accepts God's will, God's view, and is subject to God. As God moves within, her will submits to God's will and her mind accepts God's thought. She does not care for herself. This can be compared to the Chinese proverb which says, "A husband sings, and the wife follows."

We need to be subject to God, but this does not mean that we do not have any consciousness, choice, preference, or thought. In a strong and spiritual church, the believers are full of choices, preferences, and thoughts; however, their choices are God's choices, their preferences are God's preferences, and their ideas are God's ideas. Outwardly it may seem as if only the church is moving, but actually God is mingled with the church and moving in the church. As far as such Christians are concerned, God is mingled with them in their living and moving. Their move is the move of God with man; the two have become one. Therefore, as far as the church is concerned, she is truly both man and God. No matter how we look at her, there is a special flavor of both God and man. We always should remember this point.

If we go to a certain place and discover a group of zealous Christians, we should not praise them quickly, saying, "All the churches should have this kind of zeal; this is the proper condition of the church." We should not react quickly. Instead, we should ask, "Is this zeal only of man, or has it been stirred up by God's love in them?" These are two different sources. Some expressions of zeal come solely from man, but other expressions come from man's love for God and from his subjection under God's hand which are the result of God's operation in man. The two expressions are different; one comes from man's zeal, the other from the mingling of God with man. The former is not of the church, but the latter is of the church. This is a great matter and crucial principle. We must keep this principle.

If we want to know whether a church in a locality is the church, we must hold on to the principle that the church is the mingling of God with man and that the move of the church is the move of the mingling of God with man. It is not a simple and easy matter to make a judgment based on this principle, and if we are careless, we can easily make mistakes. We should take this as a basic principle but not make any judgment according to this principle in a loose and careless way.

## THE CHURCH NEEDING TO PASS THROUGH THE FILTER OF THE BIBLE

If a group calls itself the church, its inward condition, activities, and everything about it must be according to the Bible. According to the Bible, a local church should not have a special name, a special belief, or a special fellowship. Regrettably, most Christian groups today cannot pass these three tests as a filter.

First, almost every group has a name. We know that the moon is the moon; we do not need to add a special name to it. Similarly, the church is the church; she does not need another name. If people ask us what church we are from, we should tell them that we are in the church. If we reply, "I am from the Church Assembly Hall," it will puzzle people and cause them to wonder exactly what the Church Assembly Hall is. We need to see that the church is one. The name of the church is simply the church; other than this, the church has no other name.

We need to see that "Church Assembly Hall" is not our name; it refers to the place where we meet. For example, the house where Mr. Chang lives is called "Chang's residence." This refers only to a place. We do not use "Church Assembly Hall" as our name, but government regulations require us to register a name. Thus, we are forced to use this. We do not have a choice, but we do not designate ourselves by this.

We do not want to use a name, because the church is simply the church; she cannot have any other name. If someone puts a sign in front of Mr. Chang's house, saying, "Chang's Residence," it would not be a problem, and it would be all right if there were no sign. However, it would be very strange if someone puts up a sign that says, "Wang-Chang's Residence" or "Liu-Chang's Residence." We should never call ourselves Church Assembly Hall, because that is not our name; it is only where we meet. Furthermore, we are not members of any particular church; we are members of the Body of Christ.

God does not want believers to say, "I am of Paul," "I am of Apollos," or "I am of Cephas." He reproves all these things (cf. 1 Cor. 1:12). God is not pleased with any special name. God does not approve of this. We are gathered into the Lord's name (Matt. 18:20); we are saved because we believe into the Lord's name. The place where Jehovah establishes His name is the center of the gathering of God's children. The matter of a name is a great thing in the universe. We should not have any name other than the Lord's name. There should not be a Lutheran Church, Wesleyan Church, Anglican Church, Presbyterian Church, or other type of "Church," because none of these names are according to the Bible.

We should never let the enemy deceive us and think that the matter of name is unimportant. If Mrs. Hwang is called "Mrs. Chang," her husband would be furious because such a thing is not acceptable. Just as we cannot give someone a name in a careless way, we cannot name the church in a careless way; God does not permit this. Those who really know the church and the truth concerning the church would never dare to give a name to Christians. The apostles were on the earth several decades after the Lord's death and resurrection, and many of them were greatly used by the Lord. However, if we read church history, we will realize that none of them ever put a name on the church. They did not dare to carelessly give a name to the Body of Christ; it is absolutely forbidden because it is not according to the Bible.

Not only is a special name a serious matter but so are the matters of a special belief or a special fellowship. These three tests are completely according to the view of the Bible. Thus, if we want to know whether a church is on the position and ground of the church, we should place every situation under the light of the Bible and measure each one with the Bible. Furthermore, we should never compromise or accommodate in our measuring.

About four or five years ago, I met a brother who is the most compromising and accommodating person I know. If a four-foot-tall person was walking beside him, he would squat down to walk with him. Only if a person was seven feet tall would he be unable to accommodate him. After several years, this brother's greatest improvement was realizing that he should not compromise. We need to see that compromising is man's way of neutralizing things; man always likes to neutralize the truth. God's truth is absolute; if it is yes, it is yes, and if no, no. It should never be neutralized. Every compromise is a neutralization. Man thinks that it does not matter very much if the church has a name and that we do not need to be so particular as long as we are zealous for the Lord. This is wrong because the truth should never be compromised; the truth is always absolute.

Those who like to compromise are usually not very absolute. Those who like to compromise may have been touched by God, but they do not want to be absolute. An absolute person never compromises. It will be easy for us to compromise with others and not be absolute if we dismiss God's inward touching and are unwilling to obey and deal with Him.

## THE CHURCH NEEDING TO PASS THROUGH
## THE FILTER OF CHRIST

If a church does not have any special name, special belief, or special fellowship and has passed all three tests of the Bible, we still need to investigate further to see if it is full of Christ and the element of Christ. This is the second filter.

The first filter is the Bible, and the second filter is Christ. When the saints gather together, do they have more of the element of man or more of the element of Christ? Do they take man as the head or Christ as the Head? A Christian group may not have a special name, special belief, or special fellowship, but if they have too much of the element of man, they are merely an independent group in their locality. They may say that their group does not have a special name, special belief, or special fellowship, but they may also not have any genuine fellowship in the life of Christ with other members of the Body of Christ. They can be independent in a locality. If a Christian group has more of the element of man than the element of Christ, this certainly will be their situation. This is a fixed principle.

The saints in a certain church may not have a special name, special belief, or special fellowship, but certain people may have a special position which nullifies the position of Christ. Consequently, the church will be full of independent opinions and doctrines. In contrast, if we learn to reject our self and allow Christ to have the position as Lord, we will desire fellowship with saints in other localities. This is a certain fact. The more a person lives in the self, the more he feels there is no need to fellowship with others. However, the more a person lives in Christ, the more he feels a need to fellowship with others. This is true both of individuals and of churches.

If a church seems to be according to the Bible outwardly, but the saints do not like to fellowship with Christians in other localities, this shows that they have more of the element of man than of Christ. The more a church is in Christ, the more the saints in that church are eager to receive fellowship from others. Whenever we are secluded and try to serve God by ourselves, we should remember that we are being independent and sectarian. Thus, we need to filter the condition of the church with Christ.

We have told the co-workers many times that we would not allow man to have the top position among us even if it meant stopping our work and shutting everything down. Everything must come from the amount of Christ we have within. We should allow only Christ to pass through us; we should never allow anything of man to pass through us. Only those who have received more of the element of Christ, who have known, experienced, and gained more of Christ, and who are filled with Christ have the ability to bear responsibility. Such a person spontaneously manifests his position. People in the world look to ones who have wealth, education, and social status; however, we do not have such things in the church. Among us, we do not distinguish people by wealth, position, or fame. Among us, we have only Christians, and we have only Christ as everything. What is a Christian? A Christian is one who is full of Christ. This is the church. The church is not like human society. People in society determine a person's position based upon human observations, human desires, and human views, but the only factor for such a determination in the church is Christ.

## THE CHURCH NEEDING TO PASS THROUGH
## THE FILTER OF THE HOLY SPIRIT

If we want to determine whether a group is the church, the Bible is the first filter and Christ is the second. Furthermore, we also need the filter of the Holy Spirit. Some people may ask, "Is Christ not the Holy Spirit? Why do we need the filter of the Holy Spirit?" We need to realize that Christ is the life of the church, but the Holy Spirit is the move and operation of the church, both of which involve the authority of the church. The outward appearance of the church is based on the Bible, the content of the church is Christ, and the move of the church is the Holy Spirit. The church must not be only scriptural and full of Christ. It must also be completely spiritual and under the Holy Spirit's ruling, the Holy Spirit's moving, and the Holy Spirit's operation. The Holy Spirit must be everything in her.

A local church may be according to the Bible outwardly and have some measure of Christ inwardly, but when it actually moves and operates, man is ruling over it. This is very different from the Holy Spirit's ruling. We emphasize Christ in the aspect of the life and nature of the church, but there is also the aspect of authority in the church, which is an aspect of the Holy Spirit's move and operation. The nature of a local church may be Christ, but her move is often not of the Holy Spirit. Instead, her move, administration, and authority may be according to man's hand, not God's hand. Therefore, the Bible, Christ, and the Holy Spirit are three essential matters to the church.

These three filters or safeguards lead us to conclude that human views, ideas, opinions, manipulations, abilities, and everything worldly must be stopped because they are of no benefit in the church. In order for the church to be scriptural, human views, manipulation, abilities, and worldly methods must be stopped. Then the Holy Spirit will have a free rein to exercise His authority.

I want to ask the responsible brothers in each locality whether they lead the saints to serve by the Spirit or by their own methods and manipulation. Human manipulation must not be present in the church. Nevertheless, even those whom we think are spiritual can be manipulative. For example, a certain brother may be causing much trouble for the responsible brothers in a church. As a consequence, they may feel that one of them should visit him. After discussing this matter, they realize that he will be happy if a certain responsible brother visits him, but he will be unhappy if a different brother visits him. Therefore, they decide to send the brother who will make him happy. Some may think that this is wise, but actually it is not; it is human manipulation.

What does it mean for the responsible brothers to allow the Holy Spirit to operate? It means that the responsible brothers should bring the difficulties they encounter to the Lord and say, "O Lord, this is Your church, and this difficulty is Your difficulty. How do You want us to deal with this problem and solve this problem?" They should bring everything under God's mighty hand and see how God would lead them. They should not involve their views, thoughts, and human manipulation. There is a great difference between these two ways of dealing with difficulties.

A local church once had to provide hospitality for many saints, and they felt that the burden was quite heavy. So the responsible brothers came together to discuss the situation, and they expressed some hope that the elders would contact and fellowship this burden with some of the wealthier saints. When I heard this, I said, "I beg you to accept what I say. No one should contact anybody concerning the expense for this hospitality. At the most, you should make an announcement." I stopped the brothers' discussion to show them that contacting different ones in this way is human manipulation. At the very most, we can make an announcement to let the saints know about this matter, but we should allow the Holy Spirit to rule in this matter. Perhaps this local church was according to the Bible outwardly and full of Christ inwardly, but in the matter of material offerings, it did not pass through the filter because the brothers did not allow the Holy Spirit to rule in the church; instead, they tried to use human hands to accomplish things. This is not according to the nature of the church.

The church is an organic entity of God mingled with man, of man completely submitting to God, living completely in God, and moving fully with God. Hence, all the things of man, including his opinions, views, ideas, and methods, should not be in the church. In the church everything that is of man and the world should be stopped.

The Lord has been very merciful to us because He has shown us what the church is and how to use the Bible, Christ, and the Holy Spirit to consider the nature of the church. If we apply all these filters and a church passes through them all, we should bow our heads and say, "Lord, here is Your Body, Your dwelling place, and a place where You can rule." Otherwise, we should submit ourselves to the Lord and ask Him to forgive us and to rescue us from human methods and manipulation and from worldly views.

### ADDITIONAL NOTES
### FROM THE WORKERS' MEETING

We need to look at the condition of each local church, placing all the problems of the churches before the Lord and studying them together. This will help us discover difficulties in each locality and among the serving ones. In order to see the difficulties and shortages, we must look at these crucial matters in each locality. We also need to look at the difficulties brought into the church service by individuals.

## Four Crucial Matters Requiring
## Our Attention in the Church Service

Concerning our service in the church, we must pay attention to the following four matters. First, we should not neglect the gospel. Second, we must strengthen the perfecting work in the truth and in our knowledge of the truth. Third, we must experience life. Once a person is saved and brought into the church, we should immediately help him to know the truth and experience life. Fourth, we need to help him also to learn to serve. These are four necessary matters.

Some churches are not so strong, rich, or capable, and they cannot take care of these four matters at the same time. For example, when a local church is first established, it mainly emphasizes the preaching of the gospel. Helping the saints in the matters of knowing the truth, experiencing life, and learning to serve may also be considered, but the primary emphasis is on preaching the gospel. During the past few years the saints in the church in Taipei placed more emphasis on preaching the gospel, but now they are paying more attention to pursuing life. Strictly speaking, it is best when we emphasize these four matters at the same time.

Under normal circumstances, after the church emphasizes the preaching of the gospel, the saints should be led to study the Word, to perfect the new believers, to pursue life, and to enter into the church service. Sometimes the church is short-handed and cannot take care of everything, but we still should not emphasize only one thing, such as preaching the gospel, and neglect the matters of truth, life, and service. This is not so good and proper. Even if we are not so strong or rich, we should learn to help and lead the saints in each aspect. Let us consider the church in Taipei as an example. Last year, much emphasis was placed on pursuing life. However, we should not think that we can neglect the gospel because we are emphasizing the pursuit of life. Although we may not be able to focus on all four things at the same time, we still need to do our best to take care of every aspect, making some effort to seek the Lord's leading and to make practical decisions.

If the church decides to preach the gospel, the saints should study how to preach the gospel and how to lead people to receive the Lord. They should pay attention to whom they are preaching the gospel. For example, preaching the gospel among the family, at the campus or factory, and among the young people all need to be studied and considered. Only after studying and seeking can we know to whom we should preach and how we should preach. At the same time, we need to study how to coordinate the brothers and sisters together. For example, who should lead the singing, who should give the message in a gospel meeting, how should we prepare gospel tracts, and who should take care of transportation to and from the gospel meeting? We need to consider these matters.

When the church wants to preach the gospel, we cannot expect people to come if we peacefully sleep at home and then suddenly rise up and shout some slogans. We must consider everything in detail and adequately prepare everything in order to be on track and to produce results. We must carefully study which gospel tracts to use and which hymns to sing. This is the meaning of doing the Lord's work. We must be like this in the work of the gospel, and we must also be like this in the perfecting of the saints in the truth. We must take one step at a time to help the saints to know the basic truths, and then little by little we must take the saints deeper and deeper into the truth, just like a curriculum in school.

It is not possible to preach any truth without some preparation, nor will we develop this ability by peacefully sleeping at home. We can release a truth only after studying the Word, collecting spiritual books, and logically organizing our thoughts to determine the sections. This requires much labor.

Once I was fellowshipping with a brother concerning the matter of service, and I told him, "There must be some procedures in the service of your locality. You should not be like the Chinese proverb which says, 'Bandage the head only when it hurts, and bandage the foot only when it hurts.'" This will not work. We should serve as if we are doctors. When a patient comes to us, we should conduct a diagnosis by examining his whole body and then treat his illness step by step. At the same time, we should estimate how long it will take to treat the illness. Similarly, when people set up a school, they must have some procedures, whether it is a secondary school or a university. When we manage the church, we should be like a careful, methodical gardener. Even when we invite people to eat a meal, there should be a particular order in our serving of food. We must be like this even more in the Lord's work.

No worker should sleep peacefully at home every day; a good worker and a good responsible one must be a person who studies every day. Once a brother came to Taipei and, after observing us, said, "Every time I come, I see some change in your way." In doing the Lord's work and in serving the Lord, we must have an attitude to study and improve. If we do not practice this and only copy others, our work will not be effective. We can take other people's work as a reference, but their work cannot replace our own labor.

In the spring of 1934, when I began to learn to do the Lord's work, several other brothers also began serving the Lord. None of us slept peacefully at home; instead, we tried our best to study and labor every day. If anyone working for the Lord is able to sleep peacefully every day, he will be useless, and there will be a big loss to the Lord's work.

We all need to see the importance of these four things: the gospel, truth, life, and service. This word is not for any particular church. Every church should study these matters so that it will be on track in preaching the gospel, in perfecting the saints in the truth, in advancing in the experience of life, and in serving. Through the preaching of the gospel in the church in Taipei, people have been brought into the church in groups of three to five hundred. However, we still need to learn more about how to lead and strengthen the saints in truth, life, and service. Every item of the gospel, truth, life, and service is crucial, and every item needs to be carried out. If we can carry out these four crucial matters, then the church will have a firm foundation after four or five years. No matter where we go in the future, we should do more than simply preach the gospel. We should also have a firm foundation in truth and in the pursuit of life. Then spontaneously our service will be weighty. We need to bring these four items back to our locality and try our best to practice and carry them out. We should have the attitude of a climber who tirelessly advances up a mountain, and we should not sleep peacefully and be at ease. Finally, we should ignore every difficulty and press on fearlessly.

## Paying Attention to Cultivating Talents

In addition to the previous four points, we need to pay attention to cultivating the talents of the saints. Concerning this, we need to pay attention first to the young people, and among the young people, we should concentrate on the students. If the work in a locality cannot gain the students who are there, then their work is a failure, and this kind of failure means that there is no future. We do not despise older people, but if a church has only older people, something is missing. If we look at society, we can see that any work or business must pay attention to the young people in order to have a future. After hearing this word, please do not feel that this is unfair and wonder why the future of the church depends on the young people. In the church life, the function of the young people is very different from the function of children and older people.

Teenagers are still quite young, and older people are often forgetful. If the older saints in the church can pass on the lessons they have learned in the Lord throughout the years to the younger saints, regardless of whether it is a burden for the gospel, knowledge of the truth, or a portion in the service, this would be wonderful. In this way, the older saints can rest and sleep in peace, the young people can function appropriately in the church, and the teenagers and children can grow up healthily in the church. On the one hand, we need to advance faithfully in the gospel, truth, life, and service so that we can maintain and solidify the condition of the church, but on the other hand, we must cultivate and gain the talents.

Moreover, we should give middle-aged saints and those in other age groups particular leading and perfecting. This does not mean that we are ignoring certain ones and paying more attention to others. However, the future of the church and the Lord's work must have a way to go on. Some may say, "Because God is not a respecter of persons, we should treat old and young people alike. Even if a person is talented, God may not use him." I do not want to argue in response to such a word, but we should ask the Lord to open our eyes to see His needs and to see what is fitting according to our portion. If we do not see this, it will be difficult for us to help the people around us. If we do not exercise any discernment in helping others and use the same way regardless of whether one is old or young, there will not be much future in our work, because we will not be able to produce useful ones or cultivate a useful second generation in our service.

From the account of the Epistles in the New Testament, it is doubtful that Paul taught Timothy and Titus the same way that he taught other brothers and sisters. Even when the Lord Jesus was on the earth, He treated the disciples differently from the way He treated others who served Him. The

Lord served the multitude by preaching the word to them. However, the Lord brought His followers to a high mountain, a special place, where He could bring them on in order for them to meet His need one day. It was the one hundred and twenty disciples who were able to meet the Lord's need at the beginning of the church age in the New Testament (Acts 1:15). We need to learn how to lead the work into the future and not merely watch others doing things.

In the matter of cultivating talents, we need to exercise discernment in our work. Some work is more general, and some work is more specific. Sometimes when the Lord was on the earth, He would speak to thousands or even tens of thousands of people, but eventually the Lord brought only a few people to the high mountain with Him, and only three people saw the Lord's transfiguration (Matt. 17:1-2). No matter where we work, however, we should not have any preferences. If we must make choices, we should not base them on our feelings; instead, we should base them on a person's function before the Lord and how much the Lord can have a way in him. We may need to pay special attention to the condition of some saints, even allowing some to stay in the same condition for the moment. Even within a garden there is some differentiation. Some flowers grow on the edge of the garden, and some flowers grow in the middle. This is absolutely not a matter of despising certain ones or even esteeming others more highly; we must be able to give the saints nutrients based on the needs of their particular function.

We should not leave any work to its own fate. Instead, we must work by the Holy Spirit, and the Holy Spirit needs our cooperation. Every worker, every elder or responsible brother, and even more, everyone who loves and pursues the Lord must learn this. As we lead the saints in the church, we should lead them according to their condition before the Lord, and we should be balanced in every aspect. In this way, our work will become effective. If we do not study, we will not know how to handle anything. Every fisherman studies the best way to catch fish; it requires much learning and studying.

When we work, we should even study our contacts. For example, we need to study the kind of people we can gain and the kind of results we can produce. We will become effective in our work only when we produce some useful ones. If we pay attention only to quantity, the results of our work will not be very useful. Thus, in the service of all the churches, we must advance in the four points that we spoke of earlier. We need to pay attention also to the matter of talents. If a person has the portion of an elder, we should train him; if a person has the portion of a deacon, we should diligently help him as well. Then in our work, we will not only have many who are saved but also many who can serve. Furthermore, we will cultivate some useful ones, such as elders and deacons. We need to learn these things.

We cannot leave these things to work themselves out when we do the Lord's work. I hope we would all pray for these matters. The basic reason for the lack of useful people in the church life is that we have not learned enough and also that we have not taught others enough. Many people have been saved, and the work has been raised up, but we do not have workers. This shows that we must catch up; we all need to learn. After we have learned some lessons, we need to teach what we have learned to the brothers and sisters so that they can teach others when they go to different places (2 Tim. 2:2). In this way, we can produce useful people. Eventually, everyone will be able to do the work.

## Concerning the Problem of Individuals

Concerning the problem of individuals, let us use Brother A and Brother B as an example. When Brother A does something, he focuses and concentrates on it; however, when Brother B does something, he often considers many different things. It is very interesting that the Lord often places these kinds of brothers together. Although Brother A concentrates on what he is doing, he does not have much consideration; consequently, he is fast. In contrast, Brother B is slower because he has more consideration. Such a situation causes each to learn a different lesson.

Since Brother B takes a long time to decide, this is a great hindrance. Therefore, he must learn some lessons. This does not mean that he should not have any consideration; instead, he must be quicker in his consideration and be willing to sacrifice and pay the price. If both the kingdom of the heavens and the lake of fire are before us, we should not have to think about the choice. If we want to enter into the kingdom of the heavens, we should forget about the lake of fire immediately. If we take the time to think about it, we may be too late. In some matters, we need to be simple and determined. Before the Lord, we must learn to exercise our judgment properly, quickly, and promptly. This does not mean that we should not think when we work; rather, we need to learn how to discern what is more important and what is less important, and we need to learn to make sacrifices.

We need to give much consideration to the matter of cultivating talents. Today if we put all our effort into small things, we may reap some benefit; however, we should focus more of our time on cultivating the talents. This means that we need to make some sacrifices, because we cannot possibly do everything. If we want to do the Lord's work, we must weigh the importance of each matter. If the Lord wants us to go east, we must go east. At such a moment, we should not even look to the west, no matter how important it may seem. When we are clear about what is more important and what the Lord wants us to do, we need to drop everything else. We must learn to give up some things and to sacrifice. If we cannot drop certain things and stop working for the Lord, we cannot take up other things and truly work for the Lord.

When we meet a certain brother and say, "Brother, this is a very important work," he may reply, "Yes, but we cannot neglect that work." Or when we say, "We should take care of this person," he may reply, "Yes, but we should also take care of that person." It seems as if he cannot make a decision and does not have a definite goal. He considers every person about the same and all work as being equally important. However, those who are more experienced can quickly pinpoint a goal in an accurate and strong way and then act accordingly. I hope that we can all learn these matters.

# CHAPTER TEN

# THE TYPES OF THE TABERNACLE, THE ALTAR, AND THE ARK IN THE CHURCH

Scripture Reading: 2 Chron. 1:1-13; 1 Kings 3:4-12, 15

In our speaking about the church, we have been able to touch only a few points, because the matter of knowing the church is a broad topic. Nevertheless, the points we have spoken of are very crucial. I hope we would all grasp these crucial points before the Lord and seek clear light concerning them.

## THE CONTENT OF THE CHURCH

The church is the Body of Christ (Eph. 1:22-23), and she is joined to Christ as one (5:31-32); this is a tremendous light. If we want to test any Christian group with the Bible, we need to see the crucial point that Christ is the content of the church. In addition, there are also several other crucial points, such as the reality of the church, the authority of the Holy Spirit, the administration of the church, and the move of the church. The more we go on before the Lord, the clearer we become that these points are great filters for any Christian group and even for us. We must ask, "Are we meeting according to the teaching of the clear word in the Bible? Is there anything among us that contradicts the truth in the Bible? Is our intrinsic move truly based on the living Christ as everything in us? Does our administration and move truly come from the Holy Spirit's operation and ruling?" We should not only examine other meetings; we also need to examine our own meetings with these points.

When we consider these points, we will arrive at one conclusion—the church is Christ Himself. Hence, the church requires us to put off everything of man, the world, and religious organization. Everything related to man, the world, and religious organization needs to be put off completely. We need to put off all the confusion issuing from Christianity because many things of man, the world, and religious organization have been brought into the church. The Bible shows that the church requires us to put off everything of man, the world, and organization. Whenever the elements of man, the world, or organization are in a local church, the church loses Christ's position and nature. I hope that all the brothers and sisters can firmly grasp these crucial points, studying them one by one and putting them into practice.

## TYPOLOGY IN THE OLD TESTAMENT

We need to consider an important point based upon typology in the Old Testament so that we can have another source for testing and examining our knowledge of the church. During the time of the Old Testament, the center of the service of God's children to Him was the tabernacle, and the center of the tabernacle was the Ark of the Covenant. Those who have studied the Old Testament know that the Ark typifies Christ. In the original text, *the Ark of the Covenant* means "the Ark of the Testimony," and it typifies Christ as the testimony of God. Inside the Ark of the Covenant there were the two tablets of the covenant, and it is Christ who bears the covenant that God made with His people. The covenant God made with us is based upon the person and work of Christ. Thus, He is the Ark of the Covenant and the Ark of the Testimony.

We can also see the two natures of Christ from the Ark in the Old Testament, which included both the nature of wood and the nature of gold (Exo. 25:10-11). Wood refers to Christ's humanity, and gold refers to Christ's divinity. When wood and gold are joined together, they signify Christ, who has both divinity and humanity.

Furthermore, the outward appearance of the Ark, or the enlargement of the Ark, was the tabernacle. The tabernacle and the Ark shared many similarities. The Ark was joined to the tabernacle, and the tabernacle came out of the Ark. The Ark was the center of the tabernacle, and the tabernacle surrounded the Ark. From both God's perspective and the perspective of the worship of God's children, the Ark and the tabernacle could not be separated. The two were as one. However, even though they were one, there was a distinction, but even though there was a distinction, they could not be separated. This can be compared to the head and body being one; there are distinctions, but they cannot be separated. If they are separated, they are finished.

In normal circumstances the Ark and the tabernacle could not be separated when God's children were worshipping Him because the two were one. Readers of the Old Testament agree that the Ark typifies Christ Himself and that the tabernacle typifies the Body of Christ, the church; in addition, the church is Christ (1 Cor. 12:12). The outward appearance of the Ark is the tabernacle. Although there are distinctions between the Ark and the tabernacle, they are joined together; the tabernacle is the expression, location, and outward form and appearance of the Ark. Thus, the tabernacle is the Ark. Similarly, the church is the expression, location, and outward form and appearance of Christ. Christ is in the church in the same way that the Ark is in the tabernacle. The church is joined to Christ, and Christ is in the church; consequently, the church is Christ.

## THE HISTORY AND TYPOLOGY OF THE SEPARATION OF THE ARK FROM THE TABERNACLE

In a normal situation the Ark and the tabernacle should always be joined together and never separated from each other. This means that under normal circumstances Christ and His outward form and expression should not be separated. However, something abnormal happened in the Old Testament— God's children failed and the Israelites became desolate and degraded. As a consequence, the Ark was captured by the Philistines and carried away (1 Sam. 4:1-11). The captivity of the Ark is a well-known story in the history of God's children. The captivity of the Ark signifies the loss of God's testimony due to the fall of God's children. This is true according to typology in the Old Testament and also according to the reality in the New Testament. As the church began to be degraded and defeated, God's testimony in Christ was captured and lost. This separated the Ark from the tabernacle so that the tabernacle was in one place and the Ark was in another. Although the tabernacle moved from Shiloh to Gibeon (Josh. 18:1; 2 Chron. 1:3), the Ark was not in the tabernacle (1 Sam. 4:3).

In the beginning, the situation of God's children was normal because the tabernacle was among them, and the Ark was in the tabernacle. The tabernacle with the Ark inside was the center of the service of the children of God, and they kept God's testimony on the earth. God's presence was upon the Ark in the tabernacle. When their general condition declined, the Ark was captured. From that time forward the Ark and the tabernacle were separated, and even though the majority of the Israelites focused on the tabernacle, the Ark was in another place. The majority of the Israelites saw the outward tabernacle, and they continued to offer sacrifices and serve God there. However, there was a small group of people who loved God and were in God. Their eyes were not focused on the tabernacle but on God's Ark.

We must pay attention to three points. We need to ask where the Ark was during the time it was separated from the tabernacle. The Ark was in David's hand, and it eventually stayed in a tent that David pitched in the city of David (2 Sam. 6:16-17). David was not only a king; he was also a person who knew God's heart. Although the majority of God's children were in desolation, paying attention only to the outward tabernacle, there were a few people who knew God's heart and paid attention to the Ark rather than the outward tabernacle merely. David represents these ones. He was different from the thousands of Israelites who offered sacrifices at the tabernacle in Gibeon. David did not focus on the tabernacle, because he knew God; instead, he brought the Ark back and placed it in the city of David. This is the first point.

When God's children are in a proper condition, the Ark and the tabernacle are never separated. Furthermore, there should have been no distinction between the house of the Israelites and the house of David; all God's children should worship and serve God together so that the Ark is in the tabernacle, and

God is with them. When the children of Israel became abnormal, fallen, and desolated, the Ark was captured and separated from the tabernacle. At that time there was only the outward tabernacle, but there was no Ark inside of it. In other words, when God's children are in desolation, they may have an outward form without the inward reality. In terms of today's situation, we may also have the church outwardly without Christ as the reality. This is the second point.

During the period of desolation, the majority of God's children served God at the location of the tabernacle at Gibeon. Nevertheless, they served in a careless way, having only an outward form of service related to the physical tabernacle. Only a small group of people—like David, who knew God, who was according to God, and who was pleasing to God—paid attention to the Ark. This means that they did not focus on the appearance of the church but on Christ, the reality. Their eyes were not focused on outward things but on Christ. This is the third point. I hope we can all firmly grasp these three points.

When David passed away, his son Solomon became the king; however, like a child, he did not know God adequately. After he became king, he was thankful to God. However, he took oxen and sheep and all the leaders to offer sacrifices to God at Gibeon (2 Chron. 1:3). He chose the tabernacle that was far from him instead of the Ark that was near to him; he did not realize that his house was in Jerusalem and that the Ark was also in Jerusalem. He went to Gibeon because Jehovah's tabernacle and the bronze altar were there.

Outwardly, the tabernacle looked exactly the same as it did when Moses was alive. Solomon took all the leaders to Gibeon and offered thousands of sacrifices. Interestingly, according to the record in the Bible, God came to Solomon that evening and gave him a vision and a dream. God spoke to Solomon in the dream, and Solomon asked God for wisdom; thus, God granted him wisdom. After Solomon received wisdom, he immediately went back to Jerusalem, the place where the Ark was, and he worshipped God there (v. 13). Before he met God, he had an ordinary view of serving God according to an outward form. This is the reason he went to Gibeon to offer sacrifices. After he received wisdom and a vision from God, he immediately went back to the Ark in Jerusalem and offered sacrifices there. From that point forward, the Bible does not speak any more concerning the relationship between Solomon and the tabernacle; it speaks only of matters related to Solomon and the Ark.

We need to see that when the church is in a normal condition, Christ, the inward reality, and the church, the outward form, are one; the inward Christ is expressed through the outward church. However, the church became desolate and God's testimony was lost. As a result, the tabernacle and the Ark were separated. From that moment forward, those who do not have a vision, which constitutes the majority of the people, look only at the outward appearance of the church and neglect the reality of Christ. Only a few people like David do not focus on the outward form and appearance of the tabernacle but care only for the Ark, for Christ. God's eyes similarly are not on the outward form but on the reality; God does not look on the tabernacle but on the Ark. He does not regard the outward appearance of the church but the reality of Christ. From the beginning of Israel's degradation, God was interested in the Ark and its location, not the tabernacle. Similarly, God is interested in where Christ can be found, not in the outward appearance of the church.

May God be merciful to us and show us that whenever we speak concerning the matter of the church, we cannot neglect Christ. We cannot do things in a proper way according to the tabernacle but be without the Ark within. We cannot merely have an outward appearance of the church that is according to the Bible but not have Christ within. We must consider the church in our locality. Based on outward form and appearance, it may seem that it is a complete tabernacle that does not deviate in any way from the Scriptures. It may have nothing of the world, organization, and man. It also may not have a special name, special belief, or special fellowship. Additionally, the truth of Christ's death on the cross may be present, and the gospel may be spread quite effectively. Nevertheless, it may not have the Ark, Christ, within. This is similar to the situation at Gibeon, where there was a tabernacle and a bronze altar but not the reality of the Ark. This is a very serious problem. The tabernacle, the bronze altar, and the Ark were equally important.

## EXAMINING THE CHURCHES

If we want to examine the church in our locality, the best means are by the tabernacle, the bronze altar, and the Ark. The tabernacle refers to the outward expression of Christ, the church. The bronze altar refers to the cross, which is the truth of redemption, and the Ark refers to Christ Himself. In a normal situation, these three are joined together. However, if there is only a tabernacle and a bronze altar, the situation is not normal.

Outwardly, a certain church may truly look like the tabernacle, having no defects, and in addition, it may have the bronze altar, which signifies the gospel of redemption. The church may preach the gospel, bring people into the worship of God, and even help people receive Christ's redemption, grace, and salvation. Hence, both the tabernacle and bronze altar are present, and everything can look proper outwardly. Nonetheless, we still need to examine whether it has the Ark—Christ—within.

A type is like a picture; it is not like a piece of writing, which can be understood plainly. In order for us to understand a picture, we need to have some insight and intuition. Originally, the tabernacle with the altar typified Christ, but when the Ark was gone, there was only an outward form without an inward reality. These outward things can remain—for example, the truth of redemption can remain—but the reality can be gone. Originally these three things were one, but now the Ark is often missing. This picture shows that it is possible to have the outward forms of Christ and the redemption of Christ but not have Christ as the center and reality.

A local church may have the form of the church outwardly, and it may also preach the gospel, but whether Christ is present depends on whether the element of the serving ones comes from Christ or from their natural being. If there is only the element of man and nothing of the element of Christ in a church or if there is very little of the element of Christ in a church, then it does not have the Ark; it has lost the Ark. This kind of church may have the outward form of Christ, the redemption of Christ through His cross, and the name of Christ for people to be saved, but it does not have Christ as its inward reality, life, and center.

## NEEDING LIGHT AND REVELATION TO KNOW THE CHURCH

If we want to speak about the matter of the church, we must see that the tabernacle needs the Ark. Without the Ark, the tabernacle is a place that does not have God's presence. His presence is with the Ark, not the tabernacle. If those who seek God with a pure heart arrive at the tabernacle, God can still give them the vision, revelation, and light to go to the Ark. This was Solomon's experience. Solomon went to the tabernacle in Gibeon to offer up sacrifices; he had a common view, a general view, the view of most Israelites. In their concept the only place to offer sacrifices to God was at Gibeon. When Solomon went to Gibeon to offer sacrifices and worship God, he was enlightened to see that God's presence was not there but in Jerusalem. Consequently, he immediately went back to Jerusalem and offered sacrifices there (1 Kings 3:4-5, 15). Once a person is enlightened, he pays attention to the matter of the Ark. The Ark typifies Christ, who is the center of the church. The reality of the church is Christ.

May God have mercy on us so that we would not be a common and ordinary people but a remarkable people. We should not have a common and ordinary view; we should have God's revelation. Even if everyone pays attention to the tabernacle, we should pay attention to the Ark. The Bible is precious, and it shows that the Ark was not in anyone's hands but David's. Even though God's children were desolate, David knew God's heart. His view was different from the crowds of people, who could have said, "Is this not the tabernacle? Is this not the altar for offering sacrifices?" This can be compared to saying, "Do we not speak of the cross? Do we not preach the cross? Do we not speak of the precious blood of Christ?" This is a picture of today's condition. The crowds will pay attention to the tabernacle and the altar, but those who know God's heart will pay attention to the Ark, Christ. The living testimony of God is Christ (Rev. 1:5).

May the Lord grant us strong light to genuinely know the truth concerning the church. We thank the Lord that the tabernacle and the altar are in the church, but what about the Ark? Our testimony in each place cannot be only the tabernacle and the altar; we must also have the Ark. We cannot have only the outward form of the church and the doctrine of the redemption of the cross; we must also take Christ as our center, life, and reality. We must have Christ as the location of God's presence.

However, this does not mean that we do not need the tabernacle and the altar. If we read the Old Testament in a thorough way, we can see that God revealed to Solomon that he should build a more solid tabernacle for the Ark, the temple (1 Kings 5:3-5). In addition, he also made a bronze altar and a great molten sea of bronze. This means that we should not neglect the altar; that is, we should not ignore the teachings concerning the cross and redemption. However, if we have only the outward form of the church and the doctrine of redemption without Christ as our center and life, then in God's view, the church is still void and empty of reality. This is because the center—Christ—is missing.

We need to see that the Ark at the center in the tabernacle is the mingling of acacia wood with gold. Acacia wood signifies humanity, and gold signifies divinity. The center of the church is the mingling of God with man—man being subdued before God, being mingled with Christ, taking Christ as his life and person, taking Christ's heart as his heart, taking Christ's emotion as his emotion, and taking Christ's will as his will. The church is not simply man, but man mingled with Christ. This is the Ark.

If every move and idea of a certain church come only from man, this church does not have the Ark. If the brothers serve God by placing themselves in the incarnated Christ and if they take His mind as their mind, His will as their will, His emotion as their emotion, and His life as their life, giving Him the ground to be their center and everything and submitting to the living Christ, then that church has the Ark.

The tabernacle is the outward form of the church, the altar is the truth of the cross and the spread of the gospel, and the Ark is Christ as the life and reality in the church. We should never despise the tabernacle and the altar. Even if there were only the Ark, we would still need to prepare a better temple for the Ark. Merely having the Ark without the tabernacle, the outward form, is not sufficient. We even need to prepare an outward form for the Ark that is larger and more solid and secure, which is the temple. We must see both sides of the truth.

Today many people in Christianity care only about Christ but not about the outward form. In other words, they do not care about the church; they care only about Christ. Because of the church's desolation, they believe that they will lose Christ's presence if they care about the church. Nevertheless, if we read 2 Chronicles 3 and 4, we will discover that the Ark needs an outward form; the Ark is not complete without the tabernacle. Just as Solomon needed to build a temple for the Ark, we need both sides of the truth—the outward form and the reality.

In the situation among the churches today, the greatest shortage is in the aspect of the Ark. The only excuse for neglecting this matter is ignorance. The tabernacle of the church is the outward form, and the altar in the church is the redemption of the cross. However, the root, the center, of the church is Christ as life and reality. He is the Ark.

## THE TABERNACLE, THE ALTAR, AND THE ARK BEING EQUALLY IMPORTANT

Today orthodox Christians can be divided into three main groups: one group focuses on the tabernacle, another group focuses on the altar, and yet another group focuses on the Ark. However, there are not many who pay attention to the Ark.

One brother told us recently that fifty young people from the United States suddenly volunteered to go to Japan to preach the gospel. These young people were paying attention to the altar. Another youth organization came to Taiwan several times as well. At the most, their work was related to the altar. They tried to bring people to the Lord by playing basketball. However, if people can be brought to the Lord by playing basketball, it is also possible that people can be brought away from the Lord by playing basketball.

Preaching the gospel by playing basketball can bring a Christian only to the altar; it can never bring a Christian to the experience of the Ark. We dare not say that no one can be saved through this kind of basketball gospel preaching, but one thing is certain—we can rarely find anyone who is saved in this way who is willing to forsake the world, bear the cross, take the Lord's life as his life, and follow the Lord to walk in the way of the cross. This is the meaning of having the altar without the Ark.

Today there are many mission boards that preach the gospel zealously; however, they do not have the tabernacle and the Ark. They have only the altar. We humble ourselves before the Lord and say that we absolutely do not have the intention of criticizing others. We need to speak of these examples because we want to help everyone understand the Lord's way.

In her proper condition the church should have the tabernacle, the altar, and the Ark at the same time. In other words, she should have the church, the redemption of the cross, and the glorious Christ as her center. We should have all three at the same time, and we should stress them equally. We should not ignore or overemphasize any one of them. On the island of Taiwan, especially in the church in Taipei, there is no problem concerning the tabernacle, and the matter of the altar is adequate. However, the matter of the Ark concerns us very much. I hope that everyone who has an ear to hear would be able to open his heart and spirit for the sake of the Ark. We should never despise the Lord's gospel, and we should exalt the Lord's redemption in order to make the bronze altar brightly shine. Moreover, we should never despise the matters related to the church, such as our coordination in the service and our meeting and worship together, but we must pay attention to Christ as our center and reality.

History shows that when God's children are in desolation and confusion, there is a danger that many with a heart for God will focus only on the tabernacle and the altar and ignore the Ark, which is the desire of God's heart. This is the reason we want to help the brothers and sisters to know the Ark— Christ. This does not mean that we despise the tabernacle and the altar. Instead, it means that the reality depends upon having the Ark, Christ, as our center and life.

In conclusion, there are three major points in this message. May the Holy Spirit enlighten us to see that when God's children are in desolation and when God's testimony is affected by man, we must pay attention to these three things simultaneously: the tabernacle, the altar, and the Ark. According to typology, we must focus on the matter of the church, the matter of redemption, and the matter of Christ as life at the same time.

If we consider the condition of the churches in the localities today, we are satisfactory in respect to the tabernacle and the altar, but we are very short in respect to the Ark. This means that the churches do not have any problem with the outward form of the church and the redemption of Christ, but their knowledge of Christ is poor and inadequate. May the Lord have mercy on us so that we would know Christ more, have the Ark as our center, and not despise the matter of the church with its coordination and service. Furthermore, we should not despise the Lord's redemption on the cross and His gospel. We must preach the gospel everywhere, help people to believe in the Lord, and help people to gain Christ as their life. We should not have any bias; instead, we should pay equal attention to the tabernacle, the altar, and the Ark.

# CHAPTER ELEVEN

# THE BUILDING UP OF THE BODY OF CHRIST

Scripture Reading: Eph. 4:12-13

## THE GENUINE BUILDING UP OF THE CHURCH

After seeing the types of the tabernacle, the altar, and the Ark, which signify the outward form of the church, redemption, and Christ, we must see how to measure the church. In other words, we must see how to measure the spiritual worth, weight, and position of a church. Since the Ark represents Christ as the inner substance of the church, we can measure the church only by Christ Himself. Ephesians 4:11-12 also speaks very clearly of apostles, prophets, evangelists, and shepherds and teachers who perfect the saints unto the work of the ministry, unto the building up of the Body of Christ. All the gifts that Christ gave to the church are for the building up of His Body; the goal of the building up is for the Body of Christ to become full grown and to attain to the measure of the stature of the fullness of Christ (v. 13).

We need to see what it means to build up the church. To build up the church is to build up the Body of Christ. The goal of the building up of the Body of Christ is for the Body of Christ to become full grown and to attain to the measure of the stature of the fullness of Christ, that is, for the church to arrive at the measure of the stature of the fullness of Christ. Hence, the matter of the church involves Christ. If the church does not have Christ inwardly, the church is void, empty, and without reality. Consequently, if we want to evaluate the church, we must not do it according to anything other than Christ Himself, and we must see that a group of Christians has the inward stature of Christ.

Anything that does not match Christ and is not of Christ should not have any place in the church; it should be completely eliminated and destroyed. In the church there are only Christ's position, ground, and element. If we look at the church from the outside, there are many persons and matters, but these persons and matters should be mingled with the element of Christ. This means that every responsible brother and serving one should be mingled with Christ inwardly. In other words, all the responsible brothers and serving ones need to submit to Christ and allow Christ to mingle with them. In this way, even though we are still human, we will have the mingling of Christ within; we will be humans who are mingled with God. All our service and work should be mingled with the element of Christ.

Sometimes we hear people from certain Christian groups saying that they are truly God's church because their beliefs are orthodox and their worship is according to the way of the Bible. However, if we examine them more deeply, we may discover that Christ is not mingled with them and that the Holy Spirit does not have the ground to rule in them. On the contrary, we may be able to touch only people and things. When we genuinely want to live in the Spirit and allow Christ to be the law of life in us, some may attempt to "pour cold water" on us by saying that this will not work. In such circumstances, however, it is not we who are being blocked and hindered; rather, the Holy Spirit is being blocked and hindered.

We should never be like this in the local churches. No local church should allow man to overstep Christ and the Holy Spirit. No local church should prevent a person who lives in the Lord from working with them. If a local church cannot enable someone who lives in Spirit and who follows the Holy Spirit to go on together with them, such a church is undoubtedly ruled by man, allows man to have the top position, and has more of the element of man than the element of Christ. The Lord does not approve of such a situation.

We must adhere closely to this principle: the normal condition of any local church is to establish Christ so that Christ can be built up in the church, so that the stature of Christ can grow daily in the church, and so that the Holy Spirit can become more active in the church as He lives more in the church. In a normal local church the Holy Spirit is able to lead people to learn and accept the breaking of the cross, to put themselves aside, and to submit to the authority of the power of the Holy Spirit. In other words, a normal church life involves living in Christ and allowing Christ to lead us to learn the lesson of the cross so that we can learn how to build up the church as the Holy Spirit increasingly lives in us.

### THE STANDARD OF THE CHURCH BEING CHRIST

The standard of the church is simply Christ. We cannot conclude that the church has made progress and has grown simply if a church in a certain locality increases from four hundred brothers and sisters to six hundred in one year. In reality, the church may not have grown at all. Even when a church increases in number, we cannot determine whether the church has been enlarged and made progress merely by looking at these outward numbers. We must see whether Christ Himself has increased within a church. When Christ increases within a church, it has truly been enlarged and made progress.

When we visit a church, we may discover that even though it has increased in number, the element of man has increased as well so that the church is full of man's ideas and opinions. According to the proper measure, this church has not made any progress. Even though these saints may have some experience and do not directly confront or offend one another, we can sense that they have their own opinions. Such saints do not submit to the Holy Spirit and do not allow the Holy Spirit to reign in them; instead, it is possible to meet people who are only experienced in the ways of the world. In other words, we can touch only man's element and self-cultivation but not much of the element of Christ. It is possible for saints to be very weak even when a church increases in number.

If there is an increase only in number, we will touch only weakness and activity in their service. We will not touch the authority of the Holy Spirit, and we will not find people who are under the Holy Spirit's authority, who abide in life by the Holy Spirit's operation in them, and who serve the Lord by allowing Him to rule. Such a church will not have much of the stature of Christ. They may increase in number, and the responsible brothers may be full of human experiences and not argue with one another; however, we cannot touch Christ in them. This kind of church is a church in name only; it lacks reality.

If the responsible brothers and the saints remain like this, sooner or later the Holy Spirit will be forced to raise up another group of people. The Lord will raise up a group of people who will submit to the Holy Spirit's authority and who will have much fellowship with Him. Then when people contact them, they will sense the Lord's presence and taste the flavor of Christ in them. Thus, the Ark—the testimony of God—will be among this group of people.

David was a man who knew God's heart, and he brought the Ark to the house of Obed-edom because he knew God's heart (2 Sam. 6:11-12). However, the house of Obed-edom was neither the beginning nor the destination. The beginning was the tabernacle, and the destination was the temple; Obed-edom was only a part of the building process.

Over twenty years ago, the meetings that began in many places in mainland China were like the house of Obed-edom. When I first started serving God, the local church where I met was a "house of Obed-edom." The house of Obed-edom, however, can last only a short period of time. Those who know God will not leave the Ark in the house of Obed-edom; instead, they will bring the Ark and set it in the city of David. The Ark can stay in a certain person's house for a short time, but eventually it needs to enter into the temple. Thus, it is not sufficient simply to have the Ark; we also need to build up a temple for God's Ark.

The stature of the church is Christ. When we build up the church, we cannot build with anything other than Christ; we can build only with Christ. Several years ago we visited a certain church and realized that the brothers did not know very much of the truth and were not clear about God's Word. When we visited them this year, all the brothers were able to stand at the podium and speak for the Lord. Some might say that this church has made progress, but we can say only that they have made progress in the truth; we may not be able to say that the church has made progress. A church has made progress only when there has been an inward increase and growth of Christ. A church may increase in the knowledge of the truth outwardly, but she may not have much increase of Christ inwardly. We need to be able to discern this difference.

Many Christian organizations have studied the truth and published magazines for many years, but they have merely human views and ideas. It is difficult to find anyone among them who is under the breaking of the cross, who allows Christ to rule, and who lives in the Holy Spirit. If our church is like this, we have not grown much in Christ; instead, we have grown only in our mind. Even the truth cannot be used to measure the church; we can measure the church only by Christ.

Sometimes even the truth can replace Christ. The church in Taipei has been in the exercise of the four stages of the spiritual life, in which the third stage concerns the discipline of the Holy Spirit. Many saints have the concept that the discipline of the Holy Spirit involves losing something, being physically injured, having a car accident, or becoming sick. However, few of us truly see that the discipline of the Holy Spirit causes us to experience the breaking of the cross to allow the Holy Spirit to have ground in us and rule in us. Often we have the doctrine of the discipline of the Holy Spirit but not the reality of being ruled by the Holy Spirit. Hence, the stature of Christ may not be established in us. Among today's Christians, there are too many substitutes for Christ; anything can be a substitute for Christ. However, only the things that come out of Christ have the element of Christ and are of Christ Himself.

Some Christians pay more attention to spiritual cultivation than to Christ, but spiritual cultivation is not Christ. Similarly, the things we think are related to the discipline of the Holy Spirit may be unrelated to Christ. Sometimes we visit seminaries and see people holding Bibles in their arms, walking slowly, and looking up to the heavens every few steps. It seems as if they are very pious. Such a pious demeanor conveys a sense of spiritual cultivation, but spiritual cultivation is not Christ. The result of this kind of spiritual cultivation is not spiritual growth but the growth of the flesh; instead of the spirit, the flesh is strengthened.

Spiritual cultivation may seem very real outwardly, but actually it is very false. Many seminary students and preachers behave and conduct themselves very differently at school than at home. When they are at home, their true nature is manifested, and they act like different persons. We can be like this as well; we can act like two totally different persons when we are with the saints and when we are at home. Just as our natural life can be expressed in our pride, it can be expressed in our meekness. Just as our natural life can be expressed in our "wildness," it can be expressed in our refinement. All the things that people think are good and virtuous may not be spiritual or of Christ.

We may have the term *the discipline of the Holy Spirit* without any real knowledge and experience of it. This can be a substitute for Christ in us. As a result, we may receive some discipline, but we do not gain Christ or experience Christ. We need the discipline of the Holy Spirit in the church life, but we cannot use this item to measure the church. We cannot use anything but Christ to measure the church; we can use only Christ to measure the church. The degree to which a person knows Christ, allows Christ to rule in him, gives ground to Christ, and allows Christ to operate in him is the degree to which he has gained Christ.

In the church the goal and purpose of the gifts are to build up the church so that the church would have the measure of the stature of the fullness of Christ. The church has no other work.

## THE AUTHORITY IN THE CHURCH

In the church there is not only the matter of life but also the matter of authority. Some may ask where the matter of authority in the church is spoken of in the Bible. It would require much time and effort to list every reference in the

Bible. Here we will use only Romans 12 as a proof. Romans 12:3 says, "I say,...to everyone who is among you, not to think more highly of himself than he ought to think, but to think so as to be sober-minded, as God has apportioned to each a measure of faith." This means that one may receive grace to be a hand, someone else may receive grace to be a finger, yet another person may receive grace to be an arm, and some other person may receive grace to be a foot. Although every member is different in size, everyone is a member. We should not be proud and think more highly of ourselves than we ought to think. If one is a hand and thinks more highly of himself by considering himself to be an arm, he will cause trouble. This is because the hand serves under the arm and also functions above the fingers. Thus, the arm is above the hand, and the hand is above the fingers; this is to be balanced and in order.

The more a church receives the Lord's grace, the more she has the element of Christ within, and the greater is her stature of Christ; at the same time, more authority is manifested in that church. Today we live in an age of democracy, and people everywhere talk about democracy. However, there is neither a dictatorship nor a democracy in the church. In the church there is only the order of life and the authority of the Holy Spirit, because the church is not an organization; the church is an organism. Worldly society is a matter of organization; consequently, people either talk about autocracy or democracy. The church, however, is not an organization but an organism; therefore, the administration of the church is not a matter of organization but a matter of life.

In the Bible the church has a very good name: the Body of Christ (Eph. 1:23). It is very easy to understand the Body. Let us use the members of our body as an illustration. If all of our members want to hold a meeting to discuss equality, would they even have a way to be equal? The only way they can be equal is for the body to die and for all the bones to be detached and scattered.

We all know that a living body stands upright. When a person stands up to speak, his body must be upright. The stronger and more active a person is, the more upright his expression is. When a person becomes sick and lies down, he becomes flat. The members of his body are on the same level only when he is dead and his bones are detached.

Sometimes when we look at the condition of a so-called church, it seems like a bunch of scattered bones. The brothers speak about being equal among themselves, and the sisters do not submit to the brothers. Everyone talks about equality, but this is actually a situation of scattered bones. The church is the Body of Christ. On the surface the body seems to be organized, but in reality it is an organism. All the different members of the body cannot talk about being equal, and furthermore, they must stand upright. Once the members stand upright, however, there is surely a matter of order. There are some who are above and some who are below. Consequently, there is the matter of authority.

I hope that the saints who are responsible and serving in a locality could receive this word. This does not mean that a person who receives this word wants to be in control in the church. Anyone who wants to control others will assuredly not receive grace from the Lord. Everyone who has received grace and who knows God does not like to control others. When we first spoke of the matter of order and authority in life, an older sister asked, "Will the brother who ministers the word use this message to cause others to submit to his authority?" Actually, the person asking such a question may be the first not to submit to authority.

Those who want others to submit to them do not know grace. Those who truly know grace do not hope or desire that others would submit to them. In the church we should not have people who desire to control others, and we should not have people who do not have a heart to submit to authority. Both such people lack grace. The church is the organic Body of Christ, and it should not have people who want to control others.

Every person who has received grace and lives in the Spirit of life will find his place in the Body of Christ, and he will find his order among all the members. There is no hierarchy in the church, but there is an order; there is no control of others in the church, but there is submission to one another (5:21). Ephesians does not speak of the rank of each member, but it does speak of functioning according to the operation in the measure of each one part (4:16). How can we give our arm and wrist hierarchical names? There is no hierarchy with respect to the hand and the arm, but there is an order between them. If the hand could speak, it would say, "If I offended everyone in the world, I would not be afraid, but I am afraid of problems between my arm above and me. If there is a problem, I will be in trouble." If we live in life, we will surely know our position.

The authority of the church that we speak of is entirely different from the authority of the pope in the Catholic Church. If someone asks who our authority is, we should reply that it is the brother next to us. The brothers who coordinate and serve with us are our authority; we do not have a leader among us like the pope who has authority over everyone. We have no such thing. Our only Head is Christ; He is our unique authority, and we are members one of another (Rom. 12:5; Eph. 4:25). The only difference among us relates to the matter of order and authority in the Body. We need to realize that the saint closest to us is our authority; he or she is our authority. Because the closest member to the fingers is the hand, the hand is the fingers' authority.

If we come into a normal, living church that lives in the Spirit and has the full-grown stature of Christ, we can see immediately that the members have the expression of the Body. They are members one of another, they are joined to one another, and they know their own order. Everything is upright and full of life, not flat and weak.

When there are many opinions in the church, there is no solution other than to submit to the cross and receive its breaking; only then can we know whom we should listen to according to the authority and order in Christ. A proper church is an upright church, and the brothers and sisters serving there know their position and relationship to one another. When we go to some local churches, the elders are sitting in the business office like department or section heads in a government agency. When the deacons come to see the elders, they behave like subordinates coming to receive orders from superiors. This kind of situation makes us sad. Actually, this is the condition of degraded Christianity.

In the church there are elders and deacons, but the elders should not put on the airs of an elder, and the deacons should not consider themselves lowly and insignificant. My arm is higher than my hand, but my arm does not show off its strength, thinking that it is higher than my hand. Similarly, my hand does not think that it is smaller and without much use. Some deacons have this concept when they are with the elders; they think that they should simply take orders from the elders. This erroneous concept comes from Hades and the world.

If God appoints us as elders, we receive the eldership through His grace in life; therefore, we do not have anything to boast in or any reason to feel lowly. We should realize that we are people under the ordering of life in the church, the Body. This is what is spoken of in Romans 12:3, which says that we need "to think so as to be sober-minded, as God has apportioned to each a measure of faith."

There is no dictatorship or autocracy in the church; neither are there democratic or hierarchical positions. In the church the brothers and sisters coordinate as one organic body. The church is not organized but organic. The proper church life is the move of an organic body. Apostles, elders, and serving ones are all members, and each functions according to his portion and stands in his position in one organic entity. They all know life and authority, and they all keep the order of life.

I hope that all the brothers would learn the lessons of knowing life, knowing our order in life, and knowing authority by learning this order. We do not have a centralized authority among us. Instead, the brothers around us are our authority; the members who serve the Lord with us are our authority.

If five brothers who coordinate together want to preach the gospel, do they need to hold an election to see who will be the director and leader? We may be concerned that if they do not have an election, there will be no one leading them and no one who will be responsible and give the message. So what should they do? They should submit to one another and work together. Activities in human society always require prior arrangements, such as voting for a president and a vice-president. However, it is not the same in the church life; all the brothers and sisters should live in life and allow the Holy Spirit to be the Ruler. Everyone should submit to the authority of the Holy Spirit and keep the order of life. If this is the case, each one will know his position and what to do.

If there are five brothers in a family, it is not necessary for them to come together and vote on who is first and who is second. The order among the five brothers in the family is determined by life. The first brother does not need to feel proud, and the youngest brother does not need to feel inferior. Their order is based on a natural course. The oldest brother is the oldest brother, and the youngest brother is the youngest brother. This is the order of life.

Similarly, when we are with the brothers, we immediately know our place. A sensible child obeys his father, mother, oldest brother, second oldest brother, third oldest brother, and so on. Marvelously, this is the way in every healthy and normal family. The oldest child knows that he is the oldest child and that he should have a certain responsibility and conduct; at the same time, when he gives a command, all the rest of the children obey him because they know their birth order. In a healthy family, not only is the father the authority, but the mother is an authority as well. Furthermore, the oldest brother is an authority over the second, the second brother is an authority over the third, the third brother is an authority over the fourth, and the fourth brother is an authority over the fifth. There is a certain order in the whole family.

Every authority is a protection, a support, and a supply. For example, when a family eats together, the youngest child typically gets the most food because everyone loves him. The older children often envy him and feel that he is the most privileged. Nonetheless, the youngest child may say, "I am not the most privileged, because everyone regulates me." This illustration shows that there is an order of life among the members of the body. Although order comes with restrictions, it also comes with a supply. If we live in life, keep our position, and respect the position of others when we do anything in the church, we will be able to coordinate with one another in a proper way.

When the brothers and sisters take care of the cleaning service in the church life, we have discovered two kinds of situations. Some saints have truly made progress. When they clean, they have no ideas and opinions. They simply follow the responsible one who tells them how they should clean, what they should use, and what their responsibility is. This shows that they have truly learned some lessons. However, when other brothers and sisters clean, they do not fellowship even though they do not argue. When the responsible brothers try to tell them how they should do it, they may say, "I will do my part, and you should do your part. Please do not bother me." Of course, some people may not say this, but they display this kind of attitude when they clean. This represents a lack in knowing the order of life and a lack of learning the lessons of life.

## BUILDING UP THE BODY OF CHRIST

The more a person lives in the Holy Spirit and in life, the more he knows his position, the order of life, and the authority in life. Such brothers and sisters are a definite strengthening to the Body of Christ. If my little finger rebelled and refused to stay in its place, wanting instead to become a foot and to walk, what kind of situation would this be? The entire church often suffers loss when a small brother or sister refuses to keep his or her place in the church. On the contrary, if a person keeps his place, he will be a strengthening to the Body. In other words, the members who strengthen the Body are those who keep their place.

Ephesians 4:16 says, "All the Body, being joined together and being knit together through every joint of the rich supply and through the operation in the measure of each one part, causes the growth of the Body." Every joint in the body has its own measure, which is developed through life, and it is able to supply all the members richly. When everyone functions according to his function, the body is built up. A church becomes strong and is built up when all the saints know the order of life and stay in their place.

Thus, the matter of the church involves strict requirements; it requires us to be separated from the world, to reject the self, to deal with the flesh, and to deny the natural life. It also requires us to be separated from independence and individualism. It is not sufficient for us to be separated from the world, the self, the flesh, and the natural life, because we may still live according to our independence and individualism. Independence and individualism are the main factors that cause the Body of Christ not to be built up. In order to have the church, we cannot have individualism, and in order to have the Body, we cannot have independence. In the Body there is no individualism, no individual idea, judgment, decision, inclination, choosing, or preference. Anything individual hinders the building up of the church and damages the Body of Christ.

Every believer has his own personality and characteristic; God's salvation does not nullify our personality and characteristic. On the one hand, we have been shown mercy to be in God's family. In a family an older brother may be bigger, but he is still a person, and a younger brother may be smaller, but he is also a person. This is the situation in a family. On the other hand, when we speak of the church as the Body of Christ and ourselves as the members in this Body, our person does not exist. In the Body we have only one person, and this is the person of Christ the Head. If all the members in our body were their own person, we would be in great trouble, and we would not be able to live.

Although a body has many members, there is only one person, the head. When our head feels tired and wants to sleep, all the members lie down together. If our head feels tired and wants to lie down to rest, but our hands do not want to rest and instead keep moving and working, our whole body will become sick.

There are always two sides to a truth. As far as being a brother in God's family, every believer is a person; however, as far as the Body of Christ is concerned, his person does not exist because there is only one Body. Consequently, there can be only one person. Some brothers and sisters insist on being their own person in the Body, and as a result, they prevent the Body from making any move. They must realize that they are members in the Body. If they try to be an independent member, they will become the ugliest members in the Body, but if they remain in their proper order, they will be the most beautiful members.

The key to all these points depends on the level of life in us. If our life is sufficiently abundant, it will require us to give up our individual person and give up our individualism, independence, prejudice, and pride. This is the way for the church to reach the measure of the stature of the fullness of Christ, the way for the church to be strong, and the way for the church to express the fullness of Christ.

# CHAPTER TWELVE

# THE PROPER WAY TO FOLLOW
# THE BIBLE AND THE INNER LIFE

Scripture Reading: Eph. 1:22-23

After we spent time before the Lord seeking His will concerning the different aspects of the church, the Lord in my spirit has given me the sense that we should touch the matter of the church according to the actual situation of the saints. In principle we can divide this topic into two aspects: the first aspect concerns the Bible, and the second aspect concerns the inner life.

## EXAMINING AND DECIDING BASED ON THE BIBLE

Every genuine Christian has a Bible in his hand. To us the Bible is so clear, secure, and reliable. As long as God's children have some reverence and godly fear in their hearts, they will never object to the Bible. Everyone must respect the position of the Bible before God and treasure the authority of the Bible among God's children. We need to praise God for giving us the Bible outwardly as our greatest heritage and a priceless treasure. The Bible has been passed down to our hands and translated into our language so that we can easily understand it; this is a great blessing that the Lord has given us. Hence, when we speak of the matter of the church, we must check with the Bible concerning the condition of the church. We should examine the Bible when we measure a church. All the children of God who are godly must confess that we cannot accept anything that is not according to the Bible, that cannot stand up to the scrutiny of the Bible, or that clearly violates and is against the teachings of the Bible. Thus, every person who is godly and belongs to God must eventually examine the matter of the church according to the Bible.

## Coming Back to the Bible

About one century ago, the Lord raised up a group of brothers in England. Because they had many questions concerning Christian groups, they began to check whether their condition was according to the record and teaching of the Bible. After comparing the situation with the Bible, they discovered that all the Christian groups they encountered had some problems. These Western saints had a simple slogan: "Back to the Bible!" They hoped that the condition, content, and activities of the church and all of their work would be according to the teaching of the Bible. However, after these brothers passed away, their so-called church degraded into unseemly Christianity, which has gone astray from the Bible in many things and does not match the Bible.

One hundred years ago the Holy Spirit raised up a group of brothers to come back to the Bible. They wanted to drop everything that was not in the Bible, and by the Lord's grace, they wanted to recover everything that was in the Bible. Even today, both in the East and in the West, there are still many godly people among God's children who are answering the Holy Spirit's call and bringing the matter of the church back to the Bible. They want to drop everything that is not in the Bible and recover everything that is in the Bible, according to what they have seen in the Bible and according to the grace that they have been shown. The church must be according to the record of the Bible. Whatever man can see and touch related to the whole condition and situation of the church should be according to the teaching of the Bible.

Today, in this age of confusion in Christianity, the first question we should ask, regardless of which Christian group we contact, is whether their condition is pleasing to God. We should not quickly accept that they are on the ground of the church. We should compare the condition of every Christian group with the Bible. This means that we should use the Bible to determine the matter of the church. If we judge according to the will of man, we get into trouble because everyone has his interpretation and view. If we try to answer the question of the church according to man's view, we will only become more and more confused. We must all learn to drop our views, cease from our opinions, and bring the question of the church to the Bible.

Some people may say that even though there has been one Bible throughout the ages, everyone has different interpretations of the Bible and different definitions of the meaning of its words; therefore, there will still be many arguments. This word sounds very logical, but actually it is not. In the past twenty years we have met thousands upon thousands of people who belong to the Lord. We can testify that as long as a person has a godly fear before God and is willing to put himself aside, not having his own prejudice or opinion, then when the Bible speaks of the number ten, he will not read it as nine or eleven. Unless a certain person has some prejudice, his reading of the Bible will not be different from what it actually says.

For example, there are two methods of baptizing in Christianity: one way is to baptize by sprinkling water, and the other way is to baptize by immersion, burying a believer in the water. If a person reads the Bible without any prejudice, he should not have a second view concerning this matter; he would surely regard the view of baptism by immersion. In the past I was baptized by sprinkling. I had no feeling at the time, and because I was not serious, I did not pray. Strictly speaking, I was not saved. My name appeared on the list to be baptized only because I passed an interview with the pastor and attended a communion worship service. I stood before the crowd, and as I held a bronze basin, I was sprinkled with a few drops of water and then received the communion. However, I was not saved. The following year, however, I touched the Holy Spirit and was genuinely saved. Then I began reading the Bible. Because of the Lord's grace, I desired the Lord's word like a newborn babe who desires milk (1 Pet. 2:2).

One day I saw the matter of baptism in the Bible. When I read that the Lord was baptized into the water and came up from the water (Matt. 3:16), I began to wonder, "Have I not been baptized? Why did I not go into the water and come up from the water?" I went to my pastor and asked him. He answered that it was proper to be baptized by immersion, but some people think that baptism by immersion is too troublesome and that it is more convenient to be sprinkled with water. He said that when the weather gets cold, and both men and women need to change clothes, it becomes troublesome. This reply did not satisfy me, but I did not want to argue with him, because I was a young person. So I asked, "Is it not true that we should follow the Lord's footsteps? If we do not follow the Lord in the matter of baptism, on what matters should we follow the Lord?" This pastor was very eloquent in answering, so he said, "If you truly want to imitate the Lord, you should go to the Jordan River." I did not answer him, but inwardly I was not happy, and I felt that he was arguing irrationally.

After I went home, I read the Bible again and discovered that John the Baptist was baptizing in Aenon "because there was much water there" (John 3:23). This shows that baptism does not have to be in the Jordan River, and "much water" undoubtedly indicates that the people were baptized by immersion, not by sprinkling, because baptism by sprinkling does not require much water. Then I read in Acts 8:37-39 that Philip baptized the Ethiopian eunuch, and they both went down into the water and came up out of the water. I felt that I had more ground, so I went again to the pastor. After he listened, he did not argue, and he said, "There are two ways in our church. If someone wants to be baptized by sprinkling, we baptize them by sprinkling, but if you want to be baptized by immersion, we will baptize you by immersion." I could not be satisfied with his answer, and I could not agree with him inwardly because the truth can be only one, not two. If the Bible says that we should baptize by immersion, we should not baptize by sprinkling, and if the Bible says that we should baptize by sprinkling, we should not baptize by immersion. I could not agree with his way of speaking, because once we practice this, it will only produce problems, including problems in matters other than only baptism. There are many areas in which we might not be according to the Bible.

From that day on, I stopped trusting what that pastor said,

and I listed all the situations that I saw and compared them one by one to the Bible. Because I began to look into the matter of baptism in the Bible, I began to look into many other matters, including the church. As a result, I found that many items were not according to the Bible. One day I read in George Müller's biography that he too had been baptized by sprinkling. When a sister spoke to him concerning baptism by immersion, he did not agree with her. She only asked him to read the Bible thoroughly, and because Müller paid attention to the Word of God, he read the New Testament again. Müller concluded that the Bible speaks concerning baptism by immersion more clearly than it speaks concerning prophecies. Therefore, he was baptized by immersion. If we bring a matter to the Bible and put aside our own views and opinions, and if we examine and compare the matter with the Bible in a thorough way, we will become clear and understand it without any dissension.

## Confusion Being Caused
## by Man's Opinions and Ideas

Today the confusion in Christianity is not because the record in the Bible is confused; instead, confusion is produced by man's opinions, ideas, and ways of doing things. If we are careless, we will be led in circles by the confusion of Christianity, but if we are serious, we will bring all the matters concerning the church to the Bible and compare them with the Bible. We should accept everything that is in the Bible, and we should reject anything that is not in the Bible. If we have a fear of God, and if we compare all the matters of the church to the Bible, we will discover any situation in Christianity that is not according to the Bible. If we are not serious Christians, there is not much else to say, but if we want to be serious Christians, we must fear the Lord and respect His Word, bringing all the matters concerning the church under the light of the Bible to obtain God's rule and standard. Then we will have God's final decision. Everything other than this belongs to man's opinions, views, standards, and ways of doing things. Anything that belongs to man or follows the world will be rejected by God. The Bible is great and divine;

everyone who fears God should come back to God's Word in this way.

## MATCHING THE TASTE AND DEMAND OF THE INNER LIFE

The most precious thing to a Christian is that we have not only the Bible outwardly, but the life of God inwardly. Every life has its particular demand and taste. As God's children, we have God's life with its demand and taste in us. For example, a chicken has a life with a demand to eat. If we try to feed a chicken unclean things, however, it will refuse to eat because they do not match its taste. A duck likes water, and its life demands that it be in water because water matches its taste. Every life has its particular demand and taste. Similarly, as saved ones, we have Christ's life in us, and His life demands that we receive supply and satisfaction in the church; furthermore, this demand also has a taste.

After I was saved and began to read the Bible, I compared the denomination where I was with the Bible, and I found that there were many situations that were not according to the record in the Bible. I still went to meetings, but I felt depressed and uneasy after every meeting. Before I was saved, I had always felt quite good after a meeting because the chapel was very quiet. It was much better than the theater. After I was saved, I began to pray, pursue, and have fellowship with the Lord, and I realized that the life in me truly had a demand and taste for receiving the supply of life. The messages in those meetings, however, could not supply me inwardly; I could not receive food there, and I was not satisfied inwardly.

One winter at Christmas, everyone was celebrating in the chapel. Although I was saved, because I was still young, I went to see the show with everyone else. Afterward, however, I felt very sad inwardly, and I decided that I would never go there again. This was due to the taste and demand of the life in me.

Within every saved person, there is a taste and demand related to life. This is just like the life in a little child that spontaneously causes him to want to eat. Furthermore, he has a certain taste. If he is given food that is stinky and tastes bitter, he will spew it out, but if he is given food that smells good and is sweet, he will eat all of it. The taste of life in genuine Christians tells us where we should meet to please the Lord—where there is spiritual food, where there is the Lord's presence, and where God feeds His children. There is a demand and a taste in us. We cannot merely judge the matter of the church outwardly according to the doctrines of the Bible, but also we must judge it inwardly according to the taste and demand of life.

When I gave some messages in Tsingtao, someone asked, "Which Christian group is right? Every group says that they are right, so how do we judge?" I answered that we first need to measure a group with the Bible. If we cannot find anything wrong in this regard, we must judge it according to the demand and taste of life. For example, there are many groups in Tsingtao. If a group preaches the gospel, has the Lord's name, and helps people to be saved but lacks the element of the Lord within, its testimony will not be bright. When a person is newly saved, he may feel good about going there because the Lord's name is there and because he received help to be saved and know salvation. Nonetheless, since it gives only a little ground to the Lord, he cannot receive any deeper grace. Even though there is only a small amount of the element of Christ, he can still be satisfied with this kind of group because he is newly saved.

However, a need in him will increase, and when he grows and knows the Lord more, he will not feel satisfied in these meetings. One day he may go to another group, and it may be that this group gives the Lord a little more ground, and their leading ones may be consecrated and pursuing the outpouring of the Holy Spirit. After this brother experiences consecration and pursues the outpouring of the Holy Spirit, he will feel full of the Lord's presence and able to touch the Lord's presence more than in the first group. This will temporarily satisfy his taste. However, after a while there will be a further need in him which cannot be satisfied, so he will look for another group. The third group may truly be more spiritual and have more of the Lord's presence. But after a year or two, a need will again arise in him. Then he will find a fourth group that has more spiritual weight which satisfies him. Eventually, he will be led to where the Lord wants him to stay. The taste and demand of life will tell him that he has reached the highest place, the place where he can touch the Lord's presence the most and receive the most life supply.

## BEING ACCORDING TO THE BIBLE AND TAKING CARE OF THE DEMANDS OF THE LIFE WITHIN

Full-time servants of the Lord should never argue with people about which place is right or wrong. We need only to show them the principles of being according to the Bible and according to the inner demand of life. If people fear the Lord, they will bring the matter of the church to the Bible and resolve it according to the Bible. They will also take care of the taste and demand of the life within them; they will go wherever this life requires.

In 1947 in Shanghai, there was a brother who often criticized the church. In one meeting he was openly critical of the church. After he spoke, I stood up and said, "Brother, I dare not say that we do not have the shortcomings which you spoke of, but if you can find a place in all of Shanghai that is better and more correct, I will surely follow you." He shook his head and stated that he could not find such a place. Then I said that he should stop his criticizing if he could not find such a place. This word seems so simple and unsophisticated, but I want to present it to you because it is the simplest and easiest way to measure the matter of the church.

On one hand, with a godly fear we should put aside everything that is not according to the Bible, and on the other hand, we must touch the inward sense to see whether we are supplied and can touch the Lord's presence in fellowship. We cannot merely measure everything according to the Bible in an outward way and ignore the existence of the inward spiritual reality and the Lord's presence. We need to know the Lord's Spirit and life, and we need to allow the Lord to rule so that the cross can break us more deeply. If we do not have this, we merely have some outward rituals, and we are according to the Bible merely in an outward way. By themselves, these things do not have much value. We should allow the cross to break us inwardly and to dig into us more deeply so that Christ can have more ground in us and so that the Spirit can have more authority in us. Then when people come into our meetings, they will be able to touch the living Christ and the heavenly reality. Only this is the genuine church.

Outwardly, the church must be completely according to the Bible; inwardly, the church must be completely filled with Christ and the Spirit. If we want to test whether a church is according to God's desire, we must test according to these two aspects. We need to use the Bible outwardly and the Spirit inwardly; we have the light of the Bible without and life's demands and tastes within. We should not despise either of these two aspects; both aspects are principles for solving the question of the church.

## OUR NEED TO STOP OUR ENTIRE BEING

Since the church is the Body of Christ, the church is Christ Himself. Christ is the embodiment of God, and He is God becoming flesh, taking the likeness of a man, and living the life of a man. Anything that relies upon man's ability, organization, and way of doing things cannot reach this goal. Whenever we touch the matter of the church, we need to stop our whole being. When people touch the matter of the church, all of the *I*s, like "I think," "I view," "I want," and "I will," begin to come out. We need to stop them. We should not say, "Baptism is indeed according to the Bible, but I think…" This should not be our response.

In the past there was an older sister in a certain locality. She was very educated, bold, and eloquent; furthermore, she loved the Lord very much. One day she came to me and asked, "Why does 1 Corinthians 14 forbid women from speaking?" When I heard this word, I replied in a calm way because I sensed that something was not right: "I only know that this is clearly recorded in 1 Corinthians 14, but just like you, I do not know the reason." Then I asked, "Although neither of us knows the reason, is 1 Corinthians 14:34 the commandment of the Bible? If it is not the commandment of the Bible, it can be removed, but if it is the commandment of the Bible, what can we say?" Then she said, "But I think…" I responded, "You do not need to think. Who needs you to think? If we need to think, there would be no Bible." These words truly shocked her, but is our view worth anything? Do we have the position to give an opinion? If we had the position to give an opinion, we could abandon the Bible. We must all learn the lesson of stopping our reasonings and simply saying Amen to God's Word without anything else.

Often those who ask why do not want to submit, and usually those who ask why are proud and arrogant. This kind of person will say, "I think," "I view," "I thought," "I want," "I decide," and "I want to do this." This kind of attitude is not from the heavenly Jerusalem but from Babylon, the abyss. Those who fear God will not say anything before His Word, and they know that only what God says counts. We may not understand the reason, but we must still bow and confess that He is the Lord, that we are His servants, and that our attitude is simply to receive.

Whenever we touch the matter of the church, we should prostrate our whole being, because if man is present, there is no church, and in order for there to be the church, there cannot be man. If we are, there is no church, and if there is the church, we cannot be. The Bible is a strong, outward requirement; however, there is something stronger within us—the Holy Spirit and life. The requirement within us is more subjective and personal, and it touches us more. In the case of the older sister spoken of earlier, I used the Bible to calm her down, but I also asked her, "Sister, does the feeling within you agree with me or does it agree with your words?" She replied that her inward sense was not in agreement with her view and that its demand was for her to accept 1 Corinthians 14 even though her outer man did not want to accept it. This shows that although I used the Bible to deal with this matter, the life within her was dealing with it as well.

## CONCLUSION

Concerning the church, the Bible is the standard, and life is the demand. Often people argue with us about the matter of the church, but as they argue with us in their mind, the feeling in them agrees with us and speaks for us. Consequently, we sometimes need only to point out certain things and then let their inward feeling continue to speak to them. If we want to touch the matter of the church, we need to drop everything of the world and everything of human relationships, organizations, methods, views, and opinions. We should not give these things any ground, because neither the Bible nor the Holy Spirit gives them any ground. The Holy Spirit has only the demand of life.

We do not need to argue concerning the matter of the church; instead, we need only to discern. Discernment requires an inner feeling. If we fear God and pursue the Lord, we should use the Bible as the outward standard, and we should use the taste of life within as the inward demand. If we want to meet the Holy Spirit's requirements, we must walk according to the truth of the church. If we do not want to pay the price and if we care about human relationships, positions, or the acceptance of the world, trying to maintain ourselves in Christian organizations, we can only look to the Lord for His mercy. May the Lord be gracious to us so that our hearts would remain clean, our spirits would remain open, and we would keep following life and taking the proper way of the church.

CHAPTER THIRTEEN

# THE SPIRITUAL REQUIREMENTS
# OF A CHRISTIAN AND THE STANDARD
# FOR TESTING THESE REQUIREMENTS

Scripture Reading: Rom. 12:3-5

## THE SPIRITUAL REQUIREMENTS OF A CHRISTIAN

Everyone who follows the Lord must realize that there are certain spiritual requirements in every spiritual matter. Some requirements come from the outward teaching of the Bible, and others come from the inward sense of life. A Christian who is living and who is according to the proper standard will be sensitive to these requirements. If we have been shown mercy and love the Lord, and if we are willing to learn to live before the Lord, then spontaneously our heart will turn to the Lord and love Him. We will also want to please the Lord. In this way we will be in fellowship with the Lord inwardly. In our fellowship we will often encounter spiritual requirements from the outward teachings of the Bible and from the inward sense of life.

### The Requirement of the Word of the Bible

Before a sister is saved and begins to pursue the Lord, she may always set herself over her husband and take the lead in everything at home. She can rule over her husband with her opinions and completely disregard his opinions. In such a situation, she is the leader and the head of the house. As she begins to pursue the Lord and fellowship with Him, however, she will read Ephesians 5:22, which says, "Wives, be subject to your own husbands as to the Lord." When she reads this word, the teaching of the Bible will be full of power and touch her being, and light will come forth to shine in her whole being. At this moment the teaching of the Bible will require her to subject herself to her husband. If she truly loves and pursues the Lord, it will be difficult to ignore this requirement and not accept it.

All the brothers and sisters who have had this kind of experience understand what I am saying. If we do not accept this requirement, we will immediately sense that there is a barrier between us and the Lord, and we will feel as if something is wrong. Sometimes we receive a requirement in the morning. If we do not agree with the Lord, we will feel very uneasy throughout the day; it will seem as if something is missing in us. Only when we answer the Lord's requirement can we be at peace and inwardly at rest. Then our relationship with the Lord becomes very pleasant and comfortable, and we have a sweet feeling before the Lord because we are in agreement with His requirement in the Word.

## The Requirement of the Sense of Life

In the past many of us liked to gossip about others and were quite talkative. Before we were saved, we had no feeling and did not care about our talkative nature. However, after we were saved, we began to pursue the Lord and fellowship with Him. In our fellowship we sensed a demand that restricted our speaking. Although we may not have read a teaching about this in the Bible, we sensed that there was a demand from the life in us, which restricted our tongue and the words in our mouth. This demand required us to be less talkative. This is a demand from the life within. If we do not agree with this demand, we will feel that we have offended the Lord, and we will immediately be condemned by our conscience. We will remain under condemnation until we submit to this demand, confess our sin of gossiping, and agree that we are willing to learn to restrict our speaking through His grace. After we agree, we will immediately feel bright, fresh, and comfortable, and we will have the Lord's inward presence.

These two examples show two spiritual requirements. Strictly speaking, as those who pursue the Lord, we have a spiritual requirement as the standard of our walk, but how do we know if we are walking on the right path? How do we know which way to take? The standard of our walk is based on a spiritual requirement, and there are two kinds of spiritual requirements. The first requirement comes from the Bible's clear teaching, and the second comes from the sense of life. We often experience these requirements at the same time, and they correspond to an inward and outward requirement. They can be compared to a compass which directs us on the right path for our walk on the Lord's way. This compass tells us what we should do and where we should go. In other words, our Christian living should match these spiritual requirements and always agree with them. I hope all the saints would firmly adhere to this principle and realize that our whole Christian living should be a living in agreement with these spiritual requirements.

We may have been a Christian for only a week, a month, or even a year, but if we have never had a sense of these spiritual requirements, we are probably not saved, and if we are saved, we probably do not love the Lord much or fellowship with Him. If we are truly saved and fellowship with the Lord, we should sense some spiritual requirements in us every day. We should touch the Lord's requirements in His Word and the requirements from the sense of life every day. If it has been a long time since we touched any spiritual requirements, we should realize that something is wrong in us. This shows that the fundamental frustration in a Christian's living is related to these spiritual requirements. We cannot neglect these spiritual requirements.

## SPIRITUAL REQUIREMENTS RELATED TO THE CHURCH

### Life Requiring Us to Have Fellowship with All the Saints

Every saved person who lives before the Lord definitely has some spiritual requirements within him. Based on this principle, we need to know the requirements that are related to the church. As soon as we begin to live before the Lord, we can sense a spiritual requirement within to fellowship with other saints. This is a true fact, and we cannot avoid it. The Lord and His life within require us to fellowship with other saints. The life we have received, which is in each one of us, is not an individual life; rather, it is the Lord's life, a great life. We are not the only ones who have received this life; many other people have received it as well. This life in us requires us to fellowship with other saints.

The saints meet together all the time in the church in Taipei, and they see each other frequently. Thus, they may not have much consciousness of the fact that life requires fellowship, and they may even feel that they have too much fellowship. Some saints have said that there are too many meetings, yet if they do not come to the meeting, they do not have peace. Some colleagues of the brothers and sisters say, "You are so busy. In the morning you are in a hurry to go to work. In the evening you are in a hurry to go home. Then after dinner you are in a hurry to go to the meeting. You are in a hurry every evening of the week, but it seems as if you never get tired of meeting. This is truly strange." In reality, this is a matter of the life in us.

Recently more than ten brothers and sisters went to visit the church in Manila. The saints there were very warm-hearted, and they invited the brothers and sisters to eat the best food every day. As a result, the brothers and sisters became tired of eating fine food. However, this did not eliminate their need to eat. The human life needs food, but people cannot eat too much; otherwise, their bodies will not be able to bear it. But if a person is without food for three or four days, he will immediately sense a need in his body for food. At such a time, it will not matter whether the food is plain rice or a gourmet meal. As long as there is a need and the food is edible, it will taste very good.

The saints in the church in Taipei attend meetings all the time; they may attend a meeting today and another tomorrow, and sometimes they even attend several meetings in a day. Thus, they may not feel that there is a demand within for fellowship. However, if they went to an isolated place and were unable to see a brother or sister for a whole week and were unable to attend a single meeting for two weeks, there would be a demand for fellowship with other saints within the depth of their being.

In the first year of the Sino-Japanese War, some brothers and sisters and I visited a place in northwest China. Before we went there, we often broke bread with many brothers and sisters to remember the Lord. Since we broke bread often, we took it for granted and did not feel that it was very special. However, when we were in northwest China, we had to wait for a long time before we could attend a bread-breaking meeting on the Lord's Day. All of us inwardly longed for the bread-breaking meeting. This was something related to the requirement of life. We need to realize that the Christian life is not an individual life; the Christian life is a corporate life. Christians cannot be alone. This can be compared to the fact that bees like to be together. If there is a swarm of bees, all the nearby bees want to be with it; this is a demand of their life.

Please keep in mind the reason that we need the church. A Christian needs to meet because the life in a Christian requires him to fellowship with all the saints. This is a true fact. If we separated ourselves from the saints, did not go to the meetings, and had no contact with the saints for three to six months, how would we feel inwardly? Would we feel happy or unhappy? We would immediately sense a demand within us. This can be compared to a person who wants food because he is hungry. The demand in us requires us to participate in the church and to have fellowship with the saints. This is the first requirement of life with respect to the church.

## Life Requiring Christians to Serve Others

If we live before the Lord and have fellowship with the saints, there will be a condition in us that requires us to serve and supply others. This is the reason some unbelievers think we are foolish when they see us going to meetings in the evenings, cleaning the meeting hall, or visiting saints in their homes even though we may be exhausted after working all day. They do not see that this is not a foolish matter but a matter of the life in us making a demand. Unbelievers may think we are foolish, but we feel very joyful within.

We can all testify that the life in us is truly a serving life. Around 1946 there was a sister in Shanghai whose husband was the manager of a bank. Since she was the wife of a manager, she had several maids in her house, and she did not need to do any housework. However, she liked to go to the meeting hall to mop the floor and clean the windows. After a while, her husband began to wonder why she went to the meeting hall every day. This seemed unusual to him, and he wondered what she could be doing at the meeting hall. One day he came to the meeting hall and discovered that his wife was mopping the floor. He could not understand her behavior and was very upset. Since he was a bank manager, he felt that it was demeaning to him for his wife to do such menial work. He could not understand why his wife would go to the meeting hall to mop the floor when they had several maids in their home.

We can all testify that when this sister was mopping the floor, her face was shining. The more she mopped the floor, the more the Lord's presence was with her. We could not stop her from mopping the floor. This illustrates that the requirement of the life in Christians is very wonderful. This life requires us to serve others. Some people may think that the manager's wife was silly, but actually, if she was asked, she would say that she could not be happy if she did not serve others. Her desire to serve others was like the hunger in man for food. When she served others, she was satisfied. This is a requirement of life in Christians. This requirement demands that Christians meet together and serve one another. Without this requirement, Christians cannot meet or serve together.

## Life Requiring Christians to Be Served and Supplied

Life also demands that we be served and supplied by others. This is very natural. The reason we come to break bread, pray, fellowship, or even listen to a message is because the life in us has a requirement of needing to be supplied. If we go to a meeting or listen to a message, and if the meeting is full of supply and the Lord's presence, we sense satisfaction, sweetness, and the inward presence of the Lord. This is the life in us that requires us to be supplied.

When we come to the bread-breaking meeting, sing hymns, or listen to prayers, we become inwardly satisfied. There was a gospel friend who attended our bread-breaking meeting, and he was quite puzzled by what he observed. He knew almost all the people in the meeting—some were university professors and some were college students. The meeting lasted for one and a half hours, but there was no message, no exhortation, and no story-telling. Instead, the people only sang hymns and prayed prayers. Consequently, he could not understand why everyone seemed happy and joyful by the time it was over. Were they truly satisfied or only superstitious? He had many questions because he knew most of the saints, many of whom studied science and had doctorate degrees in chemistry, but he could not understand the situation.

This is similar to eating at a well-known restaurant in Taipei. Whenever people go there to eat, they wait in line. Even managers and chief executives wait in line, but they are willing to do this because the life in them has a need to be supplied. When we attend the bread-breaking meeting, we may only sing a few hymns or pray some prayers, but inwardly we feel that we are in the heavenlies; we feel satisfied and happy. This shows that life requires a supply.

## Life Requiring Christians to Be Spiritual

Furthermore, the life in each saint requires us to be spiritual. When we are in the spirit, we feel comfortable within. In other words, when we follow the inward requirements to forsake the world, reject the flesh, and deal with our self, we immediately feel inwardly pleasant. However, if we indulge our flesh, love the world, and try to preserve our self, we feel inwardly uncomfortable. This proves that the life in us requires us to be spiritual. This requirement, however, does not only apply to us; it also applies to others.

When a person acts in his flesh and self in our meetings, there is no need to say anything because the life in the saints feels very uncomfortable about this fleshly activity. Similarly, when a saint moves according to the Holy Spirit when he prays, speaks, or chooses a hymn, all the saints sense that they are touching the Spirit inwardly. This is a definite fact.

If anyone has been shown mercy, he has had this experience to some degree.

### Life Requiring Christians to Exalt Christ

The life in us requires us to always exalt Christ and uplift Jesus. If we meet a saint in our daily life who lives before God, who exalts Christ, who has been broken in the self, and who allows the Lord to flourish, we feel glorious, bright, joyful, and sweet. We also feel pleasant in our spirit. However, if we meet a saint who boasts in himself and who expresses himself and his flesh, we feel uncomfortable. This relates to a requirement of life.

### Life Requiring Christians to Do God's Will

Life also requires us to do God's will. When we follow God's will and desire to do God's will, the life in us feels sweet and pleasant. Sometimes we may disobey and oppose God's will, but the life in us still requires us to follow God's will. This requirement is so strong that even if we fail and do not follow God's will, we still feel sad and depressed in our spirit when we see others not following God's will. This is a requirement of life in us.

### Life Requiring the Church to Live Out Christ and to Allow the Holy Spirit to Rule

The highest requirement of life is that we live out Christ, let the Holy Spirit operate in us, and allow Christ to rule in us in the Holy Spirit. All the requirements of life are related to the church. If we care for these requirements, it will not be difficult to touch the way of the church and see the genuine condition of the church. If we care for the sense of life, we will be able to easily discern whether a Christian group is truly in the reality of the church; this is a crucial matter.

### THE STANDARD FOR
### TESTING THE REQUIREMENTS OF LIFE

### Testing the Requirement of Life for Fellowship

Now we must see something regarding the standard for

testing the requirements of life. We have spoken of the fact that life requires us to have fellowship. However, when we go to a Christian group, the people we meet often do not match us, even though we are open and eager to have fellowship. We do not have fellowship with them and are even unable to have fellowship with them. At such a moment, we should examine the reason for this. We should examine it from two sides. First, we should check whether there is a problem with us that prevents us from fellowshipping with others. If we do not have any problems, such as loving the world, living in sin, or caring for the flesh, then the problem is not with us. Although people in this group may say that they are Christians, we need to check whether they allow the Lord to reign in them and whether they live in the Lord. This is a very practical matter.

In the spring of 1937 I was invited by a Christian group to speak. After I gave the message, they invited me to fellowship with them. At the time I felt as if I was in the Arctic Ocean, because they did not understand me, and I did not understand them; we were totally incompatible with one another. Nevertheless, they spread a feast for me, and some even said, "Mr. Lee, the message you gave truly helped us. We truly appreciate you." However, deep inside I was grieving because we could not truly blend and fellowship with one another. Even though they called themselves Christians and were a Christian group, I realized that they did not live in the Lord or pursue Him enough, despite the fact that some of them had the Lord's life. I went back to northern China after the meeting, and later I heard from others that an elder and some of the deacons and preachers in that group did not understand my words. Then I understood why we did not have anything to fellowship about and could not fellowship with one another, even though they praised my message.

The life in us truly requires others to live in the spirit so that there can be fellowship. Hence, we should never assume that it is enough for some people to say that they are Christians or that they are a Christian group. This is not enough for us to believe them and conclude that they are a church according to the Bible. We must apply the requirements of our inner life, one of which is the requirement of fellowship. Based on this demand, we must check the genuine condition of any group. What is their condition before the Lord? If we live before the Lord, love the Lord, and reject the world and sin, yet we feel uncomfortable and cannot fellowship with them, this shows that they have lost Christ and the ground of the church and that the Holy Spirit is not ruling in them. They may have the Bible in their hands, but the word of the Bible does not have much ground among them or in them. The requirement for fellowship enables us to test whether a Christian group is taking the way that pleases the Lord.

## Testing the Requirement of Life
## for Christians to Serve Others

The second requirement of life is that we serve others. Sometimes when we go to a Christian group, we cannot serve even though the life in us wants to serve. We may want to serve, but we may not be allowed to serve or our service may be rejected. On the one hand, every saved person has the desire to exercise his gift and supply others according to the requirement of life. On the other hand, some Christian groups can hinder the believers from manifesting their true function according to the requirement of life. We may be in a certain church and sense the requirement of life to serve others, but if we are not allowed to exercise our function and service, there are definitely some problems in the church.

However, before coming to such a conclusion, we need to check to see whether we have any motives in our service. Are we coveting something? Are we serving by our flesh, preference, or self? If any of these things are present in us, the church is correct to reject our service. However, if the church rejects us and our service, even though we do not have anything of the flesh and self nor any motive, covetousness, or preference in our service, we can conclude that this church is not according to the Holy Spirit. It is merely an organization of Christianity. A church that allows the Holy Spirit to exercise authority and has the presence of Christ will be eager to let the saints function and serve. This kind of church affords the greatest opportunity for the saints to minister the grace they have received. As they manifest their functions in the church, they benefit the church.

It is impossible for us to manifest our spiritual function in organized Christianity. In 1938 I was in northern China, and I met a Western missionary from the China Inland Mission. He was a little younger than I, and he loved the Lord very much. He was an American, and he lived in a big guest house owned by the China Inland Mission where many other Western missionaries, who were mainly from England, also lived. We did not know one another, but after fellowshipping a couple times, we began to know one another in the Lord. One day he came to fellowship with me and said, "Brother Lee, there is something that I cannot tell anyone, but I feel that I can tell you. Deep within I am very clear how the Lord wants me to serve, but everyone in my mission has risen up against me. Although I tell you these things, I still cannot say too much." He told me that he had received some spiritual things and that he wanted to supply and minister what he had received to people in the Holy Spirit. However, he encountered difficulty and persecution in his mission; he was bothered to such an extent that he needed to come and fellowship with me, and he asked me to pray with him. At that moment I became clear that there were some problems in his mission because his service to the saints through the Spirit was encountering opposition and being hindered. His mission was not under the authority of the Holy Spirit, and it had lost Christ's presence and the Holy Spirit's operation.

If we look only at a church outwardly, we may find nothing that is against the Bible outwardly; nevertheless, we still have to look at its inward condition to see whether it is ruled by man or whether the world has any ground in it. When we live in life, life will require us to serve, but if we encounter opposition and difficulties in a certain place, we can conclude that it has lost Christ's presence. If we live before the Lord, reject our flesh, and allow the Spirit to rule, but we are still unable to serve, we can conclude that the Christian group is not in the Holy Spirit, nor does it exalt Christ. We need to see the many aspects of the requirements of life.

Once I was in Taiyuan in the Shansi Province, and I ate

something very sour. I thought it was vinegar, but after tasting real vinegar, I realized that the two were quite different. Many things that appear to be the same may not be what we think they are; we can know if there is a difference only by tasting them. We need to see that the taste of life is accurate. One kind of vinegar looks similar to grape juice, but if we taste them we will know the difference; one is sweet, and the other is sour.

The church is not merely a matter of letters or doctrines according to the Bible. It is also a matter of life. When we live in the Spirit and in life, the sense of life, the demand of life, and the taste of life within will tell us whether the activity of our Christian group is of life, of Christ, and of spiritual reality. We will know inwardly; this is a principle.

## Testing the Requirement of Life
## for Christians to Be Served by Others

Although life requires us to supply others and for us to be supplied by others, we sometimes cannot receive any supply or give any supply to others in certain meetings. For example, we may attend a Holy Communion meeting, but the element of ordinances and the religious atmosphere may be much greater than the supply we receive. It may be so strong that we do not receive any supply at all. We may also be in a prayer meeting and hear some very long prayers but not touch any spiritual reality in them. Thus, we can conclude that this church is not proper.

## Other Tests for the Requirements of Life

Although some groups call themselves Christian, we can sense only human activity, human ruling, and human position there. The requirements of life demand something spiritual, but there is nothing spiritual there. The life in us requires us to exalt Christ, but Christ is not exalted there. In these groups there is nothing spiritual; instead, we can see only human methods, organizations, relationships, and positions and even human ability, piety, and reputation. We cannot touch Christ and the Holy Spirit's work there. This indicates that these groups do not have the presence of Christ and that they are not under the Holy Spirit's authority. Thus, we can conclude that they are not churches according to God's life.

## CONCLUSION

We must see one principle: no matter where we go, we should not judge whether a Christian group is the church, whether it pleases the Lord, and whether it is standing on the ground of the church merely by appearance or outward things. We need to love the Lord, turn to Him, reject the flesh, and not love the world. When we live this way before the Lord, we will be able to discern through the sense of life whether a group allows the Holy Spirit to rule in them, whether they have Christ's presence, and whether they are truly the church.

We also need to discern the church according to the Bible. In this way, no matter where we go, we will always have a compass and a standard to help us know whether a church has the Lord's presence and the Holy Spirit's ruling and whether it is in the position and way of the church.

# CHAPTER FOURTEEN

# THE REALITY OF THE CHURCH AND THE EXPERIENCE OF THE CROSS

Scripture Reading: Eph. 2:15-16; Col. 3:9-11

Ephesians 2:15-16 clearly shows that the Lord created the Jews and the Gentiles in Himself into one new man through His death. Through His death on the cross He created Jewish and Gentile believers into one Body. There are at least two significant points here. First, the Lord's death on the cross not only accomplished redemption and dealt with our sins, but it also created two peoples, Jews and Gentiles, into one new man. Second, the new man that the Lord created through the cross is His Body. In Ephesians 1:23 Paul speaks of the church as His Body. Then in chapter 2 Paul indicates that the Body is the new man that the Lord produced on the cross; it was created by Him through His cross.

The church as the Body of Christ is the new man, a new creation, and it was created by Christ through the cross. The new man created by Christ through the cross is a corporate man. There are not many new men; rather, the many believers have been constituted into one new man through Christ's cross. This new man is the Body of Christ, which is His church.

Colossians 3:9-11 speaks of the new man having the same image as the Lord who created him. Verse 11 says, "Where there cannot be Greek and Jew…" *Where* refers to *the new man* in verse 10. In the new man "there cannot be Greek and Jew, circumcision and uncircumcision, barbarian, Scythian, slave, free man, but Christ is all and in all" (v. 11). This is a very crucial verse. Verse 9 says that those who are saved, who belong to Christ, and who are in the church have put off the old man. Then verse 10 says that we "have put on the new man, which is being renewed unto full knowledge according to the image of Him who created him." In other words, the new man and the Lord have the same image.

Verse 11 says that "there cannot be Greek and Jew, circumcision and uncircumcision, barbarian, Scythian, slave, free man" in the new man, "but Christ is all and in all." In other words, the new man is not composed of different people who no longer have certain distinctions; rather, there cannot even be different people. In the church as the one new man, there cannot be the highly educated or the uneducated, and there cannot be slaves or free men, but Christ is all and in all.

The church must be according to the Bible and according to the life in us. From an outward perspective, a church that is on the proper ground blessed by the Lord and on the path under His leading, must be according to the clear teaching of the Bible. From an inward perspective, the church must be according to the sense of life within the saints. Therefore, when we examine and study the condition of a church, we must consider the Bible from an outward perspective and life from an inward perspective. A church that matches the teaching of the Bible and the inner sense of life is a church that is on the pathway of God. This is the most basic principle we must apply when examining a church.

## CHRIST BEING THE ESSENCE OF THE CHURCH

The church is the Body of Christ. She shares the life of Christ, and she is joined and mingled with Christ as one. Therefore, the church is Christ Himself. However, I am afraid that the brothers and sisters may not understand this simple yet crucial word in a deep and thorough way. If we have a deep and thorough understanding, we will realize and see that the church is Christ Himself. For example, because this podium is made of wood, its substance is wood. Because this microphone is made of metal, its substance is metal. Because the church comes out of Christ and is formed by the life of Christ, the essence of the church is Christ. Since this podium is made of wood, its substance is wood. Since the church is constituted with Christ, her essence is Christ.

In the past some have said that the church is an aggregate of all Christians. This means that the church is the aggregate of all those who believe into Jesus. Based on this, it would seem that the church is composed of Mr. Huang plus Mr. Chang plus Mr. Lee plus everyone else who has believed into Jesus. Many people have this impression of the church, but actually this is not true. It may be correct to say that the church is the aggregate of all the Christians, but what is a Christian? This is the crucial matter. Being a Christian is not simply a matter of a title and should not be used lightly. *Christian* refers to people who have Christ mingled with them. A Christian is one who is mingled with Christ.

According to the Greek text, *Christian* may be rendered "Christ-man," but what does *Christ-man* mean? A Christ-man is one who has been mingled with Christ inwardly. Before tea is added to a cup of water, the water is plain water; however, after tea is added into the cup, it becomes tea-water. It is called tea-water because tea has been mingled with the water. In China there are many tea shops around the region of Nanking and Hankow. These tea shops mainly sell tea-water, yet they are not called water shops but tea shops. Even though people are drinking water, it is called tea because tea is a crucial element in it.

In the same principle, those who believe into Jesus are called Christians. We are Christ-men, but the crucial element in us is Christ. Although we are humans, Christ has been added into us. Hence, we are human, but Christ is the primary element. Our humanity is not the main element. We all need to see that after believing into the Lord, we become Christ-men, and the aggregate of all the Christ-men is the church. In other words, the church is produced by the aggregate of Christ in many people. The church is Christ. The essence of the church is Christ.

## THE CHURCH BEING
## A MYSTERIOUS CORPORATE NEW MAN

Colossians 3:10 tells us that the church is the one new man. In this new man there cannot be this one or that one, but Christ is all. In the church life we often address each other by our surnames, such as Brother Huang, Brother Chang, and Brother Wu, but actually there should be no Brother Huang, Brother Chang, or Brother Wu in the church, because this is all part of the old man. Every saved person should be a Christ-man, a person who is full of Christ inwardly, who is mingled with Christ inwardly, and who is filled with Christ. The aggregate of all the Christ-men is the church. The church is the Body of Christ, which is a mysterious corporate new man. In this new man there cannot be you and I; there can be only Christ. Christ is all and in all. This word may sound simple, but we need to let this word saturate the church. This is not the word of man but the word in the Bible, the word of God.

The essence of the church is Christ. Through His death on the cross Christ released His life to produce His mysterious Body. This mysterious Body is a corporate new man. In this new man there cannot be this kind of person and that kind of person, but Christ is all and in all. The condition of the church is according to the nature and essence of Christ.

### THE CHURCH BEING CHANGED IN NATURE AND BECOMING DEGRADED BECAUSE OF THE ADDITION OF MAN'S ELEMENT

Regrettably, the condition of the church today is totally different from the church revealed in the Bible. The condition of the church today is full of man's element; thus, the church has many things that come from man. We all know that human beings are very troublesome. If a place has never been visited or inhabited by people, it retains its natural scenery. However, once it has been visited and inhabited by people, its condition quickly changes. A certain mountain area may have many trees and flowers and look very beautiful. After people begin to live there, however, it gradually becomes disorderly and different. When people first live there, everything is still quite clean. After a while, however, it becomes messy. The longer people live there, the more it resembles a marketplace that has many things of man. This shows that man is the source of uncleanness, and man is a troublesome problem. Once the church contains the things of man, there will be trouble and disorder in the church. Once *man* is in the church, the church begins to resemble a market. This is abnormal.

The church is Christ, and the essence of the church is Christ. In today's so-called church, however, the exact opposite is the condition. This is because man, not Christ, is in the church. The church is filled with man, not Christ. If Christ is in the church, the church is pure, clean, spiritual, heavenly, and full of life. However, today's church is full of human elements. Human feelings, human thoughts, human views, human ways, and human organization have come into the church, and even the society of the world has come into the church. The things of man, the natural being, and everything attached to man have been brought into the church by man. Thus, there is mixture in the church, and she has lost the essence of Christ.

When Christians speak of the matter of the church, not many of them will take the Spirit as their goal. When they speak concerning the church, they are all mixed with man's element. Some Christians who truly love the Lord even say, "I am very clear that the place where I worship does not please the Lord, and I do not receive any spiritual help and supply there, but I cannot help but go there. What should I do?" It is better for us not to answer such a question, because they already know the answer. We should not be foolish. What they need to know, they already know, and what they should feel, they already feel. Nevertheless, they cannot do anything because they care for human feelings and human friendships. There is no cross, and there is no Christ. This is the flesh, this is human feelings, and this is the world in disguise.

## THE CROSS PUTTING MAN'S FLESH TO DEATH

Such people do not see that human feelings, the flesh, and the world have all been put on the cross. As a rule, those who love the Lord should put all these things to death by the Holy Spirit through the cross; they should be condemned and put to death on the cross.

The church is Christ, and the church is under the cross. Wherever there is the cross, there is Christ, and wherever there is Christ, there is the church. Today the church has lost her reality, and her nature and form have changed because man rejects the cross and does not allow the cross to deal with his feelings, face, and worldly ways. When the things of man remain, Christ is gone, and the church is changed in nature. We need to see that once we touch the church, we must touch the cross. The church is joined to the cross.

### THE CROSS DEALING WITH MAN'S ELEMENT

When we touch the church, do we touch Chinese, Japanese, British, or Americans? None of these should be in the church. Some people say that the local Taiwanese and the people from the mainland are very different in temperament. However, when we consider the matter of the church and touch the matter of the church, there cannot be local people or mainlanders. Furthermore, there cannot be Chinese, Japanese, and British, because all have been crucified on the cross with Christ.

If the cross cannot do a breaking work in us, the church can never be manifested in reality among us. With the cross, Christ will come forth, and the church will be a reality. Without the cross, Christ will be gone, and the church will lose her true nature. This is a true and concise word concerning the church. If there is the cross, there is the church; if there is no cross, there is no church. When there is no cross, man comes in. This means that you can come in, I can come in, and anyone else can come in. When we all come in, Christ leaves, and there is no church. When Christ is gone, the church loses her true nature, and she becomes the church in name only but not in reality. If we want to keep the true nature of the church, we must touch the cross.

A person once came to see me and said, "After I heard your messages several times, I truly felt the Lord's presence, but something happened recently. In the place where I worship, I have been elected to be an elder and a board director. I am in a dilemma. What should I do?" I did not answer but instead asked, "How do you feel about this?" He replied, "Well, if people want to give me the position of a board director and an elder, it is impolite and difficult to refuse." I did not say anything. It seems that we could speak concerning anything, but whenever we spoke concerning the church, we could not go on. Although this person loved the Lord, the cross had no effect in him through putting him to death. We should realize that people use political tactics to retain and gain people for their place. Using the so-called position of an elder or board director is just a political tactic to retain people and prevent them from going to other places.

If a church treats people in this way, it should be chastised by God, because all she has is human politics, human tactics, and human methods but not God's principle. A person who knows the Lord and lives in the Lord would never be willing to do this, ask others to do this, or allow others to do this to him. Nevertheless, in Christianity today there are too many stories like this.

## THE CROSS PRODUCING THE CHURCH

We need to see that once the human element is present, the church is gone. In order to have the genuineness and reality of the church, man must be terminated. There is no way for man to be terminated other than through the cross. The cross is the place to terminate and end man. The cross has two effects: it terminates man, and it releases Christ's life. This is true even today. Whoever has the cross has been terminated, but at the same time, Christ's life can flow out from him. If the cross works in us, our person will be broken and terminated. At the same time, Christ will flow out from us. Because of these two effects, the cross produces the church. When the cross works in us, our person is terminated, and at the same time, Christ has the position in us. In this way the church is produced. With the cross, man is terminated and Christ comes in, and when Christ comes in, the church is produced. We must know this.

When we touched the church, we felt that the church was quite good. We sensed the Lord's presence, touched the Lord in our heart, and enjoyed meeting here. However, after several months something surely happened to expose our unbroken flesh and active self. Even though we feel the Lord's presence and are uplifted inwardly, it becomes hard for us to bear the situation after being offended and hurt by a brother or sister. Such things happen all the time.

Two weeks ago a certain brother said to the responsible brothers, "I truly praise and thank the Lord that He has brought me to this church. I truly feel the Lord's presence and blessings here. I have received much help." A week later he came and told the brothers, "I feel that our meeting hall should make a change here and an alteration there." Because his suggestions were not proper, the brothers could only listen to him but not do as he suggested. When he came to the meeting hall several days later and discovered that his opinions had not been accepted, he stopped coming to the meeting because he felt that he had lost face. When the brothers went to visit him, he said that he was ashamed to come because the brothers did not accept his suggestions. This brother was more open than most. When we visit with some, they will not even speak truthfully about the reason for their absence. They only give strange reasons. This shows that they truly have not been gained by the church.

It is possible that a person may love the church today and hate the church two weeks from now. This is because of man's face and man's self. If the cross has not done a breaking work in a person—breaking his flesh, self, natural being, and person—he will not be able to be touched or endure any setback. Instead, he will withdraw immediately. Sometimes this kind of brother or sister needs to be disciplined by the Holy Spirit for several years and receive some chastisement and suffering in order to learn the lessons. Then they will begin to regret their past Christian life, a life in which they suffered and encountered many difficulties after leaving the church and Christ. Gradually they will realize that they left the church because they wanted to keep their face, to boast in themselves, and to express their flesh. When they become enlightened, they will come back to the church in shamefulness and humility. At this time, even if we do not speak the word of the cross, they will have some experiences. Thereafter, even if they want to praise the church, they will not be so quick. Many of those who praise us often become the ones who oppose us the most. Therefore, when we go out to work, we should not be moved by man's praises. The people who praise us today may become the ones who oppose us tomorrow. A person who has learned the lesson and has been broken will not praise others easily. Even if we have received the greatest help from a certain brother, we still need to learn not to be so quick to praise.

The brother with the opinions about altering this and that has come back. He has truly received some help and advanced, and he is serving the church humbly. It is safe for us to say something because he is able to receive it. He knows that he needs to be broken. He rarely gives suggestions and opinions because he has been dealt with and does not dare to speak carelessly. He has been dealt with by the Lord to such an extent that he says, "O Lord, I have said these things. May You guide the brothers in their acceptance, and may You also make me joyful in whatever the outcome may be." This person has Christ, not himself, and he will be able to remain in the church.

## THE CHURCH LIFE REQUIRING
## THE EXPERIENCE OF THE CROSS

Anyone who does not receive the cross will eventually have problems in the church. Anyone who has not been broken by the cross will eventually be stumbled by the brothers and sisters. The church is produced through the cross, maintained through the cross, and, even more, expressed through the cross. When the cross is present, man goes out and Christ comes in, and when Christ is present, there is the reality of the church. Please remember that the church is the one new man produced by the cross of Christ. In the new man there is no *man;* there cannot be this kind of person or that kind of person. There cannot be you, I, he, or anyone else. In the new man there is only Christ. Only Christ is all and in all. This word may sound simple and easy to understand, but in order to practice it in our real living, we must go through the cross. The experience of life will not be manifested in reality in anyone who is short of the cross.

Only those who are under the cross can know the church, only those who have been broken by the cross can be in the church, and only those who allow the cross to break them and cross them out are qualified to examine the church. When a person has been terminated by the cross, that is, his flesh has been nullified by the cross, his emotion broken by the cross, his opinion and ideas rejected by the cross, his ability torn down by the cross, and his tactics eliminated by the cross, he will be in the reality of the church. He will be able to understand the church, touch the nature of the church, know the essence of the church, and discern the church. He will be able to judge the church accurately, and his view of the church will be according to the Bible and life. These three—the cross, Christ, and the church—cannot be separated. When the cross is present, there will be only Christ; when there is Christ, there will be only the church. All three are closely related.

# CHAPTER FIFTEEN

# GOD'S WORK OF REDEMPTION—
# THE MINGLING OF GOD AND MAN

Scripture Reading: Rom. 11:36

Romans 11:36 says, "Because out from Him and through Him and to Him are all things. To Him be the glory forever. Amen." Some versions translate *out from Him* as "of Him," and others translate it "from Him." The meaning in the original language is "out from Him." *Through Him* may be translated as "passing through Him." This is similar to someone needing to pass through a bridge in order to cross from one side of a river to the other side. *All things* may be translated as "all," including persons, things, and affairs. All persons, events, and things are out from Him, pass through Him, and eventually are unto Him.

## KNOWING LIFE AND THE CHURCH,
## AND EXERCISING TO LEARN
## HOW TO WORK AND HOW TO DO THINGS

We need to know the Lord's way in order to know how to serve Him. This requires that we know life and the church and have a proper exercise in order to learn how to work and how to do things. These are two crucial exercises. In order to do anything, we must first prepare material. For example, if a farmer wants to grow a plant, he must first have seeds. If he does not have any seeds, he cannot do anything. Even if he has seeds, however, he still may not know how to plant them. Therefore, once we have the material, we need to study the way. Our knowledge of life and the church is the material, and our learning how to work and do things is the way. Our knowledge concerning life and the church is the capital and material for us to serve the Lord. If a businessman wants to do business, he must first obtain capital and then study the way to do business. If he has both the capital and a way, he will probably succeed in business.

By the Lord's mercy, we have a desire to serve the Lord; therefore, we must pay attention to our material and our way. We cannot work for the Lord merely because of our zeal and love for Him. We need to consider the kind of work to do, the kind of material to use, and the kind of capital we possess. These are critical issues. If we do not have any material and capital, we might as well forget about serving the Lord. However, if we have capital and material, we still may not have the way and, thus, may not know how to serve. Therefore, when we speak of knowing life and the church, our purpose is to help the brothers and sisters obtain the necessary capital and material. This can be compared to the need for the builders of the temple to go up the mountain to gather wood (Hag. 1:8). Our perfecting of the saints can be compared to gathering wood from the mountain. If we want to do the Lord's work, we must know life and the church in order to obtain the material for the service of the Lord.

Following this, we need to know the way. After we have material, we still need to consider how to do the work in different places and how to make arrangements for various matters in the work. The brothers who administrate the church in the different localities and who serve the Lord full time know from their experience that there is a great difference between one who knows how to work and one who does not. One brother may go to work in a certain place, but there is no result. When another brother goes to work in the same place, however, there is an immediate result. Even though God is the same, the Lord is the same, and the environment for the work is the same, the work of one person produces no fruit, but the work of another person can be very fruitful. The difference lies in both the *person* and the *way*. Furthermore, all our work is affected by persons, events, and things. Therefore, if we want to know how to work, we must know how to do things. In our exercise for the service, we must pay constant attention to these two matters.

The knowledge of life and the church is a matter of truth and light. In regard to the Lord's work, many churches are weak and poor because the brothers and sisters do not know how to do things. This is a serious matter. The condition of some brothers and sisters is very good before the Lord—they love the Lord, they are godly, and they pray frequently. However, once a work is placed in their hand, it is finished; once a local church is entrusted to their care, its condition becomes poor. Considering the degree of their love for the Lord and the condition of their spirituality and prayer, they should be useful to the Lord in many things. Nevertheless, the outcomes are exactly the opposite. Although they love the Lord and often pray with tears, their service is ineffective. They pray; however, the environment remains the same, and the condition of the church remains the same. This is because they do not know how to work and do things, even though they are spiritual and pray regularly. If a believer is neither spiritual nor able to work, he will be worthless. However, if a believer is merely spiritual but does not know how to work and do things, there will be no result.

A microphone needs electricity in order to produce sound. However, a microphone cannot produce sound with electricity only. In order to produce sound, there is a need for support from many other things, such as an electrical plug and wires. Perhaps there is no problem with our spirituality and prayer, but if there are problems with the way and method of our work and doing things, our work will not be profitable. We should never think that we can work as long as we are spiritual and know how to pray. More than twenty years ago I thought that as long as we read the Bible diligently, prayed frequently, and were spiritual, the Lord would work and do things through us. However, this is not the case. In the past twenty years the experiences of many churches and saints have proven that merely being spiritual and praying regularly are not enough. We also need to know how to work and do things.

This can be compared to a chemistry formula which requires four ingredients. If we have only two ingredients, we will not produce the expected chemical reaction. Similarly, if we are not spiritual and do not pray, and we rely simply on a method of doing things, we will also not have the results. Without electricity, a microphone will not work, regardless of its quality; furthermore, even when there is electricity, other electrical parts are needed. We need to be spiritual and pray, but we must also consider the matter of how we work and do things.

We need to pay attention to our spirituality and our way of working, just as we need to pay attention to electricity and the electrical components of a microphone. Both aspects are needed. I hope that we will all spend some time to put these points into practice. If we make the effort to exercise in these matters, we will gain some understanding. Anyone who feels that he does not know life and does not know how to serve, work, and do things should not feel embarrassed to ask. We should not focus on trivial matters; rather, we should focus our study specifically on how to serve, work, and do things, the totality of which is our service to the Lord.

### REALIZING THAT GOD'S WORK OF REDEMPTION REQUIRES MAN'S COOPERATION

Those who serve the Lord should have a basic understanding that God requires man to cooperate with Him in His plan. Everyone who has a heart to serve the Lord should know this in a fundamental way. In creation, God created everything by Himself, and in the final act of creation, God created man. After He created man, everything was complete; man did not need to do anything or ask for anything. The work of creation was done by God alone, and man did not have any part in it.

However, in addition to His work of creation, God has the work of redemption. In creation man did not need to do anything, and he had no part in God's work. In redemption, however, God wants man to work together with Him. Redemption is accomplished by a joint effort of God and man. Just as tea-water is produced by the mingling of tea and water, redemption is accomplished by the mingling of God with man. God did the work of creation through His own position, qualification, power, and authority; however, redemption is accomplished through the mingling and joining of God with man. Without God, redemption could not be accomplished, but without man, redemption could not be accomplished either.

## THE WORK OF GOD'S REDEMPTION BEING THE MINGLING OF GOD WITH MAN

When our Savior accomplished redemption on the cross, did He redeem us in His status as God or in His status as man? Is the Lord Jesus God or man? This is a very important question. We must remember that every item in redemption is accomplished through the mingling of God with man. Where did redemption begin? It began from Bethlehem. The story of Bethlehem is the story of God entering into man. Incarnation shows that God's redemption requires the mingling of God with man. Redemption cannot be accomplished only by God Himself, and redemption cannot be accomplished only by man. Redemption can be accomplished only by God entering into man and by the mingling and joining of man with God.

It is certainly true to say that Jesus is God, and it is equally true to say that Jesus is a man. Jesus the Nazarene is the result of the mingling and joining of God and man. When He was on the earth, His thoughts, His work, and even the direction of His footsteps were all for redemption. His every footstep was the footstep of God with man, and His every action was the action of God with man. We need to be clear that the One who was born in the manger in Bethlehem and was worshipped by man is God yet man. The One who dined in the house of the Pharisee is God yet man. The One who was crucified on the cross at Golgotha is God yet man. The story of the Gospels is the story of God's redemption through the mingling of God and man.

When the brothers lead the churches or give messages, are they only in themselves? If they are, this should be disapproved. If a brother is giving a message in himself, this is no different than the practice in Islam, Taoism, or any other religion. When we give a message in the church, God should be speaking through us. In whatever we do, God should be doing it through us and God should be mingled with us. If I speak without being mingled with God, I should be cursed.

When the Lord Jesus was on the earth, He was the son of Mary and the brother of James, but within He was the Word of God; He was God. God Himself was in Him. This is the great mystery of godliness (1 Tim. 3:16). The redemption of Christ began from Bethlehem, and the significance of Bethlehem is incarnation, which is the mingling of God and man. From the day that the Lord Jesus became flesh until now, this principle remains: God desires to enter into man and mingle Himself with man as one. If we want to serve the Lord and work for Him, we must see this great and basic principle.

When we serve the Lord, it is not enough to be zealous, to give some material offerings, and to pray some prayers; the basic principle of serving the Lord is to see that God does everything in redemption through the mingling of God with man. He wants man's cooperation. Once we see this principle, we will be able to solve the following three matters.

## All Work Being of God, Not of Man

Since God needs man's cooperation in His work of redemption, all work is of God, not of man. In our exercise we must seek to act according to the principle established by God. God's desire that man work together with Him has been initiated by God, not by man. God initiates His work, but it is carried out by man's cooperation with Him. We could never even dream that redemption requires man's cooperation and needs to pass through man. This thought is not of man. If we do not see this principle, we will definitely have many deficiencies in our work. All works require man's cooperation with God, but no work is initiated by man. All works originate from God as the source and are carried out with the cooperation of man. We need to see this principle: All work begins with God, not with man.

This is the source of the confusion in today's Christianity. The main reason Christians are divided into many denominations and sects is that many things among them have been initiated by man, not by God. The point of initiation is not God but man. Every person who serves God should submit to Him and say, "O God, although You cannot do anything without me and although You need me to work together with You, everything must originate from You, not from me. I will not move unless You move; I want to move only in Your move."

What is the difference between the church and religion? No religion has been initiated or advanced by God. In contrast, the church is initiated and advanced by God. Religion is something conceived by man, who worships and serves God according to his thoughts about God. However, the church does not come from man's thinking; rather, the church comes from God. The church is the issue of God's moving and calling in man and of man's answering God's call. From the Old Testament to the New Testament, those who served God were called by God; no one served out of his own desire. Saul, who took the way of religion, persecuted Jesus the Nazarene and was zealous in all kinds of religious activities. Then one day he saw a great light on his way to Damascus, and he heard a voice from heaven, saying, "Saul, Saul, why are you persecuting Me?" He immediately said, "Who are You, Lord?" (Acts 9:3-5). At this point Saul began to know the church. The church originates from Christ and comes out of God Himself.

Religion comes from man's imagination, but the church comes from God's revelation. In religion man volunteers to serve God, but in the church man's service comes from a calling that originates from God Himself. The Lord said to Saul, "I am Jesus the Nazarene, whom you persecute." Saul immediately asked, "What shall I do, Lord?" (Acts 22:8, 10). Saul did not say, "I will do something for You." If he had said this, it would have been religion. The evil one in Isaiah 14:13-14 says, "I will," but when man submits and stops his efforts, he asks, "What shall I do, God?" Then, like Paul, he will receive a revelation: "It will be told to you what you must do" (Acts 9:6).

Nothing in the church comes from man's imagination. Rather, everything in the church should be the result of God's revelation to man, God's shining on man, God's calling of man, and God's gaining of man. God wants to gain man because He needs man to cooperate with Him. In the church God gains man to move with Him and to cooperate with His move. In religion man initiates, man decides, and man works. Although there is "service," it is of man. Today many preachers are doing man's work. In principle, only that which is of God, is called by God, and answers God's demand is the service of the church. Anyone who does not serve God according to this way serves God according to his own imagination, decision, and desire. Although these people say that they are serving God in the church, they are involved only in religious activities.

Hence, as we learn to serve God, we need to see that God's work requires our cooperation with Him. No work should originate from ourselves. The Father, Son, and the Spirit are in us. All work is started and must be started by the Triune God.

## God Needing Man in His Work

Once we see that God's work requires man's cooperation, we will realize that man has an important place in God's work. This is quite different from our prayers, which often include the thought that we are nothing and that the Lord can work without us. This is not God's thought. Instead, we should pray, "Lord, without us, You cannot work." This is a prayer that is according to the truth and according to God's heart. Although God the Almighty created the heavens and the earth, those who know God will say, "God, You can work only when You have us. Without us, You cannot work at all." If there were no people on the island of Taiwan, how could God preach the gospel? Throughout the years we have realized from our experience that even though God is almighty, there are things that He cannot do. His inability to do certain things relates to us in our experience. Although God can do everything, He cannot force us to move. He may move in us for many years, but we still may not rise up to take action. God can do everything in the universe, but He cannot force us to rise up early or read the Bible. God needs our cooperation; He cannot do many things in us because, even though He is almighty, there are many limitations in us.

With God there is eternity past; with man there is eternity future. As God journeys from eternity past to eternity future, there is a bridge of time. This bridge of time is really man himself. God wants to cross from one side to the other through man, but many people have a sign that says Not a Through Street. When God makes a demand on us, we often shake our head to indicate that the road is blocked. When God makes a demand, we often respond, "But I have a wife, children, and..." Our "but" means that God cannot pass through us. In eternity God is not under any restriction, but in time God is restricted. If we will not allow God to pass through, God cannot do anything in the church life. We restrict God the most.

Nevertheless, God is patient. When He cannot get through in us, He will wait patiently and call us again. If we do not listen to Him, He will wait some more. He is very patient. He will wait until we are touched by Him and say to Him, "O God, I will say yes to You. I will no longer say but or Not a Through Street. I will only say Amen." When we hear the Lord's word and forsake everything to follow Him, we will not be like the disciple who said to the Lord, "Permit me first to go and bury my father" (Matt. 8:21). God's principle in redemption is that man would cooperate with Him and that man would be a bridge for Him to pass through.

We should never consider this as a doctrine only. On the whole earth, regardless of when or where, God will be expressed as long as we are willing to say, "God, I am here. I want to be a smooth way to let You pass through." God always works in the principle of incarnation, that is, in the principle of God mingling with man.

Some brothers like to ask, "How do we give a message and speak for God?" We can study this matter and discover thousands of requirements, but we cannot ignore this one basic question: Do we allow God to pass through us and mingle with us? If we do not have a clear understanding about this point, regardless of how well we speak, our speaking will be useless. We must see that God requires man to cooperate with Him in His work; man's cooperation is indispensable. Without man's cooperation, God's way is blocked. If we prostrate ourselves before God and allow Him to pass through us, God's glory will be expressed.

In our fellowship with God and in our reading of the Bible and prayer before the Lord, will we answer His call unconditionally when we hear His voice? Or will we say however and but? How many of us can say yes to the Lord, or "Lord, I will take this way"? Our usefulness in the Lord's hand depends upon how much we cooperate with Him; how far He can go in us depends entirely upon how absolute our Amen is to Him. We are sinful and corrupt, we tend to lose our temper, and we always blame others. From our experience in following the Lord, we know that these are hindrances to the Lord. However, our unwillingness to submit to the Lord absolutely is the greatest hindrance.

Some brothers and sisters never offend others, but they are not useful to the Lord because when they respond to Him, they say yes and then say but. This is like a bridge that is well-constructed and clean but with a sign that blocks it, saying Not a Through Street. Do we want to be this kind of bridge? Another bridge may be old and broken, but the Lord can still cross over because it is open for passage. Some believers may be like a broken bridge, but the Lord can still pass through them.

There was a sister in Shanghai who was born of a high-class family. Both she and her husband were highly educated. Before she became a Christian, all her relatives and neighbors praised her meekness and elegance. Later, she believed in the Lord and continued to conduct herself in a well-tempered way. Another sister was bad-tempered before she was saved. After she was saved, she still quarreled with others frequently, and she was far inferior to the meek sister in the way she treated her husband. Thus, this sister truly admired the meek sister for her elegance and gracefulness. The rough sister loved the Lord very much, and she would come to every meeting, often praying with tears because of her realization that she was short in many things. One day the meek sister complained to the brothers about the rough sister. She pointed out that the sister would put on a head covering and pray very spiritual and inspiring prayers in the meeting but then fiercely quarrel with others at home. While we should not quarrel or argue, is anything gained by only being meek and by refraining from quarreling? Although the meek sister behaved very well, she always said but when the Lord made a demand on her. What is the difference between this and being quarrelsome? We may be perfect, but what good is it if we cannot be a bridge to let God pass through?

I am not saying that we should be rough, but I want to illustrate that God wants a person who will let Him pass through and cooperate with Him. We absolutely must see that God is not looking for meek and perfect people in His work; rather, He needs people who will cooperate with Him. Without man's cooperation, God cannot do anything. May we not be proud but pray: "O God, You can work without me, but if You have me, it will be easier for You to work. I do not want to delay Your time." God truly needs our cooperation.

## Man Needing God in God's Work

If we have seen that God needs our cooperation, we will realize that we cannot be independent from God in anything. On the one hand, we know that if God does not have us, He cannot get through; on the other hand, if we do not have Him, we cannot move. We need to tell Him, "O God, I thank You that I have been shown mercy. Because of Your creation and redemption, I have You and I am even becoming You, but I am still a man. God, You cannot work without me. You need me, and You need man." We should all lift up our head and be encouraged to pray in this way by God's grace. Furthermore, we need to tell Him, "Without You, I cannot do anything; I need You."

### CONCLUSION

When we put these three matters together, we will arrive at one great principle: God's work of redemption is carried out by God and man working together. All work originates from God, not from man. Man is needed in all His work, and God cannot do anything without man. God is needed for all His work as well, and man cannot do anything without God. The most important matter for one who serves the Lord is his relationship with God. The degree of our cooperation with God determines the degree to which we can touch and contact Him. The second matter is morality. We need morality to maintain our position before man. If we do not have morality before man, regardless of how much knowledge we have before God, we will not have any position to speak before men. As we serve and work for the Lord, we should spend much time to fellowship with the Lord. When we do anything, we should continually contact the Lord within and continually consecrate ourselves to the Lord and cooperate with Him.

# CHAPTER SIXTEEN

# ALL SERVICE BEING INITIATED BY GOD

Scripture Reading: Job 38:1-2; 42:1-6

## ALL WORK BEING INITIATED BY GOD

Those who serve the Lord must see that God's redemptive work is accomplished through man's cooperation. If we see this, we will have a clearer realization that all our work must be initiated by God, not by us. All our service and work should be initiated by God, not by us. Although we may know this in doctrine, it is not easy to experience.

All of us who work for the Lord in various places and all the responsible brothers in the churches must consider how much of our work in serving God is initiated by God and how much is initiated by us. Regardless of how well it was done, how much of what we have done in the past has been initiated by God? This is truly a great matter. All our work and service in the church must be initiated by God and must be according to His desire.

## ALL SERVICE INITIATED BY MAN BEING RELIGIOUS ACTIVITY

Anything that is initiated or started by man, regardless of how much it is for God, is a religious activity. In God's eyes, this kind of activity is not His service or His work. God considers only what He has initiated and started as a service and work to Him.

God wants man to cooperate with Him, but He does not want man to initiate anything. Anything that is initiated by man is a religious activity. To an unbeliever, any kind of Christian activity is a religious activity, but according to our knowledge of God, there are two kinds of activities: one is a religious activity, and the other is an action initiated by God. The second type is not a religious activity. An action initiated by God will come from God's prompting within man. Often a man has no thought of God and no heart to serve God, but God comes to him, prompting and touching him, revealing Himself, giving him a command, a calling, and a leading, so that he receives something of God and cannot help but take action. This kind of action is not related to religion; rather, it comes from God and is initiated by God.

## THE SCRIPTURAL BASIS
## FOR SERVICE INITIATED BY GOD

### Abel Offering Sacrifices by Faith according to God's Revelation

The Bible shows that the first generation that served God after Adam included his sons Abel and Cain. Cain was the older brother, and Abel was the younger brother. Outwardly speaking, both of them had a concept of God. Both Abel and Cain brought an offering to Jehovah (Gen. 4:1-5). Abel's offering was not a religious activity, but Cain's offering was a religious activity. Even though both were serving God, Abel's offering was not a religious activity because his offering was of God, not of himself. God wanted a sacrifice according to Abel's way. Hebrews 11:4 says, "By faith Abel offered to God a more excellent sacrifice than Cain." According to Romans 10:17, faith comes out of hearing; therefore, Abel's offering came out of hearing. He believed in God. His offering of a sacrifice came in response to God's word; he offered because he heard God's word. Abel received a revelation through God's word; he heard God's word. Then he believed, and by faith he offered a sacrifice to God.

After Adam's fall, God showed man redemption through the shedding of the blood of a sacrifice. Redemption through the shedding of the blood of a sacrifice was initiated and instructed by God. Because Abel heard, saw, and understood this, he offered a sacrifice according to God's instruction. Abel's offering was not of himself but of God; it was revealed, commanded, and ordained by God. Hence, Abel's offering was not a religious activity. By obeying God's command, Abel offered a sacrifice according to God's instruction and rendered service to God.

## Cain Serving God from Himself according to His Own Will

Conversely, Cain's offering was not of God but of himself. Although he knew God, thought of God, and worshipped God, his offering of a sacrifice was according to himself. Thus, it was a religious activity. He offered the fruit of the ground to God; this was not according to God's charge, commandment, or ordination; it came from his own thought. Cain's offering was entirely a religious activity. He must have thought, "If I offer the work of my hands to God whom I serve in all sincerity, He will be pleased with me. Since I worship Him, I should offer what I have labored on to Him." Cain's way of doing things according to his opinion was not of God but of himself.

In the church life, when we see someone who is very zealous for God, we usually admire and praise him. However, someone who has been enlightened by God will be concerned whether this zeal comes from God. It may seem that a person works much and is consecrated to God, but his zeal for God can be of man, not of God. It is quite possible to offer something as Cain did and not as Abel did. According to our natural understanding, we think that God will be pleased as long as we work for Him and preach the gospel to save sinners and present them to God. However, God is concerned whether we are doing this according to our opinion or His revelation. Is our zeal toward Him, and is our offering of sacrifices for ourselves or for Him? This is God's concern.

Cain was not rejected by God because he sinned but because he did not worship and offer sacrifices according to God's way. We may think that God will accept us and be delighted in us as long as we preach the gospel, serve Him, and fervently work for Him. This is a religious concept. A person who has been enlightened by God dares not to think or view things in this way, and one who has been enlightened by God will examine himself, asking, "Is my zeal of myself or of God? Is my preaching of the gospel and working for God a profit or a damage to the church? Does my consecration for the church and my work for God originate from God? Is my service like Abel's, or does it originate from myself like Cain's?" Only those who examine themselves in this way can serve God properly.

Genesis shows that Cain did not commit the sin of murder immediately; rather, he committed murder some time later. Cain did not kill his brother Abel at the very beginning. Cain served God, was zealous for God, and gave offerings to God. However, his service, his offering, and his zeal originated from himself, not from God, so God disregarded him. In all our service, do we really have a regard for God and fear God? Are we fearful that what we do for God is not of God but of ourselves? Do we fear that our pious activities may be considered rebellious and sinful in His eyes? God has ordained that we work in a certain way, but do we reject God's command and work in another way? Are we fearful of offering the fruit of the ground rather than animal sacrifices to God? Are we afraid that our work and service are not of God but of ourselves? Just as we fear our temper, do we also fear our preaching of the gospel, our zeal, our service, and our consecration? We should be as fearful of these as we are fearful of sinning and falling.

If we are enlightened, we will be fearful in our service. We may see that our service is like Cain's, not Abel's. One who serves the Lord must be fearful that his work, even the ability to preach and cast out demons, is not a service to God. A religious activity is any service and worship that does not originate from God's revelation, command, and leading. A man may know of God and be zealous in doing things for God according to his own view, but this is only a religious activity. Anything that is not revealed, commanded, or called by God is a religious activity, even if it is for God. Beginning with Adam in the Old Testament and continuing to the end of the New Testament, the activities of one who serves God must originate absolutely from God, not from man.

### Noah Serving God according to God's Command

Noah did not build an ark because he had a dream and

then became zealous. Genesis shows that Noah did not have such a thought or idea at any time. Rather, God came to Noah one day and told him to build an ark. This was the origin of the building of the ark (Gen. 6:14—7:5). The building of the ark was not even in Noah's consideration; neither could he imagine that a flood would come one hundred and twenty years later. Even the measurements and methods of building the ark were not according to Noah's imagination but to God's determination (6:14-16). This shows that Noah's service was of God.

## Abraham Serving God according to God's Appearing

Let us continue with Abraham. Did Abraham serve and worship God because his fathers served and worshipped God? Did he serve and worship according to the traditions of his fathers? No, the Bible shows that Abraham was from the land of the Chaldeans, who were involved with idols (11:31; Josh. 24:2). Later he left his country, a land of idolatry. Abraham, however, did not leave voluntarily; neither did he initiate the move. While he was still living on the other side of the river and worshipping idols like the Gentiles, God came to him and called him, saying, "Go from your land / And from your relatives / And from your father's house" (Gen. 12:1). Abraham had no thought of leaving; rather, he was urged to leave by God who came to call him. All the moves in Abraham's life reveal the particular characteristic of Jehovah's appearing. God's appearing was the motivation for all of Abraham's actions. All his actions were controlled by God's appearing. Except for his going down to Egypt and falling (12:9—13:4), all his actions were accepted by God because they were of God as a result of His appearing.

## Moses Serving God according to God's Instruction for the Deliverance of the Children of Israel

Moses feared and knew God, and he was very zealous for the children of Israel because he was educated by his family. He even struck an Egyptian for the Israelites (Exo. 2:7-12). According to the record in the Bible, however, all these things were useless to God. Moses was dealt with by God in the wilderness for a period of forty years to the extent that all his human capabilities were taken from him. At this point he had no interest in any of man's intentions or in any religious activity. Being nearly eighty years of age, he surely must have wondered whether he could do anything other than shepherd a flock. He no longer thought of worshipping God or of delivering the children of Israel. To him, these things meant nothing.

When he felt that everything was over, however, God came to him and called him, saying, "I will send you to Pharaoh, that you may bring My people, the children of Israel, out of Egypt" (3:10). God came to send Moses. Moses' deliverance of the children of Israel did not originate from himself but from God. Furthermore, all his actions related to the deliverance of the children of Israel were according to God's instruction. The actions of the children of Israel, such as slaughtering the lambs, keeping the passover, and crossing the Red Sea, did not come from Moses' imagination or idea but from God's instruction. God personally led the children of Israel through every station they passed.

When Moses came to the foot of Mount Sinai for the building of the tabernacle, he followed the pattern God showed him on the mountain; no deviation was permitted (ch. 40). This shows that genuine service can come only from God, not from us. Anything that comes from us is a religious activity; only that which comes from God is service according to revelation.

### David Fearing God, Cooperating with God, and Letting God Work

Now we should consider David who truly believed in God. He overcame all enemies by trusting in God's grace, and he was made king and lived a peaceful life in the palace. Looking at his situation, he felt that he owed something to God because he lived in such a good palace while God dwelt only in the tabernacle. He felt that this was unfair to God, so he was zealous to build a temple for God (2 Sam. 7:1-3). Did God accept David's idea? His desire to care for God and love God was accepted by God, but his intention and determination to build a house were rejected by God, who immediately sent

Nathan the prophet to David to ask, "Is it you who will build Me a house for Me to dwell in?" (v. 5). God rejected David's good intention.

No matter related to our service to God should be determined by us. It is right for us to love God, but God does not want us to think about doing something for Him. Our heart to serve Him is acceptable, but our decision to do something for Him is not acceptable. God said, "Is it you...?" God does not want us to decide anything on His behalf. It was not up to David to decide whether or not to build the temple. Nothing should be initiated by us; only God can initiate something. God replied to David, "Jehovah declares to you that Jehovah will make you a house" (v. 11), as if to say, "David, you do not know what you are saying when you speak of building Me a house. It is I who will build you a house."

David was one who truly feared God. He was not like some Christians today who build a "church" whenever they please. Such people think that as long as they have money and a heart, they can do what they want when they want. In David, however, we see one who feared God. Although he had the opportunity, saw the need, and had the ability to build the temple for God, he stopped. The building of the temple seemed necessary, just as preaching the gospel seems good. However, if something is initiated by man, God will say, "Slow down." When man's initiation ceases, God initiates and gives a command.

When we read the Bible, we must see the light in these examples. In the matter of service, no one can initiate anything for God. There is no limit to how much we should love God or turn our heart toward Him. What God demands of us is our love and our heart, but we cannot overstep the boundaries. We can love Him and consider Him but not decide what to do next. God is the One who decides, and we must wait. When He gives a command, we can work. We should love God and wait for His command; we should seek His will and wait for His revelation. Just as the slaves in the Old Testament loved their masters and allowed their ears to be bored through with an awl to a doorpost, we must focus on waiting for our Master's command (Exo. 21:6).

Many Christians not only love God but also love people, the

world, and their family. When they become zealous for God, they immediately desire to do things for God. This is the situation in today's Christianity. The confusion in Christianity is not caused by lukewarm ones but by zealous ones. Out of their zeal for God, they build one chapel after another; out of their love for God, they establish one school after another. The confusion in Christianity would be less if fewer Christians loved God; the confusion in Christianity increases as more Christians love God. It is right to love God, but in spite of a proper love for God, many Christians are walking on the wrong way. We should only love God; we should not initiate anything for God.

I truly admire David's condition before God. If David did not fear God, after listening to Nathan's word, he might have thought, "What are you talking about? I am in the palace; I have both money and authority. There is a need, and I want to cooperate by taking action. Is this not God's will?" He might have said to Nathan, "I know that you are a prophet, but does only your speaking count? Does no other speaking count?" Because David feared God, however, he did not react to Nathan; rather, he stopped. It is not a small thing to stop. The act of stopping the building of the temple is a great matter.

Sister M. E. Barber said, "Whoever cannot stop working for the sake of God cannot work for the sake of God." This is a good word of experience. David knew that God needed a temple, but when God's word came to him, he immediately stopped his work. His stopping was not related to need or ability; rather, he stopped because God did not want him to work. The ability of David not to work for God shows his spirituality. If we were David, could we have stopped? Opportunities will come, but God's word may also come, saying, "Do not do anything. Slow down. Change your plan. Only My decision counts." Many who are zealous for God cannot hear such a word. This is the reason many workers of God cannot work for God. May God open our eyes.

David's stopping established a twofold testimony in the universe. First, all the work in the universe should come from God, not from man. Second, all that matters is what God does for man, not what man does for God. David wanted to build a temple for God, but God said that He would build a house for

David from which a kingdom would come forth. Even after God spoke this word to David, he fell twice. First, he murdered Uriah and usurped his wife Bath-sheba (2 Sam. 11:2-17, 26-27). Second, he numbered the children of Israel (24:1-10). It is amazing that after the murder of Uriah, Bath-sheba bore David a son, Solomon, and after David was chastised by God for numbering the people, he offered sacrifices on a piece of land, as instructed by God, which later became the site for the building of the temple (vv. 18-25; 1 Chron. 21:1; 2 Chron. 3:1).

The son and the site for the building of the temple both came out of David's being forgiven of his sins. Those who can see this will bow their head and worship God, saying, "It is not we who can do something for You, but You who does something for man." We must learn deep within that God wants only our cooperation; He does not need us to do anything for Him. Even if we could do something for God, He does not need it; He needs only our cooperation. We must stop all our opinions, decisions, and ideas; we need to let Him speak, let Him come in, and let Him command. All we need to do is cooperate with Him.

### Peter Learning to Simply Listen to the Lord's Command

In the Old Testament there are many such examples, and we cannot cover all of them. However, there are two examples in the New Testament. On the Mount of Transfiguration, Peter saw the Lord's face shining like the sun, and His garments became as white as the light (Matt. 17:2). Peter was stirred up in his zeal and said to the Lord, "I will make three tents here, one for You and one for Moses and one for Elijah" (v. 4). This shows that our opinions always accompany our zeal. When someone loves us, there will be hardships, because opinions always come when someone loves us. Those who love us always bring their opinions in addition to their heart.

When I labored for the Lord in mainland China, many people knew that I liked to eat steamed buns rather than white rice, but the Southerners did not know how to make steamed buns. In 1934 I went to preach the gospel in Pingyang in Chekiang Province. The brothers and sisters there loved me very much. They entertained me every day and made steamed buns for every meal. They even hired a cook to make steamed buns, but I could not eat the raw, hard steamed buns because of a stomach problem. I gave messages three times a day, but I hardly had any energy because I could not eat much. One day, when I could stand it no longer, I politely told the brothers that it would be better for me if the steamed buns were cooked a little longer. The brothers immediately replied that the steamed buns had been made by an expert. I could not respond. After I labored in Pingyang for three weeks, my body collapsed completely. The brothers were full of love, but they also brought their opinions, telling me to eat this kind of food and that kind of food. If these brothers and sisters had asked me what I could eat and had prepared it accordingly, the situation might have been entirely different. Many wives bring similar hardships upon their husbands because of their love.

On the Mount of Transfiguration, after seeing the Lord's transfiguration, Peter felt good and suggested making three tents. Immediately there was a voice from heaven, saying, "Hear Him!" (v. 5). The Lord Jesus did not need to listen to Peter, and Peter did not need to give opinions and make decisions. We do not need to give opinions or commands; the Lord Jesus should give the command. May we never forget this: When Peter told the Lord that he would make three tents, one for the Lord, one for Moses, and one for Elijah, a voice from heaven immediately said, "This is My Son, the Beloved, in whom I have found My delight. Hear Him!" Those who serve the Lord must learn this lesson. We should not be those whose opinions and ideas come out whenever we serve the Lord; rather, we need to be quiet and listen to His command.

## Paul Serving God
### according to the Vision That He Saw

Paul was Saul before his conversion (Acts 13:9). When he was Saul, he was not a great sinner; rather, he was a Pharisee who feared God, obeyed the law, and was zealous and pious. All his activities, however, were religious activities without revelation or God's light; they were all based on his ideas. He followed the traditions of his fathers and was taught at the feet of Gamaliel (22:3). On his way to Damascus, however, the Lord met him. It was only at this point that he asked, "What shall I do, Lord?" (v. 10). Blessed is he who asks this question! We should all ask the Lord, "What shall I do?" rather than telling Him, "This is what I will do." The Lord replied, "Rise up and enter into the city, and it will be told to you what you must do" (9:6; 22:10). The Lord told Paul what to do. Paul did not decide; rather, the Lord showed him a vision. Seeing a vision is not based on our decisions. We should not decide; only God should decide.

### ALLOWING GOD TO INITIATE ALL OUR WORK

All those who serve God must see a principle from these examples: God's work needs man's cooperation, but it does not require man's initiation. No work should be initiated by us. All work should be initiated by God. He commands, He calls, and He charges. We should listen to Him unreservedly. When He charges us, we should obey; when He demands, we should accept.

### STOPPING EVERYTHING OF OURSELVES IN ORDER TO KNOW GOD'S WILL

Lastly, we must ask how we can know God's command. How can we know God's will and revelation? How do we know what God wants us to do? Job 38:2 says, "Who is this who darkens counsel / By words without knowledge?" This word has broad implications. Job was a God-fearing person; he was very pious toward God. At the same time, he truly wanted God, and even God boasted that there was "none like him on the earth, a perfect and upright man" (1:8). Even Satan could not deny that Job was a perfect man. Nevertheless, Job's view and opinion were not broken. In terms of loving God, he truly loved God, but he still had strong views; in terms of fearing God, he feared God very much, but he still had opinions. The debate between Job and his friends shows that God was quite hidden. Throughout the entire book, Job is the one who speaks the most. God came in only after all the words of Job and his friends ran out.

If we do not allow God to come in because our words have

not run out, we will not be able to understand God's will because we still have too much within. This is our problem. Our God is quite able to remain silent. When the friends of Job were arguing with him, God was very patient. He stepped aside and let everyone speak; He came in to speak only after everyone was finished. The unique prerequisite to receiving God's revelation is to stop our speaking, our opinion, our view, and our self. While it is easy to say the word *stop,* it is not so easy to stop. The best way for us to stop is to die; once we die, we stop.

God's counsel is darkened by man's words. A person's opinion is expressed in his word, and his word represents his opinion. According to God, man's words darken His counsel. Consequently, when Job spoke, God hid Himself. Later Job realized that God remained silent when he spoke. When we have an opinion and want to initiate something, God stops and hides Himself. This is what we need to see.

When the Bible speaks of Satan, it sometimes refers to man's opinion. Matthew 16 records a second incident with Peter. When Peter tried to stop the Lord from going to Jerusalem to suffer, the Lord said to him, "Get behind Me, Satan!...for you are not setting your mind on the things of God, but on the things of men" (v. 23). Then He said, "If anyone wants to come after Me, let him deny himself" (v. 24). All of this speaks of man's opinions and ideas. When Job said, "I abhor myself" (Job 42:6), he was referring to his opinions, views, and ideas. When we serve in various places to lead and administrate the churches, the greatest problem we encounter is opinions. Once a person has the heart to serve the Lord and becomes zealous, his opinions come out. At such a time, God will hide Himself and withdraw His will. Everything we initiate will be interrupted by God. In the matter of serving God, we must stop ourselves in order to give God the absolute opportunity to speak. This requires our exercise.

## THE BASIC PRINCIPLE IN SERVICE:
### EVERYTHING BEING INITIATED BY GOD

*Question: The most difficult thing in our service to the Lord is that we do not know how to understand God's will and*

*touch God's word. It is truly difficult for us to stop ourselves.
Recently we have sensed a dryness in our service. Then the
Lord added a few Taiwanese sisters, and we felt that we
should visit them, but two brothers said that we should not go.
Hence, we did not know whether we should stop or visit them.
After we prayed, some had the feeling that we should not be
too hasty and go too soon, lest the sisters withdraw. However,
we eventually went, and there was no incident. I would like to
ask, How do we know whether a certain matter is of ourselves
or of God?*

Answer: Those who serve the Lord must thoroughly see, at
least once, that their service must originate from God. Many
have not seen the Lord in their service; they think that it is
good as long as they serve God. There are many who have this
kind of thought and view. Hence, the basic problem is whether
or not we have seen, at least once, that our service to God
must originate from Him, not from ourselves.

If we all have this light, our problems will be solved easily.
Many people, however, have not seen this light. Instead, they
try to analyze whether their service is according to God's will
and whether or not their service will render help. This is to
fall into the mind. The basic matter is that we must fall down
because of God's enlightenment and see that our service to
God must come from God, not from us. Seeing and having this
light will lead us to a breakthrough in the matter of not
daring to initiate anything pertaining to the service of God.
We will be enlightened inwardly to the point that we will not
initiate anything in the matter of serving God. There is a
saying in Chinese: "A newborn calf does not fear the tiger."
This means that a young calf is not afraid of anything. It is
even willing to touch a tiger. But if a calf is frightened and
hurt by a tiger one day, it will not dare to touch the tiger
again. Some of us are like a newborn calf in the matter of
serving God. In the Old Testament David realized that he
could not initiate anything in the service of God only after
Uzzah was struck by God (2 Sam. 6:6-8).

We are not speaking of trivial principles but rather about
a fundamental issue: In our service to the Lord, we must
have a definite experience and come to a clear point of being

enlightened by the Lord to see that our service must be of God, not of ourselves. If we have seen this basic matter, it will be much easier for us in practice.

## Service from Man Having
## Man's Enjoyment, Preference, and Flavor

How can we discern what is an opinion? An opinion is something that comes from us and is initiated by us. When something is initiated by us, we enjoy and like it. Anything initiated by us will bear our flavor and be our boast. Hence, when a service is initiated by us according to our opinion, often our enjoyment, preference, and boast are associated with it. When a certain matter is initiated by us, we enjoy and love it; moreover, we often feel that it is very good.

## Service from God Enabling Man
## to Worship the Lord and
## Advance Even When Facing Difficulties

Negatively speaking, we often become upset when we encounter problems and difficulties in service or work that originates from us, especially when our service and work are ruined and overthrown. But when our service and work originate with the Lord, we can worship Him even when we encounter problems.

If I have a job, working and taking orders from a manager, I may suffer a setback and be unable to carry out my job. When I encounter any hindrance and fail to succeed, I should report to my manager, but the failure is his responsibility, not mine. Conversely, when there is a success, it is my manager's boast, not mine. However, when I initiate a matter, its success will be my boast, and its failure will cause me to reflect on my own faults. Therefore, these two tests, one positive and one negative, determine whether the work and the responsibility we bear in all the localities comes from God or from ourselves. The positive test is whether or not we receive a sense of enjoyment and boasting from our work. The negative test is whether or not we are able to eat and sleep peacefully when our work is not carried out successfully. Both of these are tests to us.

I lived in Manila for quite a period of time, and I always stayed with the same family, which included several elders and deacons. They were very clear about the work in the church, and according to their mind, I should have been very troubled about bearing the burden there. They were somewhat bothered because I could eat and sleep well when I stayed with them. However, I told them that I enjoyed every meal and slept well every night despite the heavy burden of the work. One asked me how this was possible, assuming that I did not care for them. All the brothers and sisters, however, could testify that my heart was genuinely for them; otherwise, I would have been unable to live there for so long. I told them that even though I was bearing the burden, I was clear that the responsibility was not upon me. I was not doing a work of my own in Southeast Asia. I was there because I was sent by the Lord. Therefore, I was not doing my work but the Lord's work. The burden I bore was His burden, not mine.

## Service from God Enabling Man
## Not to Be Anxious or Quarrelsome

Moreover, there is other indirect evidence that shows whether a work is of God. If a certain work is not of God, the brothers and sisters often are not willing to carry it out. However, if a certain work is of God, the brothers and sisters are able to labor together. This is very good, but even if the brothers and sisters have some difficulty in laboring together, this is not necessarily a problem, because the work is not their responsibility. Those who are sent by the Lord are often quite patient. When a person is doing his own work, he will be anxious for success, but if he is doing the Lord's work, he will not be anxious, because it is the Lord's business. If we want to determine whether a person's work is of God or of himself, we only need to see if he is anxious in the work. If a person's work is according to God's sending, the sent one will not be anxious, and there will not be many opinions.

When I was in Manila once, I truly sensed that a certain matter was of the Lord because of the Lord's moving without any initiation on my part. Then a sister asked, saying, "Brother

Lee, since this matter is of the Lord, why do you not do it?"
I replied, "I need to wait until the saints also have the assurance that it is of the Lord." Then she said, "You should lead the saints. If you lead the saints, they will listen to you."
I said, "If you sense that this matter is of the Lord, there is no need for you to be anxious." As a result, there was no dispute among the brothers and sisters. If the brothers and sisters wanted to do a certain thing, and I had said no, or if I wanted to do a certain thing, and the brothers and sisters had said no, there would have been a quarrel. Anything that gives rise to quarreling is of the self, not of God.

These three tests speak of our relationship with God in our work and whether or not our work is of God. We serve in many ways, but what the Lord does through us, whether it is a success or a failure, should not give us much feeling. However, if a work is initiated by us, we will have a deep feeling regarding its success or failure. May the Lord have mercy on us and teach us in these matters so that we may see whether our work is of man or of God.

If a brother sees an improper condition in the church and is not able to eat or sleep well, this will become a problem. When our heart is set on the Lord's work, we should be able to eat and sleep well, no matter how difficult the environment. However, if a brother is able to sleep peacefully when the sky is "falling" simply because he has no real care or concern, he is useless to God. My family knows that there is not a single burden or work of the church that can press me to the point of making me unable to eat or sleep well. There is much work and burden within me, but I am clear that this is the Lord's business. Since I am here to cooperate with Him, I do not need to be anxious.

For example, I recently handed over the responsibility of managing the workers' home to a brother. Many times when I inquire about a certain matter related to the home, he does not fully know. Logically speaking, I should be restless, but I still sleep peacefully. Conversely, even if people praised the arrangement of the workers' home, I would not feel that this was my glory, because everything is up to the Lord. Hence, I can eat and sleep well, and I have no opinion on the success or failure of any matter because I know that everything originates from the Lord.

### LEARNING TO BEAR RESPONSIBILITY AND
### BEING ABSOLUTELY FAITHFUL BEFORE THE LORD

Sometimes after we hand over certain matters to the co-workers, they make excuses when they are asked about what they have done. Such people are not competent, and they should not sleep peacefully. It would be quite strange if one was entrusted with the job of bookkeeping but was unable to say at a later date what had been done and could only speak of studying the Bible and giving messages. If one wants to give messages well, work well, and even study the Bible well, he must be serious in whatever he does. An irresponsible person is useless in God's hand. When someone entrusts us with a certain matter, we must realize that this is a matter of responsibility; we should not say that we do not know.

Therefore, we must all learn to bear responsibility and burden before the Lord, and we must also serve the Lord faithfully. Although these matters are not decided by us nor originate from us, we must be absolutely faithful and responsible in what we do.

CHAPTER SEVENTEEN

# PREPARING OURSELVES
# TO MEET THE LORD'S NEED

Scripture Reading: 2 Tim. 2:21; Eph. 3:7, 20

In the preceding chapter we saw that all our work must be initiated by God and that we are merely cooperating with Him to meet the need in His heart. Hence, we need to carry out all our service by the power of the Lord. We need to rely on the Lord because we have no way in ourselves. Relying on the Lord actually means that we carry out our service by being joined to the Lord and by being in fellowship with Him.

In all our service we should work together with the Master and meet His need. When a person serves his Master, the first question we should ask is whether the service originates from himself or from the Master. The second question is whether he can meet the Master's need and fulfill His demand. In 2 Timothy 2:21, Paul told Timothy that he needed to be "useful to the master." The word *master* indicates that what we are doing is initiated not by us but by our Master. However, after knowing our Master's will and having His command, there is still a big question of whether or not we can carry out our Master's need and fulfill His demand.

## SERVING THE LORD REQUIRING
## THE SERVING ONE TO STOP HIMSELF

One who serves the Lord must first ask himself whether his service is of himself or of the Lord. Once this question is settled, he must ask himself whether he can meet the Lord's need. If Brother So-and-so is working for the Lord in Ping-tong, he must ask himself whether his work is of the Lord or of himself. Once he is clear that his work is of the Lord, the first question is settled. At this point he must ask a second question: Can he meet the Lord's need and fulfill His demand in the work? This is a big question.

These two questions require us to put ourselves aside and also require our full cooperation. The first requirement of the work is that we stop; we must stop all our activities and restrain our opinions, thoughts, and ideas. Everything of ours must be stopped. We must stop because the Lord's work does not originate from us but from Him. Once we stop, we will know whether our work is of the Lord. Then we need to be able to meet His need.

In Matthew 17 Peter spoke of several matters. Although these matters are quite meaningful, we may have never considered how they are related to the things revealed in chapter 16. In chapter 16 the Lord said, "Upon this rock I will build My church" (v. 18), but in chapter 17 Peter told the Lord that he would make a tent for Him (v. 4). The Lord said that He would build His church, but Peter said that he would make a tent for the Son of God. At Pentecost, God began to build the church. The church is not merely a tent but a house. Peter's suggestion to the Lord was according to his own concept, not according to God's purpose for His Son, Christ. Peter ultimately did not make a tent, but he did gain much material for the building of the church. Peter's word shows that man's opinion sometimes can be quite similar to God's concept. Regrettably, however, God's will is often interrupted because of this similarity.

God desires to build the Body of Christ so that His Son may obtain a dwelling place. The body of a person is his dwelling place; likewise, the Body of Christ, which is the church, is Christ's dwelling place. As far as God was concerned, Peter needed to gather the building materials, and Paul needed to build these materials into a house so that Christ would have a dwelling place.

Peter's proposal of making a tent for the Son of God was of himself. Apparently, it was the same as God's purpose, but actually, it was against God's determination. God often decides to do certain things in us, the called ones. However, we can contradict, replace, and even damage His determination because our proposals, thoughts, ideas, and opinions are quite similar to His will. This is the reason there was a voice from heaven, saying, "Hear Him!" (v. 5). This indicates that it is not appropriate for us to utter something, to speak a word, to make proposals, and to give our opinions. Instead, only He should speak, and we must hear Him.

The first point we must pay attention to in our service is to put ourselves on hold; that is, we must stop our entire being. We must see that before we were touched by God, we had no interest in the things of God, but that once we were touched by God, we were full of opinions. As soon as God leads us to the Mount of Transfiguration and we see His glory, we have many proposals and opinions. This experience is not related only to a great revival or even to a small revival. Even when we are praying at home, many ideas come as soon as we touch the Lord. Consequently, we want to do many things for the Lord. None of these ideas were present before we went to the Mount of Transfiguration; we did not care about such things. However, once we have been touched by the Lord and truly receive a spiritual burden, we immediately want to use our ideas to do something for the Lord. This is the first problem we have in the matter of serving the Lord.

Many denominations on the earth today have been produced out of Babel. Critics point out that a denomination is produced after every great revival among Christians. Church history confirms this. After every great revival, something of man is produced. When someone goes to the Mount of Transfiguration and his eyes are opened to see God's glory, his opinion and self-approbation immediately come out. This is the result of inadequate learning.

The Lord's intention is to build His church, that is, to build His church as His dwelling place, but Peter suggested making a tent. Such a tent is symbolic of many denominations. God desires to build a dwelling place for His Son, which is the church. Yet many "Peters" have gone to the Mount of Transfiguration, seen the Lord's glory, and given their opinions one after another, instead of stopping themselves. As a result, many tents, many denominations, have been produced. A tent signifies a denomination, which apparently is similar to the church. A house is according to the Master's determination, whereas a tent is according to a servant's proposal. Matthew 16 shows the Lord's determined counsel, whereas chapter 17 shows Peter's instantaneous proposal. The moment Peter presented his proposal, he was interrupted. Today because many people have not allowed the Lord to interrupt their proposals, there are many "tents." Hence, being unable to stop ourselves is the first problem in serving the Lord.

## SERVING THE LORD REQUIRING
## THE SERVING ONE TO RISE UP

One who serves the Lord must be one who also rises up. It may seem contradictory to say that we need to stop and then say that we need to rise up, but it is not. We need to restrain our opinions and stop our proposals, but we need to rise up to meet the Lord's need and fulfill the demand in His work. The work of redemption was not accomplished merely by God Himself. God needed man in the person of Jesus Christ to work with Him to accomplish His redemptive work. In redemption, fifty percent is carried out by God, and fifty percent is by man. Without God, there could not be a redemptive work, but also without man, there could not be a redemptive work. The work of redemption was accomplished by the joining of God and man. God desperately needs the cooperation of man. Hence, no part of the work of redemption can be accomplished apart from man. Whenever God wants to do a work, He reveals what He wants to do to man and requires man to stop his opinions and all that he is; then God requires man to cooperate with Him. This cooperation requires man to rise up.

I do not know how much we understand or how deeply we realize this point. Before his conversion, Saul served God, yet he was full of opinions. On his way to Damascus, however, God met him, and he fell on the ground (Acts 9:4). He had been very active, but now he was unable to move. His entire being was stopped so that he could receive God's revelation and see that his service should come only from God, not from man. God wanted him to see that all his efforts as Saul of Tarsus were according to man's imagination. Hence, God met

Saul on his way to Damascus to stop his entire being. However, this was not the end of God's work. From that time forward, God enabled Paul to rise up so that he could meet His need and be of use to Him. This second requirement is often more difficult to deal with than the first. While it is not easy for us to stop, it is even more difficult to rise up. Even though it is not easy for us to stop, nevertheless, we still must rise up to meet God's need and fulfill His demand once we stop. This is more difficult.

Among us there is a brother who has difficulty stopping his opinions and ideas. Whenever we discuss a matter with him, he has ideas and suggestions. For example, if we ask him to help sweep the floor, he replies that the windows need to be cleaned. If we ask him to clean the windows, he says that the floor needs to be swept. This shows that he is a person whose thoughts and opinions cannot be stopped. However, if he wants to serve the Lord, he must stop his ideas and thoughts.

This may be compared to the relationship between a servant and his master. If the servant acknowledges that he is a servant, he must listen to his master's word. If his master wants him to sweep the floor, he must obey his master by sweeping the floor before cleaning the windows. A servant also may hear his master's word and know that he needs to sweep the floor but goes to sleep after hearing the word. When he wakes up, he still may not move because he is waiting for someone to buy a broom. The person who is supposed to buy the broom, however, is waiting for someone to give him money, but the person who takes care of the finances cannot get any money because the person who opens the cash box is in the shower and cannot come immediately. This is not something I made up; it is an actual situation.

This shows that in the Lord's service, it is not easy for one to stop, nor is it easy for one to rise up. When a person truly meets the Lord, he will stop his entire being and ask the Lord what He wants. If the Lord says, "Sweep the floor," he should immediately sweep the floor with his undivided attention. He will consider everything related to sweeping the floor and give it his full attention. In the service of the Lord, there is a great deal of human opinion, yet very few meet God's standard. According to man's disposition, whenever people discuss something, they always have many opinions, but then they go home and sleep peacefully without any further consideration. This is truly troubling. This is one of the reasons that the elders in the church do not like people to express too many opinions.

If we learn these essential lessons, we will be very spiritual. If an elderly brother asks us to cook, we will immediately focus our attention on cooking. In dealing with this elderly brother, we must learn to stop ourselves and to rise up with our entire being. Only then can we meet the Lord's need. Our problems are related to being unable to stop and then being unable to rise up. As a consequence, we have not been very useful in the Lord's hand.

In the elders' meeting, some brothers know only how to make suggestions but not how to work. With such brothers, we should ask them to work. Since they have made the suggestion, they should take the lead to carry it out. For example, when a brother says that the sun is quite bright in the meeting hall and that it would be good to hang some curtains, I would say, "Please do it." After a few instances of suggesting but not working, the brother usually does not have the boldness to open his mouth to speak when we meet again. We do not need to reject the brothers' suggestions, but we should always ask the brothers to do it themselves. This will help them learn the lesson of not giving their opinions lightly. If they think that something is feasible, they should do it. After it is done, we can comment on it. If it is not done properly, we need to change the method. After being dealt with two or three times, the brothers will not talk so freely again. The brother who suggested hanging curtains, for example, failed to hang the curtains properly three times, and he needed to be helped in the end. Since then, he has been a different person when he has suggested something.

The Lord deals with us according to this principle. For example, when someone asked Peter whether the Lord Jesus would pay the temple tax, he replied, "Yes." However, did the Lord truly need to pay the temple tax? The Lord did not respond to Peter directly; rather, He asked him to go fishing in the sea (Matt. 17:24-27). I believe that Peter learned a great lesson through this experience. From that time on, he dared not to speak so loosely again. When facing the vast expanse of the sea while he waited to catch a fish with a stater in its mouth, Peter must have been greatly troubled. He must have thought, "All of this trouble is due to my speaking too much. When will I find a fish with a stater in its mouth?" Peter learned many lessons in a deep way. One who is learning to serve the Lord must come before Him and stop himself. What we should do is not determined by us but rather by His command. Then we must rise up to meet His need.

### ENDEAVORING TO LEARN IN ALL ASPECTS
### IN ORDER TO MEET THE LORD'S NEED

We need to rise up to meet the Lord's need, and rising up includes many aspects. A brother once said that as long as a person has a specialty, he will be able to make a living in the world. However, in the service of the Lord, we must be strong in every aspect—in our spirit, soul, and body. This is our experience. One who is useful to the Lord immediately rises up in his entire being when he receives the Lord's command. He is able to exercise his mind, emotion, and will in the same way that he exercises his spirit. He knows how to regulate, supply, and control his body. He can rise up to meet the Lord's need in great or small things.

After we are saved, we often feel that we are inadequate to meet the Lord's need and cooperate with Him when He wants to use us. It is quite good to have this kind of feeling. Because some do not have this kind of feeling, they sleep peacefully when the Lord wants to use them. This is why we say that we should not sleep and eat peacefully; rather, we need to rise up and deal with ourselves in order to meet the Lord's need.

Concerning the second point of rising up to meet the Lord's need, there are many lessons we should learn. Even though some saints talk to people, it is not easy for them to enter into their feeling or to understand them. This is due to a lack of learning. I once saw a brother who was improper in the matter of giving hospitality, and I said to him, "Brother, you must be more prepared when you give hospitality." He replied that he asked his guests about their needs, and they said that they did not need anything. I responded, "We should not be so foolish and accepting of their words. While our guests would not lie, they also do not want to be impolite." Our brother was too simple and accepting, believing everything his guests said. When they said that they could do without soap or hot water, it did not mean that they had no need of them. This brother's service shows that he did not understand people's needs, so how could he serve people well?

When the saints come to us, we often do not understand their words, and sometimes our understanding is the exact opposite of what they mean. As Christians, we should learn to speak truthfully more than politely. I have been learning this lesson for over twenty years, and I have almost learned it. When I take hospitality in a saint's house, I always tell them what I need when they ask, "Do you need to eat something?" As Christians, we must learn lessons. In particular, when we serve people, we must learn to know them, understand their words, and know their desires. Only then can we rise up to meet the Lord's need.

Some brothers like to speak with their local dialect. This is not so proper. We should learn to meet all kinds of needs appropriately; only then can we rise up to meet the Lord's need. It is not possible to give many illustrations. In short, there is much for us to learn in this second point, that is, in the matter of rising up to meet the Lord's need. The disposition of some people makes it impossible for them to serve God. If they served God, I am afraid that they would have to "peel off their skin." Not only would they need to change their clothes and make alterations, but even their skin would need to be "peeled off." If one has not learned any lesson, he will not know what to do when people come to him; he will not know how to handle a matter when it is brought to his attention. This kind of person cannot serve God.

If we want to serve God, we must learn to stop our whole being before God; moreover, we must learn to cause our whole being to rise up before God. We must learn every single point that is necessary. We cannot learn them in a day or a moment; rather, every day and every moment are needed. This is a long-term matter. If the Lord arranges for us to be responsible for receiving guests from out of town, we should consider everything related to hospitality. For example, what will the guests need when they step into the house? What will they need in their rooms? What other needs will they have? We must carefully consider these matters. Only in this way can we be useful in our service.

The condition of some young people is annoying. They read the Bible in a loose way; they miss sentences or misquote verses. How can they meet God's need? Sometimes a brother who will give a message in the meeting begins to consider what to say only at the last minute. When he suddenly remembers a verse, he cannot remember the exact verse reference; he knows it only vaguely. This proves that there has not been enough preparation. Instead of waiting until the last minute to consider what to speak, we must be so well prepared that we can open the Bible to the exact verse on which we are going to speak. This is proper preparation.

I have said repeatedly that if we want to meet the Lord's need, we must be prepared in every aspect. Serving the Lord requires us to be all-capable. We cannot say that we are fully qualified to meet the Lord's need, but the Lord requires us to be all-capable for His service. This requires us to be prepared outwardly and inwardly. Our spirit must be clean, fresh, full of the Lord's presence, and strong, knowing the spiritual way. We need to learn in all these matters. My heart often grieves when I see the saints with nothing to do. How can they have nothing to do? If we are endeavoring to learn all the time, we surely will have an endless number of things to do.

We also have read too little. Our co-workers who are in their forties and fifties, for example, read too little. In principle, we should read a new book every week. We should read books published by us and from other countries. We need to see how things are done in the United States and Japan. We should not be content with what we presently have, thinking that we have done everything well. Even if we have done well, we still need to seek improvement and consult other people. Today there are many among us who have not read even one book all year. We cannot say that we are not slothful. If this condition continues, how can we meet God's need?

If we want to serve the Lord, we must rise up and try to accomplish something. For example, if we want to clean the floor, we must study and find the proper way to clean. No one who participates in the Lord's work can be idle and unoccupied. The practice in degraded Christianity is to hire preachers to preach, but we cannot do this. One who is truly used by the Lord must be aggressive and able to accomplish great things. In the Bible nearly everyone who was useful to God was snatched out of the world by God. If they had loved and remained in the world, they would have been quite successful. Instead, the Lord snatched them out of the world and made them useful vessels in His hands.

Many people have the erroneous concept that if they are not able to do anything else, they can be a preacher. One of my classmates became a newspaper reporter when he was about twenty years old, but later he quit his job. He came to me and asked me to introduce him to the church because he wanted a job as a preacher. At that time, if a mother had three sons, the brightest one would study medicine, the next brightest would study business, and the least bright would study theology. However, service to God cannot be like this. The brightest ones must serve God, and those who are not so bright must also serve God, but they need to overcome their lack of intelligence by spending time to learn, according to the saying: "Stupidity can be remedied by diligence." We must have this kind of attitude and feeling.

One who serves the Lord cannot be idle and unoccupied. No one should be like this. Everyone should schedule his time properly, planning when to pray, visit people, clean, prepare for a message, and so forth. This requires learning. If we want to serve the Lord and be useful, we must learn every day. Otherwise, our destiny will be a dead end. Sometimes when I see some saints, I am truly bothered. For example, when I meet them on the street around 7:30 P.M., they tell me that they have nothing to do. Such people are surely useless. We must have a clear arrangement, a plan for doing certain things at certain times. If we are all willing to try this, our uselessness will turn to usefulness. Not enough people have risen up, and there are still many things that require our learning and many works that require our labor. In serving the Lord we must stop ourselves, but in meeting the Lord's need we must be absolute and rise up.

## LIFE, THE WORD, AND LIGHT

*Question: How can we touch life? Do we need a more thorough understanding of some points?*

Answer: God's work, whether in creation or redemption, is through His word. Hebrews 11:3 says, "The universe has been framed by the word of God." God created the heavens by His word; He also accomplished the work of redemption by His word. This is why there is the Bible and so many messages and spiritual publications. These are all for the release of God's word. According to the Lord's word in Matthew 13:18-23, God's word is a seed, and in this seed there is life.

We know from experience that when God's word enters into us, its first effect is to enlighten us. Whenever we have the Lord's word in us, we are enlightened. When we receive this light, it becomes life. Life is the Holy Spirit, Christ, and God. Hence, we can receive God's word by reading the Bible, listening to messages, reading spiritual publications, fellowshipping, and by the testimonies of the apostles. Sometimes the content from the Bible, messages, spiritual publications, fellowship, and testimonies of the apostles enters into our mind and memory. At a certain point, the Holy Spirit will impart the words that have entered into our mind and memory into our spirit. Then the words will impart light, and when we receive this light, it will become life, which is the Spirit, Christ, and God. Life is conveyed through the word. Once the word enters into us, it becomes light, and once we receive this light, we receive life.

*Question: If we do not have light, does it mean that we cannot receive God's word?*

Answer: The word is first, and then there is light. Whether in creation or redemption, the first step of God's work involves His speaking. He spoke, and it was done. Thus, John 1:3 says that all the things in the heavens came into being through Him as the Word. Moreover, the universe has been framed by the word of God (Heb. 11:3). God's word is great.

*Question: We have no feeling concerning the items related to prayer. What should we do?*

Answer: The question you raised diminishes the content of the speaking. Our service before God must be of God, not of us. Thus, concerning the items related to prayer, when you have the inspiration, pray, and when you do not have the inspiration, do not pray.

### PREPARING OURSELVES

*Question: One who serves the Lord must stop himself and then rise up. Is there an absolute relationship between the two?*

Answer: Let us consider a person who is learning to be a chef. A good chef is well prepared. If he needs to learn how to cook a fish when a customer asks, "Please cook a fish for me," the customer will starve. If someone wants to be a chef, he must learn as early and as quickly as possible. When he has finished learning, he should ask his master what to cook. If the master asks him to make white rice, he should make white rice immediately; if the master asks him to make steamed buns, he should make steamed buns immediately. When a chef hears the master's command, he must be able to meet the master's need in a timely way. Hence, if we have not been properly trained and have wasted much time, it will not be easy for us to receive God's command. If an apprentice has been cooking for only two days, will his master entrust him with a banquet? I believe we know that this would be absolutely impossible.

According to 2 Timothy 2:21, one who serves the Lord must first cleanse himself in order to be useful to the master. We must not have a part in any place that is improper, unclean, and full of gossip so that we will not be defiled in any way. We must learn and be dealt with every day. This is the meaning of 2 Timothy. If we prepare ourselves in such a way, we will be able to meet all the Lord's needs when the Holy Spirit commands us. Therefore, we must study the Bible properly and read spiritual publications. We must learn how to use our time so that we can meet the Lord's need even more.

## THE PROPER CHARACTER OF A SERVING ONE

*Question: My thoughts are usually confused, and I am also timid; therefore, I do not have enough boldness in judging matters. What should I do?*

Answer: Many who serve the Lord may not necessarily have the Lord's command when they first begin to pursue the Lord. According to the record of the entire New Testament, some brothers, such as Timothy, Titus, and Mark, never received a command from the Lord directly. Their activities in the work were altogether under Paul's command because they were all learners. Generally speaking, young brothers and sisters expect to immediately receive a direct command from the Lord when they rise up to serve the Lord, but first we should be learners, and then we will have a way.

Concerning our brother's question, we should learn both great and small things in our daily living. For example, we must learn to control our thoughts and train our character. If we have poor judgment, we must learn even more. If we do not learn in our ordinary living, we will not be able to meet the need when we later receive the Lord's command. We must learn in matters related to our attire and our actions, not only so that we will be detailed persons but in order to learn how to exercise our judgment.

One day, after seeing a brother's room, I told him that I was clear that he needed to learn many lessons. We should observe our living quarters, our attire, and the way we conduct ourselves in life and handle matters. If we have never been trained, we will not be able to even hold a chair properly. If we are loose in our daily living, it will be difficult for us to meet the Lord's need precisely when He gives us a command. From my constant observation of the condition of the young people, I know that their reading of the Bible is loose and inaccurate. Therefore, I implore all of us to have much exercise in our daily living.

In matters related to ourselves or others, we always seem

to do either too much or not enough; this is not right. For instance, when someone asks us to buy one hundred pounds of something, we either buy more than one hundred pounds or less than one hundred pounds. It seems that we are always too much or not enough. This is improper. We must learn to be accurate in all things.

We have more than forty brothers and sisters who serve full time, but it is difficult to find one who is accurate. It seems that everyone is loose and easygoing. This is because they have been working in a loose, careless, and easygoing fashion from their youth. This is due to an inadequate exercise in their daily living. Hence, I often say to the young people, "Your poor study of the Bible, inadequate reading of the spiritual publications, and insufficient ability to judge are due to the lack of a strict character. Once you build up a strict character, you will be thorough and effective in whatever you do."

Many full-time serving brothers and sisters have difficulty serving well because of inadequate character, not because they do not know how to do things. If the character of the brothers and sisters is improper, a task will not be taken seriously, and it will be done carelessly and sloppily. After repeated speakings, I hope we can learn these lessons in a practical way. In three to five months, I do not wish to see any serving ones among us being slothful, complacent, and sloppy. We should do things thoroughly and seriously, and we should deal with people in spirit and in truthfulness. If we do not build up our character in serving the Lord, we will be useless. Hence, we must study the Word of truth and familiarize ourselves with the Bible. Moreover, we must be diligent, serious, thorough, and solemn. Whether we do or do not do something, we must be proper. This kind of character must be built up within us, starting with the small things in our daily living.

We may use the workers' home as an illustration. When I was there for a few days, I saw that sometimes the brothers and sisters would not even close the door when they left the house. If we have not learned even this, how can we serve and lead the saints? In their small reception room, there were trays and cups near the four sofa chairs. After the trays and cups were used, however, they were not returned to their original place; everything was a mess. I can give many examples that show that we have not learned these lessons properly and our character has not been built up. Hence, I do not believe that we can study the Bible well and that our serving can be on track.

If we are willing to exercise and build up our character, we surely will have light when we read the Bible, and we surely will be effective when we serve. On the contrary, if we are not willing to properly learn about many things, our mind will be loose, confused, and useless. From now on, as the Lord so leads and has mercy on us, we must learn in a serious way. Then when we encounter a certain matter, we will not be confused or timid, but we will have good judgment and boldness. Since our mind has been trained in small things, we will be an accurate person. If we want to be used by the Lord and be useful vessels in His hand, we do not necessarily need to be very knowledgeable, but our character must be trained.

## EXERCISING IN SEVEN CRUCIAL ITEMS FOR PRAYER

*Question: We all know that there are different lines in the service of the church: the line of the gospel, the line of life, and the line of handling matters, etc. In our daily exercise, we pay much attention to rising early and finding a place to pray. Then we read 1 Samuel 1, 4, 6, and 7 and see how Hannah's prayer was answered and how she had fellowship in prayer. To summarize, there are seven items we need to pray for: first, for God; second, for the church; third, for our country; fourth, for the saints; fifth, for people to believe in the Lord; sixth, for the Jews; and seventh, for ourselves. In other words, first, we need to pray for God's kingdom to come. Second, we need to pray for the revival of the church and for the serving ones, including the elders, deacons, and responsible ones in the small groups. Third, we need to pray for our country and for those who are in authority, praying for the health and wisdom of those in high position that we may live in tranquility and godliness so that the gospel may be widely spread. Fourth, we need to pray for the prayerlessness of the saints, for those who have been lost, for the growth in life, and for the saints to join the pursuing meetings and to attend prayer meetings in groups. Fifth, we need to pray for the sending of workers for the preaching of the gospel and for the salvation of our friends, relatives, and colleagues. Sixth, we need to ask God to bless the Jews so that they may repent and believe in Jesus. Seventh, we need to pray for our enlightenment so that we will know the self, for our cleansing so that we may be delivered from sins and wrongdoings, and for our being granted a spirit of wisdom and revelation so that we may know God's will and principles. May all of us serving ones enter into the four stages of the experience in life so that we may grow in life unto maturity (see* The Experience of Life*). Is anything still lacking?*

Answer: This is good. I hope that all the serving ones and responsible brothers in the churches would not only have an actual exercise themselves but also learn to lead the saints into these life practices. We must exercise properly related to the seven items for prayer; these are truly good topics. When a person first begins to pray and cannot fully follow the sense of his spirit to pray with words, he may first pray according to regulation. Gradually, however, his mouth and mind will match each other. Then he can break away from his regulated prayer and enter into the prayer of the spirit. I hope that all the saints will try this. This way is quite good in the initial stage. It would be best if we could practice the four stages of spiritual life in every place, as our brother fellowshipped. The co-workers, elders, deacons, and responsible ones for the small groups should take the lead to exercise. In this way, all the churches spontaneously will have a living and expression of spiritual reality.

# CHAPTER EIGHTEEN

## BEING JOINED TO THE LORD
## IN THE MATTER OF SERVICE

### NEEDING TO BE JOINED TO THE LORD

One who serves the Lord must do everything by being joined to the Lord, by being in union with the Lord. In other words, he must serve by relying on the Lord. We are often unable to rise up to answer the Lord's demand and meet the Lord's need, but when we are able to rise up to meet the Lord's need, there is a risk of not relying on the Lord. It is possible not to rely on the Lord or look to Him because we are able to work according to our own capability, diligence, and earnestness. Everyone who serves the Lord must avoid acting independently. Acting independently is to put the Lord aside, not depending on Him, not praying to Him, not being joined to Him, but doing the work all by our self.

As a proper serving one, we should stop our thoughts, views, and concepts because none of our service should be out of ourselves. All our service must be of the Lord; hence, we must stop ourselves. We can receive the Lord's command and revelation only when we stop ourselves.

When a person has the Lord's command and receives the Lord's revelation, he should immediately rise up to cooperate with the Lord. Some cannot rise up because they have not been prepared adequately. For example, some have a poor character of complacency, and others are not familiar with the Bible. Both reasons prevent them from being able to rise up. Others cannot rise up because of wives, children, and parents. When the Lord came to call people, some could not answer His call because they needed to care for wives, children, parents, and even their living and safety (Deut. 13:6; 24:5; Luke

14:17-20, 26). In the same way, many have the Lord's calling today, but they are unable to rise up because of their personal concerns.

Those who are able to answer the Lord's call are simple. When James and John were mending their nets by the Sea of Galilee, they left the boat and their father and followed the Lord as soon as they heard His call (Matt. 4:21-22). Their answer to the Lord's call is the standard. There are no indications that they made arrangements for their father, their boat, and their nets. Their answer was quick, simple, and without concern for the consequences. This is truly a pattern. It is difficult to find someone who rises up to answer the Lord's call without considering his own needs first. Many brothers and sisters answer the Lord's call, yet they do it in a dragging way; they need to make arrangements for their "boats" and their "nets," and they also need to have a proper plan to take care of their "fathers" so that their relatives and friends would not misunderstand and the Lord's testimony would not be damaged. Amazingly, however, this group of Galileans did not have any of these considerations. They left their boat and nets and even were not concerned about their father; they simply rose up to meet the Lord's need.

In the Gospel of Matthew a disciple said to the Lord, "Lord, permit me first to go and bury my father," and He said, "Follow Me, and let the dead bury their own dead" (8:21-22). Whenever the Lord called someone, He did not allow him to make arrangements. If the Lord does not call, there is nothing we can do. However, once He calls, we must answer His call immediately and unconditionally. This is what is needed in order for one to rise up. Although many brothers and sisters have the Lord's calling, they cannot rise up. The first time He calls, we consider; the second time He calls, we still cannot rise up; the third and fourth times He calls, it is even more difficult for us to rise up. Throughout their lives, some Christians are called continually, but they are unable to rise up. On their deathbed, they have only regret. We need to solemnly see that when the Lord's calling comes, we must rise up immediately to answer His call and meet His present need.

## THE LORD'S SALVATION BEING HIS CALLING

In God's redemption nothing can be done apart from man. God needs man to co-work and co-labor with Him. Only degraded Christianity teaches that some, but not others, can serve God. Little do they know that in God's salvation, everyone must serve God. God saves everyone and calls everyone. As long as someone is willing to receive His salvation, He saves him; as long as someone is willing to answer His call, He calls him. The problem is not that He does not save or call but that we are unwilling to receive His salvation and to answer His call.

The Lord's salvation is His calling; all those who know God understand this. The Lord saves us to call us to serve Him. The Gospels show that when the Lord was on the earth, everyone who was saved was also called. In the Bible there is no example of the Lord's calling being separate from His salvation. The Bible does not show that Peter believed but was not called. Peter was called at the same time that he was saved. His being saved was his being called, and his being called was his being saved. Likewise, Nathanael was called at the same time and in the same place that he was saved (John 1:47-49). Paul was not saved in Damascus and called in the wilderness; rather, he was called when he was saved.

In the New Testament there is not one person whose calling is separate from his salvation. We cannot find an example in the New Testament that shows that someone was saved but called only later. If we have truly been saved, God's calling came the day we were saved. Salvation and calling are one. A genuinely saved person has a deep desire to serve God once he is saved. If a genuinely saved person does not want to serve God, his salvation is questionable. Did we not have a desire to serve God on the first day we were saved? We had this desire because God's calling is included in His salvation. God saves us so that we may serve Him. God saves everyone and calls everyone.

## ANSWERING THE LORD'S CALL

Everything related to God's redemption depends upon man; hence, without man, God cannot do anything. All the work in

His redemption is carried out through man, by means of man, and in the mingling with man, and He saves us so that we may serve Him. Our problem, however, is that we cannot rise up. We want to take care of our wives, children, parents, families, careers, futures, fame, and wealth. We have so much to take care of that we cannot rise up. We are unable to be quick and decisive. We do not have the courage and are not ready to take risks. We merely want to be a secure Christian. A Christian who is up to the standard, however, takes risks. Answering the Lord's call requires us to take risks. Some Christians seem to rise up, but because they have not been sufficiently broken and dealt with, they cannot endure and collapse after a short time. Hence, we must see that among so many Christians, it is not easy for the Lord to find some who can meet His need. Such people are rare.

A person who rises up for God needs to have the boldness to take risks and have a strong and indomitable will. A person who is timid and cowardly cannot rise up. Very often, of a hundred people whom the Lord saves, fewer than five are willing to rise up for Him. Most Christians are timid, weak in will, cowardly, and indifferent. Such ones have difficulty in rising up and are not of much use even if they do rise up. Those who rise up must have a certain amount of courage and talent. Everyone who is useful for the Lord must have a strong will, boldness, and some capability at the very least.

## LIVING IN THE LORD AND RELYING ON HIM

However, when a person rises up to meet God's need, there is another risk. Because those who rise up have some resolve and boldness, there is the risk that they will not rely on God or look to God but would rather do things in themselves. Even though they disregard many dangers and difficulties and rise up for the Lord in the face of repeated frustrations, there is a danger that they will charge ahead to do a work regardless of what the Lord is doing. They can work independently by themselves and apart from the Lord. They can put Him aside, not fellowship with Him, not abide in Him, and not be in union with Him.

In today's Christianity there are many activities and works

which have fallen into this category. As long as someone has the resolve, capability, responsibility, and boldness to take risks, he can do some work. This is the reason so many works in Christianity have lost the Lord's presence. This is truly frightening. Many things can be done without abiding in the Lord.

No matter how strong we are and how much we can rise up for the Lord, we should all be weak in every step of our work. We must say to Him, "O Lord, although I have risen up, I am still a weak person. Like the children of Israel, I need to be borne on Your wings to serve You. In people's eyes, I may be bold, I may have ideas, and I may have a strong will, but Lord, You know that I am as weak as water. If You do not uphold me and bear me on Your shoulders, I cannot walk an inch. O Lord, apart from You I can do nothing. Inwardly, I am weak in prayer. I am weak in fellowship. I am weak even in my feeling for the work." No matter how people evaluate us outwardly, thinking that we are strong, capable, and steadfast in our will, we must be weak and trembling in our inward being. We must tell the Lord, "Apart from You I can do nothing. Though You need me, I need You; I need You not only inwardly but also outwardly. Lord, in my spirit, I need Your Spirit; in my environment, I need Your hand. I need You."

## NOT BEING POLITICAL

A person who works and serves the Lord in administrating the church should never be political like unbelievers in the community and in society. In serving the Lord and administrating the church, we should never use tricks or play politics. At one time of fellowship, a brother suggested that we do things a certain way. I immediately said, "Brother, this is playing politics; this is using tricks." At another time, I heard that a brother intended to come and give me a difficult time. Someone suggested that we ask a sister to visit this brother's wife to ask her to exert some influence on him and change his mind. This is a good way for unbelievers; it can be compared to using a back door when the front door is locked. But this is altogether unacceptable in the service of the Lord and in the administration of the church.

Using tricks is a proof that we are apart from the Lord and that we have not relied on Him. Unbelievers use tricks because they do not have the Lord, but one who serves the Lord should never do this. One who serves the Lord is in the Lord. When such a one encounters difficulties, he should never turn to politics but to the Lord and tell Him, "I have no work of my own; all the work is Yours. If You permit this problem, I will accept it, but if this will cause Your work to suffer, please hinder it."

When we administrate the church, we should never use our great thoughts and excellent skills. A problem that arises in the church will become worse the more we try to avoid it. The church does not need to ask for trouble, nor does the church need to shun trouble. Whenever the children of Israel rose up to create trouble, oppose, or rebel, neither Moses nor Aaron did anything for themselves; they simply withdrew and prostrated themselves before God (Exo. 15:24-25; Num. 14:1-5; 16:1-4, 19-24, 41-45). When Moses heard the murmurings of the people, he said to Jehovah, "Why have You treated Your servant badly...that You have put the burden of all this people upon me?...From where should I get meat to give to all this people? For they weep before me, saying, Give us meat, so that we may eat! I am not able to bear all this people alone, for it is too heavy for me" (11:11-14). This is a prayer of one who knew God. Moses was a great politician, a great military leader, and a great educator; he was a man of great capability who knew how to play politics. However, if we carefully read the four books of Exodus, Leviticus, Numbers, and Deuteronomy, we will see that he never used tricks in leading the children of Israel.

Moses was an elderly man (Exo. 7:7); he was not inexperienced. He had lived in the Egyptian palace (2:10), and he had led the children of Israel to come out of Egypt and cross the Red Sea, and they obeyed him (14:31). But whenever he dealt with a problem, he never assumed a high position before men. Instead, he always fell immediately on his face before God (Num. 14:5; 16:4, 22, 45; 20:6). When the Israelites worshiped the golden calf at the foot of Mount Sinai, God told Moses, "Your people, whom you brought up out of the land of Egypt, have corrupted themselves...My anger may burn against them" (Exo. 32:7, 10). Moses immediately spoke to God of His people, saying, "Your people, whom You brought out of the land of Egypt with great power and with a mighty hand...to whom You swore by Yourself and said to them, I will multiply your seed as the stars of heaven, and all this land that I have spoken of I will give to your seed" (vv. 11, 13). Moses was saying, "O God, You must forgive them; even if You do not want to forgive them, You still must forgive them." Moses negotiated with God, and eventually "Jehovah repented of the evil which He said He would do to His people" (v. 14), and Moses was given rest (33:14).

This means that he was a man who stood up for God, but he did not serve the Lord in himself. He stood up by trusting in the Lord for his service. The Lord was his support, his surrounding wall, his shield, his banner, and his fortress. He served the Lord by being in the Lord. In the Old Testament there was Moses, and in the New Testament there was Paul, who said, "Of which I became a minister according to the gift of the grace of God which was given to me according to the operation of His power" (Eph. 3:7). Paul did not rely on his own knowledge or outward tricks but on God's inward power and outward hand.

## THREE CRUCIAL POINTS
## FOR OUR SERVICE TO THE LORD

It is difficult for a capable person to rely on God and receive leading. Nine out of ten who rise up for the Lord are bold and strong in their will. In the service of the Lord, such people need to be softened within once they rise up. One who is weak is useless, but one who is too strong is also useless. One who is weak cannot rise up, but one who is too strong does not trust in the Lord. We must always remember that serving the Lord is a matter of the Lord's work and of meeting His need in coordination with Him. Most people are weak when they should be strong and strong when they should be weak. Hence, among so many people, it is difficult for the Lord to find some who are truly useful. Some people, no matter how many times the Lord calls, cannot rise up; they are either concerned for their wives or concerned for their children. Others who rise up, however, cannot be softened inwardly. They are like a wild donkey, acting apart from the Lord.

In the matter of serving the Lord, we must be clear concerning three points, or we will be altogether useless. First, we must see that the Lord's work is carried out by His mingling with man. The Lord does not work alone, and neither can man work by himself; rather, the Lord works in union with man, and man needs to let the Lord work because He is Lord. Second, we must see that we need to rise up strongly to cooperate with Him to meet His need. Third, we need to see that once we rise up, we must immediately prostrate ourselves before the Lord. Otherwise, our zeal, our pursuit, and our desire will not match the Lord.

The Lord often wants us to stop, but we cannot stop. Furthermore, when we rise up in response to the Lord, He will say, "You should fall down in Me." Many of us cannot do this without tricks and methods. In my service with the brothers from 1946 until now, I have learned to not use tricks or human methods when we encounter problems. I fear tricks more than sins. This does not mean that we should be foolish or even that we are not tricky but that the One whom we serve does not need our tricks. Everyone who serves the Lord must learn these three crucial lessons.

It is difficult for those who cannot rise up to rise up, but it is also difficult for those who have risen up to fall down. Only those who have risen up and then fall down are useful before God. Only those who can stop in God's work, rise up in His call, and fall down in His service can serve God and administrate the church. When we sense that the Lord is not in a certain work, we should not do it. Even if it will have a great impact, we should not do it. Although we may receive people's praise, we should not do anything that the Lord is not in. Without fellowshipping with the Lord and without His presence, we should not go on by ourselves. Moses' leading of the children of Israel depended upon the Lord's presence (Exo. 33:15). When we serve the Lord, we also need the Lord's presence.

These three points—stopping in God's work, rising up in His call, and falling down in His service—seem to be contradictory, and some people cannot tolerate the changes. When we want them to stop, they cannot stop, but once they stop, they go to an extreme and even stop meditating and praying. Stopping when the Lord wants us to stop is not an easy lesson. A brother who had great enthusiasm was unable to stop no matter how much we implored him. When he finally stopped, he stopped to the point of not even acknowledging that he was a Christian. This is a problem. When we wanted him to stop, he could not stop, but when he stopped, he stopped in an extreme way. As a consequence, he lost his usefulness to the Lord. Hence, we must learn to stop ourselves in the Lord's work, to rise up in the Lord's command, and to continually fall down in His service. No matter how much the children of Israel tormented Moses, he was willing to rise up, but he also always fell down before God and let Him work.

### QUESTIONS AND ANSWERS

*Question: Although we should not play tricks when we serve the Lord, we also need to be prudent. What is the difference between playing tricks and being prudent?*

Answer: Matthew 10:16 says, "Behold, I send you forth as sheep in the midst of wolves. Be therefore prudent as serpents and guileless as doves." To be prudent is to escape the difficulty and harm that come from others; to be guileless is not to hurt others. Prudence is related to avoiding being hurt by others; hence, it is not applicable among the saints. Being prudent is different from employing tricks. Tricks are used to reach one's goals, and prudence is necessary to avoid being hurt by others.

*Question: Peter followed the Lord unconditionally because he met the Lord. However, we have not met the Lord. What should we do?*

Answer: If a person wants to answer the Lord's call, he first must experience the Lord's call. If we have experienced the Lord's call, we have met the Lord. Peter answered the Lord's call so quickly because he met the Lord. If we have not met the Lord, we do not need to answer the Lord. However,

I do not think that there is anyone among us who can truly say that he has never met the Lord. If a brother says that he has never met the Lord, he must not be saved. Every saved one has met the Lord in his spirit.

What does it mean to be saved? A brother once said that the strictness of our interview with people before their baptism should be re-examined. However, the strictness of the interview is not the point; rather, we must be able to sense that a person has met the Lord when we interview him. If he has met the Lord once, he is saved. However, if he has merely heard, believed, and received a doctrine, he is a pious person at the most. If someone has met the Lord, he may outwardly say that he does not believe, but he cannot help but believe inwardly.

Every saved one has met the Lord, but the difference is that some have met the Lord in a strong way, and others in only a more moderate way. Likewise, whenever a person meets the Lord, there is some demand within him; this demand is the Lord's calling. Our concern is not whether someone has met the Lord, but whether, after meeting the Lord, he is serious, quick to respond, and absolute. Before he meets the Lord, he does not need to answer the Lord's call, but after he is saved and has met the Lord, he should immediately answer the Lord's call.

It also is unlikely that we have not met the Lord after being saved because the Lord comes to us repeatedly, even as we are walking on the street. Sometimes when we are in the car, He comes to us; sometimes when we are shopping, He comes to meet us. He comes to meet us at different times. The real question is how we respond when He comes to meet us. Our problem is not related to being unable to touch and meet Him but in being too slow and dull in answering His call.

*Question: Was Moses called after he turned eighty?*

Answer: A person's calling has a beginning, course, and completion. If we investigate the time when Moses was called, it was before the foundation of the world. The calling of Moses was not an accidental act or idle whim of God. The name Moses means "drawn out." Long before the foundation of the world, he was drawn out. God also set apart Paul in his mother's womb (Gal. 1:15). Not only did the matter of our calling take place before the foundation of the world; even our salvation occurred before the foundation of the world.

This shows that God took several steps in the preparation of Moses. First, God prepared godly parents who infused him with godly thoughts after his birth (Exo. 2:7-9). Second, God prepared the environment of the palace in Egypt for him so that he could receive the best education of his time to lead the children of Israel (3:10; Acts 7:22). Moses' commission could not have been undertaken by someone who did not have any training. Hence, God allowed him to enter into the palace to be properly regulated and cultivated. Third, through the infusing of his parents, Moses had the godly thought and concept that he needed to rescue the children of Israel (Heb. 11:24-25). To him, this was the beginning of God's calling. Fourth, God prepared the wilderness for him in order to train his character. Although he had godly thoughts and had received a high education, his character was not fully trained, nor had he gone through any human sufferings (Acts 7:23-28). He was very strong. He had no children or any special environment, so God caused him to shepherd a flock in the wilderness for forty years so that he could be refined in a furnace like hard steel (v. 29). When all these environments had been arranged successfully, God came in and called him in a definite way. At this time, God's calling was complete (v. 30).

Hence, it is difficult to determine when God called Moses. If we consider the source, we must say that it was before the foundation of the world, but also it was in the palace, the wilderness, and the training process. Then God came in. The principle is the same with us. If we look back, we can testify that our calling was predestinated by God in eternity past. Then at a certain time, He arranged for us to be in the proper environment and did not let us go; it was at that time that we answered His call.

*Question: Does the so-called boundary of work apply only to the workers?*

Answer: In the Bible, the noun *work* has a broad and a narrow sense. In a broad sense, whatever God does in this age through the church, the saints, and the workers through their service to Him is the work of God. In a narrow sense, there are a few, such as Paul, who are chosen and called by God and commissioned by the Lord to do His work. Hence, the meaning of the word *worker* also has two meanings, one broad and one narrow. In a broad sense, all the saints who preach the gospel for God are God's workers. In a narrow sense, only those, like the apostles, who are sent by God to preach the gospel and establish churches in every place are workers of God. For example, in the broad sense we may tell the saints that everyone needs to do God's work, meaning that all the brothers and sisters have a part in the work of God. In principle, the narrow sense is included in the broad sense. For example, some answer God's call particularly and serve God in a specific way.

*Question: After hearing this kind of message, we are afraid to move in the meetings. For instance, if we think that God has not moved, we do not want to move; consequently, no one even dares to open his mouth to pray.*

Answer: This shows that you have not touched the main point of the message but instead the trivial points. It is not right if you do not move and do not pray because God has not moved during the time of prayer. If we need to wait until God moves in order to breathe and eat, could we survive? Without God moving, man should not move. This is the right principle, but you have applied it in a wrong way. Not moving without God means that our service before Him must be initiated by Him, not by us. This is a great principle.

Of course, this great principle can be applied in small matters. For example, in a prayer meeting, if God does not move, we should not move. In terms of the responsibility of the meeting, this is the right principle. However, we need to see that the responsibility for coming to the meeting is related to the burden we have received. Hence, when we come to a meeting, we should bear the burden to pray, sing, or share. This is not a matter of coming to the meeting and asking whether God is moving or whether God wants us to bear the responsibility of the meeting. Before bearing responsibility, we should first ask whether God has moved and entrusted this responsibility to us. If God is moving in us, guiding us, leading us, and wanting us to bear some responsibility, we will know what is from God as soon as we receive it. After receiving a responsibility, we do not need to wait any longer and continue to seek the Lord. If someone entrusts a child to our care, and we are clear that this is of the Lord, we must care for him by cooking for him and giving him a bath; there is no need to wait for the Lord to move further. In our service we often have the right principle but the wrong application.

In the meeting a brother may say in a very spiritual way, "If God does not move, I will not move; if I move first, it would be only a religious activity." A brother who says this, sooner or later, will become passive. We do not come to a prayer meeting simply to attend but to pray. We can first ask the Lord inwardly, "Should I go to the prayer meeting?" This can be compared to someone inviting us to eat a meal at his house. Before going, we should consider whether or not to go. But after deciding to go, we should freely eat and drink when we are at his house. If we do not eat or drink anything, people will ask us why. It would be improper for us to say that we need to consider it, because the time for consideration has passed. Therefore, in a meeting, we should actively use our spirit to fellowship with God. In this fellowship we will touch God's feeling, and we will know whether or not we should pray. We should not be passive in the meetings.

A genuinely spiritual person usually has much to minister in the meetings because he is joined to the Lord in fellowship. In a fellowship meeting, if everyone is waiting and no one opens his mouth, at a certain point someone will give a strange testimony, and then someone else will also give a strange testimony. This will damage the meeting. Everyone wants to be spiritual and wait for the moving of the Holy Spirit, but this will cause the entire meeting to fall into a kind of passivity. If we all actively exercise our spirit to fellowship with the Lord in spirit, we will have something to say, and the meeting will be living. Therefore, we should actively fellowship with the Lord in spirit in every meeting and not passively wait for Him to move our deadened spirit. We must all learn this lesson.

What does it mean to be active in spirit? What does it

mean to be passive in spirit? What does it mean to act in
fellowship? And what does it mean to act independently? We
must learn these lessons. Acting independently is religion;
acting in union with the Lord is the church. We must exercise
our spirit so that our spirit will be strong to touch God. We
should not give our opinions, but we can ask God to give us
His commands. We must be so strong that we can ask God,
force God, and urge God to issue commands. This is to exercise our spirit and to be active in spirit. This means that we
must exercise our spirit to touch the Spirit of God and allow
the Spirit of God to push our spirit. In this way, when we contact God, we will be able to touch God's will immediately. If
our spirit is living, we will cause the entire meeting to touch
the Spirit whether we are praying or reading the Bible.

# CHAPTER NINETEEN

# THE PRINCIPLE OF GOD'S BREAKING

Scripture Reading: Acts 13:22, 36

In this chapter we will see God's breaking, that is, God's breaking of man. Strictly speaking, in order to be useful in the Lord's hand and according to God's heart, we must pass through much breaking by God.

## THE MEANING OF BREAKING

Breaking removes what we originally have in our natural being, changing our original appearance and altering our original condition. We may have numerous good and noble things, but God still must tear down and destroy these good and noble things. When a structure is built, it is built according to a logical order; however, when a structure is torn down, there is no logical order, and everything is simply destroyed. Hence, in man's concept, *tearing down* or *breaking* are not positive words. However, everyone who is useful in God's hand must pass through His breaking.

For a period of time we have been speaking of the exercise of the discipline of the Holy Spirit and the breaking of the cross. Both the discipline of the Holy Spirit and the breaking of the cross are related to God's work of breaking, but they are not the breaking itself. God's work of breaking often is deeper and heavier than the discipline of the Holy Spirit and the breaking of the cross. Previously, we spoke of God's breaking in a fragmentary way; we did not touch it in a thorough way. In this chapter, we will touch the matter of God's breaking in a fuller way. Before seeing God's breaking, we must clarify several matters.

## GOD'S REDEMPTIVE WORK
### NEEDING MAN'S COOPERATION

First, in His redemptive work God needs man's cooperation. Every matter related to serving God is based upon God gaining man's cooperation. A person's usefulness in the service is based upon his cooperation with God. However, a person who has not been broken by God will not be able to cooperate much with Him. Although this is a shallow illustration, if we want to move into a house, it will need some adjustment and tearing down in order to be suitable for dwelling. Being broken is a prerequisite for God to gain our cooperation and to use us. The extent to which we are broken is the extent to which we can cooperate with God.

Sometimes we stay at a certain place temporarily. Since we are there for just a few days, we bear the situation even though the height of a door or the size of a bed does not fit our height. Outwardly bearing something in this way indicates a lack of breaking. If God does not gain our cooperation, He cannot do anything, and if we want to cooperate with God, everything that we have, according to what we are originally and naturally, must be broken. What we are originally, including our original appearance and taste, does not match God and is not compatible with God. Consequently, God must break us.

A chemical compound must be broken down in order to be combined with another compound to form a new compound. In the same way, we must pass through God's breaking in order for us to match God and to be useful to Him. We can use another example. If we want to mix cement with gravel, a process of breaking down is required. Likewise, if we want to be mingled with God, we need to pass through a process of breaking. We need to be broken in order to be useful in God's hand because we will match God only when our natural things have been removed. In order to match God, we must be broken by Him.

### ALL SPIRITUAL MATTERS HAVING TO PASS
### THROUGH DEATH AND RESURRECTION

Second, all spiritual matters must pass through death and resurrection. Anything that has not passed through death and resurrection is raw and wild. Crude iron must pass through refining and beating in order to become wrought iron and steel. Spiritual matters must pass through death and resurrection in order to be cooked rather than raw or natural. Anything that has not passed through death and resurrection is natural. God's breaking is the procedure, the process, of death. In terms of experience, it is not sufficient to merely see the death of the cross. Doctrinally, it is sufficient to see the death of the cross, but unless we pass through various breakings from God, we will not know the reality of the death of the cross. Breaking is the process of the death of the cross. One who has not been broken has not passed through death and has not passed through the cross. We may be able to clearly speak of the doctrine of the cross, but unless we are broken, we will not have any trace of the cross in our being.

The first message I spoke in Taiwan in 1949 was on the God who gives life to the dead and who calls the things not being as being (Rom. 4:17). *Calls the things not being as being* refers to God's creation, and *gives life to the dead* refers to God's resurrection power. Creation does not fulfill God's purpose; God's purpose is fulfilled through life being given to the dead. In other words, creation does not fulfill God's purpose; redemption fulfills God's purpose. For this reason, we need many breakings. Everything that goes against us is in the principle of God's breaking.

What God builds up, He also tears down. Whatever is broken by God will enter into death in order to pass through death. Once it passes through death, it will enter into resurrection; once it is resurrected, it can attain to God's goal. In order to attain to God's goal, everything that is created by God must pass through His breaking and tearing down so that what is broken and torn down can pass through death and enter into resurrection. Without being broken, it cannot pass through death; without entering into death and passing through death, it cannot enter into resurrection.

## ONE WHO IS NOT BROKEN BEING UNTRUSTWORTHY

Third, a person who is not broken can never be trusted. A person who has not been broken by God cannot be entrusted with God's work; he is untrustworthy. Such a one cannot be trusted by God or even by the elders and co-workers. A person who has not been broken, who has not been torn down by God, is untrustworthy. Such a one is a natural person, and his life is natural and false. Our natural life deceives not only others but also ourselves. If we are still living in our natural being and have not passed through God's breaking, we cannot be trusted.

I once worked in a certain place where I enjoyed the Lord's presence and blessing very much. The saints were willing to be helped, and they expressed their appreciation. Among them was an intelligent and capable brother who said to me, "From now on, I give myself completely to you and submit to your leading." I smiled and did not give him a clear answer. I simply said, "Take your time." In my assessment of him, I had the sense that he would oppose and rebel against me one day because he did not know himself. A person who is not broken can never submit to others. Usually, we submit to a brother when he fits our taste. When a brother matches our disposition, we submit to him, and when a brother allows us to vent our anger on him, we submit to him. However, when a brother rebukes us and applies some pressure, we are unwilling to submit and even rebel. If we naturally like to eat sweet things, we will not be able to tolerate sour things for even three days. We truly do not know ourselves; only those who have truly submitted to others know the rebelliousness of their natural man. After a couple of years, this capable brother completely lost his temper toward me one day. From this we can see that whoever has not been broken cannot be trusted; at a certain time he will rise up to oppose. Consequently, God cannot trust anyone who has not been broken in His hand.

## ONE WHO HAS NOT BEEN BROKEN BEING UNABLE TO DO GOD'S WILL

Fourth, a person who has not been broken cannot do God's will. A person who truly does God's will is one who has been broken by God. These four matters must be deeply imprinted in us. In order to cooperate with God, we must be broken by Him; in order to have spiritual value, we need to be broken; in order to be entrusted with God's work, we need to be broken; in order to do God's will, we need to be broken. We must be those who have been broken by God. Then we will be useful to God. We must grasp these four principles firmly.

## CHRIST BEING BROUGHT IN BY FAITH AND BREAKING

Now we will consider some examples in the Bible. The Jews highly regard two of their forefathers, Abraham and David. Although Moses is of great importance to the Jews, he is not called their father; only Abraham and David are called their fathers. In the New Testament, the very first sentence of the Gospel of Matthew says, "The book of the generation of Jesus Christ, the son of David, the son of Abraham" (1:1). This shows that the Lord Jesus' coming to the earth was made possible by two lives. In other words, God could become flesh and come among men because He gained the cooperation of two men on earth—Abraham and David. This means that the lives of Abraham and David rendered cooperation to God and brought Him from heaven. Hence, we need to examine the lives of Abraham and David.

### Abraham's Life Signifying a Life of Faith

The life of Abraham signifies a life of faith. In the Bible Abraham is regarded as the father of faith (Rom. 4:16-17; Gal. 3:7-9, 29). This shows that Abraham was the beginning of faith; the life of faith began with him. The life that can bring Christ to the earth is first a life of faith. Faith enables man to touch God and to deal with God. Hence, Abraham was called God's friend, for only a man of faith can make friends with God and deal with God (James 2:23; Isa. 41:8).

### David's Life Signifying a Life of Brokenness

David's life signifies a life of brokenness. Although we cannot find the word *brokenness* in the Bible, we can see from the biblical record that Abraham believed in God and that David was broken by God. David was under God's pressure throughout his whole life; this made him one who was according to God's heart (Acts 13:22). Consider the examples of a house and garments. The more we tear down a house, the more we can make it useful according to our heart's desire. Likewise, if a garment does not fit, we must tear it apart and alter it so that we will feel comfortable and happy when we wear it. Only after a garment has been torn apart and altered can it fit according to our heart's desire. Because David was broken by God, he was a person according to God's heart.

From the first day to the last God's hand on David was never loose. From birth, David was under God's breaking work. Jews pay much attention to the firstborn; hence, the firstborn has a prominent position. David, however, was the youngest and most despised. In God's arrangement, David was born in the least significant position. His birth caused him to be oppressed.

When Samuel went to anoint one of the sons of Jesse, Jesse kept seven sons with him but sent David away to tend the sheep. This shows the low value Jesse placed on David. It did not matter to his father whether David was there or not. On that day there was not only to be an anointing of a king but also good food, yet Jesse still sent his youngest son away. David was not as tall as his brothers in stature, so his father asked him to tend the sheep. This shows Jesse's low esteem for David.

After the seven sons of Jesse passed before Samuel, the Spirit of Jehovah said to Samuel that He had not chosen any of them. Then Samuel said to Jesse, "Are these all the young men you have?" Jesse replied, "There is still the youngest, but he is now tending the sheep." Then Samuel said to Jesse, "Send for him, and bring him; for we will not sit down until he comes here." Once David came, Jehovah said to Samuel, "Arise; anoint him, for this is he" (1 Sam. 16:1-12).

When we read this portion of the Word, we need to see the emphasis of the Holy Spirit. From the day David was born, he was despised by men, not just by others but even by his own father. Even when the whole family gathered for a feast to sacrifice to God, his father sent him away. I believe on that day, even though David did not shed tears, he must have swallowed some tears. The entire family knew that a prophet was coming and that there was going to be a feast, yet David was sent to tend the sheep. If we stay in a saint's house and are put in a situation where we cannot sleep well or we are not included among the elders and deacons, how do we react? If we were David, would we have been able to accept his treatment? We must acknowledge that everything is in God's hand. It is not up to us whether a certain matter is right or not; it is up to God. All our judgments concerning being right or wrong are expressions of our flesh; all our arguments only manifest our true condition. If David wanted to argue, he surely had the ground, but he did not argue. The Bible shows that he remained silent; he had no personal expectation or desire.

In the Old Testament David was the first man whom God found to be according to His heart. God abhorred Saul as the king of Israel because when God wanted to do one thing, Saul would do another. He did not cooperate with God. But in the house of Jesse, God found David, the youngest and most despised, and anointed him king. Although David was anointed, he did not know when he would be king. Thus, his father and brothers still looked down on him. The Philistines assembled their armies for battle with the Israelites, and Goliath defied the ranks of Israel. Saul and all Israel were greatly afraid when they heard the words of this Philistine. One day Jesse asked David to take some food to the camp and visit his brothers. When David came to the battle line, his oldest brother said to him, "Why have you come down? And with whom have you left those few sheep in the wilderness? I know your pride and the evil of your heart." This shows that even after David was anointed, his brothers still despised him (17:1-30).

David learned good lessons in the wilderness; he was tested in God's hand. When David volunteered to fight with Goliath, Saul told him that he could not go because he was too young. However, David replied, "Your servant has been tending his father's sheep; and when a lion or a bear came and took a lamb from the flock, I would go out after it and strike it and deliver the lamb from its mouth. And when it rose up against me, I would seize it by its beard and strike it and kill it…Jehovah, who delivered me from the paw of the lion and from the paw of the bear, He will deliver me from the hand of this Philistine" (vv. 34-37). David did not lie. He had learned deep lessons, and he had deep roots. After David killed Goliath, Saul kept David and would not let him return to his father's house. After more battles, women came out of the towns of Israel singing and dancing with tambourines and joyful songs and stringed instruments (18:6). They sang to one another as they played, and they said, "Saul has struck down his thousands; / But David, his ten thousands" (v. 7). This praise did not affect David, but it affected Saul. Solomon said, "A man is tried by the praise given him" (Prov. 27:21).

From that day on, Saul decided to kill David, and David had no place to hide. When we read in 1 and 2 Samuel and the Psalms of his being cast out, we can see his inward condition and the wonderful lessons he learned before God. Once when Saul was chasing him, David had no place to hide but in a cave. By the arrangement of the Holy Spirit, Saul also went into the cave. If David had wanted to eliminate the cause of his trouble, he could have killed Saul with a sword. David was not afraid of Saul, but he feared God, so he only cut off a corner of Saul's cloak as a proof to Saul. David could have killed Saul, but because Saul was God's anointed, David did not kill him (1 Sam. 24:1-15). Even with doing just this, however, David's heart smote him because he had done something out of his flesh to vindicate and glorify himself. This feeling in David's conscience showed that he had learned a good lesson.

Even after David had learned so many lessons, God still had to do a further breaking work in him. God did not raise him to the throne to be king until he was almost completely broken, because only this kind of person can reign and be God's deputy authority among His children. However, more breaking was still needed because David was still intact in his natural godliness. David's natural godliness was irreproachable. Hence, one day God arranged a situation in which David fell, causing him to usurp the wife of Uriah and to plot to kill her husband (2 Sam. 11:2-17). Without God's permission, David would not have sinned. If David's natural godliness had not been broken because of this fall, his perfection according to the old creation would have remained. However, God wanted to break his natural perfection. The tragedy that was brought in due to his fall resulted in a further breaking. God could not allow a person who was naturally godly to live in hypocrisy before Him; thus, He had to deal with the situation. This was God's breaking.

When David was escaping from his son Absalom, Shimei cursed him with words that were harsh and ruthless. The mighty men of David could not tolerate it and wanted to kill Shimei (16:5-9), but David said, "If he curses, and if Jehovah has told him to curse David, who then can say, Why have you done so?...My son, who came forth from my body, seeks my life; how much more then this Benjaminite will do so. Leave him alone and let him curse, for Jehovah has told him to do so. It may be that Jehovah will look on the wrong done to me and that Jehovah will repay me with good for his cursing on this day" (vv. 10-12). As David and his men went on their way, Shimei went along the hillside opposite him, cursing as he went, and he threw stones and cast dust upon him (v. 13). David, however, accepted God's breaking; the cursing from Shimei turned out to be for David's perfection. David felt that Jehovah had told Shimei to curse him, and the cursing was God's speaking to him.

Here we see a person who was completely torn down by God. Although he was born afflicted and oppressed, his nature by birth, his naturalness, was still not broken. At this point, his spiritual character was absolutely bankrupt. In David's household there were incidents of incest, of a son rebelling against the father, and of servants rebuking the master, all of which caused David's natural being to be terminated. In regard to being godly, David was the most godly; in regard to his status, David was a king. However, his own son and servants rebelled against him. In this situation, what did he have? He was totally bankrupt and torn down by God. He was nothing.

## MAN'S USEFULNESS DEPENDING ON BEING BROKEN BY GOD

Some saints cannot fall unless they sin; this is God's mercy. Even though the spiritual character of some is bankrupt, they still resist in their natural man. They need a great fall so that their self-praise can be thoroughly torn down. Anyone who is boastful has not been broken, anyone who blames others has not been broken, and anyone who competes with the brothers and sisters has not been broken. An unbroken person always disputes and contends with others in the church and in the work. He thinks that he can do everything and do it better than others. Those who are young and even some of the older ones are like this. When such a one hears a negative remark, he reacts immediately. This kind of person has never been broken.

Our genuine usefulness in God's hand does not depend on our capability, our eloquence, or our intelligence but on how much we have been broken and torn down by God. A useful person is one who can be broken by God. Someone who has never been pressed, mistreated, broken, depreciated, or wronged by people is raw, wild, and useless to God. Even if we have received some discipline of the Holy Spirit, we can still be useless. We may accept discipline from the environment, but if we are unable to receive an offending word from the brothers and sisters, we are still useless. We must examine ourselves in this way.

For example, when we come to the meeting, our clothes may be torn by a hook on the door. Thinking that this is the discipline of the Holy Spirit, we gladly accept it. When we enter into the elders' room or the business office, however, and encounter several unpleasant matters and hear some annoying words, we may refuse to pray and say Amen. We accept the discipline of the Holy Spirit when we are happy and pleased, but when we are upset and discontented, we become negative and cannot accept the Lord's dealing. This proves that we have not been broken by God. It shows that we have no light, have not been broken, and are still intact.

Because we have not been cracked, and the sunlight is unable to shine into us, we have no inward light. We may have heard many messages and may be familiar with the Scriptures, yet we will not have any light if we have not been cracked, and there is no opening in us. A person who has not been broken or torn down by God is most pitiful. When we are treated well, appreciated, praised, and exalted by others, we gladly receive the discipline of the Holy Spirit. However, when our being is touched and we lose our face and feel that we have been hurt, we are not so willing to receive the discipline of the Holy Spirit.

If we possess a good attribute, we want to make it known and testify to others so that everyone in the world will know about it. Furthermore, as soon as we are wronged, we want to spread it everywhere in order to gain sympathy for ourselves. In contrast to us, David was despised in his family, but he did not utter a sound or rise up to resist. Rather, he lived before God, hid in God, and learned many lessons in secret—lessons that were hidden from his father and his brothers. Here is a question: Are the lessons we learn superficial or hidden? When we give a testimony, do we disclose everything or only what is allowed by the Holy Spirit? God needs people who are broken. Only those who are broken can be according to God's heart and serve Him, serve people, and minister to people according to God's heart. Only those who are broken can administrate the church and serve the saints. Only those who are broken can be workers of the Lord, elders, and deacons. Only those who are broken can minister God's life to people in this age. May the Lord have mercy on us so that we willingly receive His breaking from within.

## LEARNING TO BE BROKEN BY GOD OUR ENTIRE LIFE

If we have truly seen what it means to be broken, we will realize that everything that comes upon us can cause us to worship God. We can let go of and accept others' despising, disagreements, and ill-treatment; we can even let go of their high regard and welcome. We must determine once and for all that we will receive God's breaking throughout our entire life. The story of David that is recorded in the Bible is not without meaning. The New Testament begins by saying, "The book of the generation of Jesus Christ, the son of David, the son of Abraham." This shows that only faith and breaking can bring in Christ and transmit Christ to others. Only such a person can be according to God's heart; only such a person can minister God's life to people.

# CHAPTER TWENTY

# GOD'S BREAKING, NOT MAN'S MAGNANIMITY BEING THE WAY OF LIFE

Scripture Reading: 2 Cor. 4:7-11, 16; 1 Cor. 4:11-13; 2 Cor. 6:3-10

## GOD'S BREAKING NOT BEING BECAUSE OF MAN'S TRANSGRESSIONS

Generally speaking, people think that a person who is in God's hand, who lives in fellowship with God, and who is acceptable to the Lord will prosper in everything and lead a tranquil life. In other words, such a person will be filled with blessing and happiness. This is a common human concept. Consequently, when we see brothers and sisters suffering afflictions and hardships, we think that they are being disciplined by God because they have committed a big mistake before God. This concept is deeply implanted in us, and it is difficult to uproot.

In 1943, after I was released from imprisonment by the Japanese, I contracted a serious case of tuberculosis, and I had to rest in Tsingtao. My illness continued for many days to the point that I was weak both emotionally and mentally. At that time one of the sisters who served the Lord with us said, "Perhaps Brother Lee has made a huge mistake before the Lord. Maybe the Lord is not going to raise him up." She thought that the Lord would no longer use me because I must have committed a huge mistake; otherwise, I should not have been so weak for such a long period of time. This is a common concept.

Sometimes brothers and sisters who serve the Lord are so much in lack that they seem to be in poverty. After eating lunch, they do not know if they will have something to eat for

dinner. When we see this kind of situation, we may think that
God is disciplining them. This is our concept. We always think
that if a person has no problems before the Lord, he will have
a peaceful and happy life. Based on Psalm 1:1, we probably
think that a person will be prosperous if he "does not walk /
In the counsel of the wicked," "stand on the path of sinners,"
or "sit in the seat of mockers" (v. 1). The psalmist even wrote
that such a one "will be like a tree / Transplanted beside
streams of water, / Which yields its fruit in its season, / And
whose foliage does not wither; / And everything he does pros-
pers" (v. 3). Thus, it even seems that this concept is biblical.

## GOD BREAKING JOB'S NATURAL WHOLENESS
## IN HIS GODLINESS THROUGH SUFFERING

On the surface this concept seems to be right, but actually
it is not. There are instances in the Old Testament and in the
New Testament which illustrate this concept. For example, in
the Old Testament there is a person who suffered very much.
Outwardly speaking, it seems that no person suffered greater
affliction and hardship than Job. However, the Bible does not
speak of any sin he committed or any problem he had before
God. On the contrary, Job feared God and did not depart from
Him. In Job 1:8 Jehovah declares concerning him, "There is
none like him on the earth, a perfect and upright man, who
fears God and turns away from evil." This declaration does
not speak of Job not fearing God and therefore being in need
of some discipline from God. Instead, this declaration indicates that there was none like Job on the earth, a perfect and
upright man, to the point that God even asked His enemy,
Satan, "Have you considered My servant Job?" Satan was
speechless before God; he was unable to accuse Job of anything. However, God still allowed calamities to come upon Job,
one after another. When they came, even Job was puzzled
because he had the same concept that most people have.

The book of Job presents the human concept. Job's three
friends thought that Job was being disciplined for his sins.
They thought that Jehovah was absolutely right, and that
God would not harm Job if he was not sinful. However, Job
refuted his three friends. The first friend said that Job was

sinful, but Job said that he was not sinful; the second friend said that Job had erred, but Job said that he had not erred; and the third friend said that Job had iniquities and faults, but Job said, "I desire to argue with God" (13:3). Job wanted to ask God, "Where am I wrong?"

Then the three friends of Job began a second round of debate with him. The first friend thought that Job had erred because God would never discipline a faultless person, but Job said that he had not erred. The second friend came and said the same thing, but Job insisted that he had not erred. Then the third friend came and said the same thing, but Job repeated that he had not erred. All these friends were debating the matter of right and wrong. The concept of Job's friends reflects our concept. However, Job was not any better than his friends in regard to his concept. His friends said that Job was afflicted because he had erred, but Job said that he had not erred. On the negative side, Job's friends said that he had erred, whereas on the positive side, Job said that he had not erred. Job's friends were not delivered from the concept that suffering means there must be mistakes, and Job said, "Cause me to understand how I have erred" (6:24). Both parties had a concept that a person is stricken only when he errs.

After they finished their debates, exhausted their words, and stopped their speaking, God appeared to Job to make him clear that his sufferings were not calamities or a response to wrongdoings. These sufferings came to Job in order tear down a person who was godly and blameless and who gave no ground for Satan's accusations. The calamities that came upon Job were not for dealing with his errors or sins but for dealing with Job himself. When he finally met God, he did not abhor his acts but himself, that is, his self which he justified and could boast of, which even God could not find fault with and which Satan could not accuse. Job said, "I abhor myself, and I repent / In dust and ashes" (42:6). It was only at this point that Job knew that God struck and afflicted him because He wanted to tear down the natural wholeness of his being.

A person who is in God's hand often suffers much affliction

and trouble. We should never think that we will have peace and blessings if we fear God. This is a religious thought, not the truth according to the Bible. A person who is in God's hand often suffers much affliction and hardship. Whether he is right or wrong, there is always breaking, smiting, and suffering. If only those who are wrong were smitten, what wrong did Job commit? The Bible said that Job was perfect and upright.

### GOD PROVING THAT PAUL WAS A SERVANT OF GOD BY CAUSING HIM TO BE IN LACK

Not only is there the example of Job in the Old Testament but also the example of Paul in the New Testament. I used to have the concept that a servant of God will not have any trial or lack if he subjects himself to God and is in fellowship with God. Consequently, I felt that he must have done something wrong if he was destitute or in lack. As I considered this concept, I could not understand. The apostle Paul's word in 1 Corinthians 4:11, however, helped me to understand. He said, "Until the present hour we both hunger and thirst, and are naked and buffeted and wander without a home." At that time, I began to ponder the experience of Paul, the top and most faithful apostle. According to my concept, since he was so faithful and perfect, he should not have had a need for food, clothing, and peace. At the most, I thought he would be suffering some persecution for the sake of the Lord's word. However, this was not Paul's reality.

According to the record of the Bible, Paul not only suffered for the Lord inwardly but also was in want outwardly. Many people spoke of him dishonorably and gave evil reports about him (2 Cor. 6:8). Even some from the church in Corinth, which he had established personally, said that Paul was crafty and that he took them by guile (12:16). Why did this kind of shame befall Paul, who was the most faithful servant of God? According to our concept, he should not have had any lack because he was God's servant. Many brothers and sisters have this kind of faith when they are called to serve the Lord. When a brother who served the Lord was asked about his living, he said, "When I serve a man, he takes care of my living. If I serve God, do you think that God will not take care of my living?" At some point, however, God truly will not take care of our living. We may ask God, "Why do You not take care of me even though I am serving You?" However, He will remain silent and supply us only after we have calmed down. Some may not accept this word, but this was Paul's actual experience.

None of us can be more faithful or have more faith than Paul, but even such a faithful one as Paul was always in lack. However, his feeling toward poverty was different from ours. He said that his lack was a proof that he was a servant of God. Some asked him for proof of his apostleship, and he replied that his poverty was his proof (6:3-10). According to our natural thought, the proof of apostleship should be a fullness of faith and an abundance of material things, but this is not the case. When a servant of God hears someone say, "God has truly caused you to abound," he will secretly say, "You do not know the hunger I have known." Our concept is altogether natural; it is the concept of fallen man, not the concept of the Bible.

### NEEDING TO BE BROKEN FOR CHRIST'S LIFE TO HAVE A CHANNEL

The most godly and irreproachable man in the Old Testament was Job; the most faithful man in the New Testament was Paul. Job did not have either a supply or peace in his sufferings, and Paul was even put in prison. At the end of 2 Timothy Paul wrote that his co-workers had left him, that those who had received help from him had forsaken him, and that no one was with him to support him at his defense—all had abandoned him (4:10, 16). His condition was desolate to the uttermost. Some surely must have said that Paul had done something wrong and was therefore being forsaken by God. Saying this is due to blindness. The stories of Job and Paul reveal that God is doing a continual breaking work in those who pursue Him and serve Him. Regardless of whether they are right or wrong, God must tear down their person. Only by being broken can Christ's life have a channel to be released; only by being broken can Christ's life swallow up all our death.

On the surface, it seems that David suffered while Saul was at ease and in peace. Saul was the prosperous one, and David was the suffering one. But was Saul right before God, and was David wrong? In reality, even when David was being chased by Saul, no fault was found in him. From the examples of David and Saul, we should realize that a person who is in God will be under His pressure and that a person who is apart from God will not experience much difficulty. Because Saul was outside of God's hand, his steps were smooth, and he was prosperous in his ways.

When we preach the gospel, we usually tell people that there is no rest and happiness in human life without the Lord, and we encourage them to receive the Lord in order to find rest and happiness. While many people believe in the Lord, they come to realize that even though they suffered before believing in the Lord, they are suffering even more after believing. However, after believing in the Lord, the feeling that we have in our sufferings is different from the feeling we had before we believed in the Lord. Sometimes we may not be happy with God because it seems that we have been deceived; nevertheless, even this feeling is good. Every believer can testify that it is truly joyful and satisfying to follow the Lord, even with all the difficulties and pressures. Many examples in the Bible show that those who are truly in God's hand will suffer affliction and be troubled; only those who are not in God's hand are at ease and in comfort.

## JACOB SIGNIFYING MAN'S RECEIVING GOD'S BREAKING FOR TRANSFORMATION

Let us consider another illustration. In the Old Testament there was a set of twins; one was named Esau and the other was named Jacob. In the Bible there is no record of Esau suffering anything; on the contrary, he married whom he liked and obtained what he wanted. Everything in his life was easy and smooth. However, Jacob was different. He made mistakes on the one hand and received dealings from God on the other. Nothing in his life turned out as he wished. Every step was difficult, and every circumstance was against him. When he saw Pharaoh in his old age, he said, "Few and evil have been the years of my life" (Gen. 47:9). Jacob's life on the earth can be described with one word—suffering.

Some may say that Jacob's suffering was a result of his craftiness. However, even if Jacob had not made any mistakes and had not been crafty, he would have suffered, because in the Bible Jacob signifies breaking for transformation. Jacob's father, Isaac, did not suffer much, but neither was his name changed. A person's name represents his person. A change in one's name implies that the person has been changed. Isaac's name was not changed because he was never broken. In the Bible Isaac does not represent breaking; he represents inheriting. In the Bible Isaac signifies that man can inherit God's blessing by faith.

Jacob's life shows that a natural person must pass through breaking in order to become Israel, that is, a prince of God. For a person to be filled with God's element, he must pass through the process of breaking. This is what Jacob represents in the Bible. He was crafty, supplanting, and full of schemes. His name Jacob means "heel-holder, supplanter" (25:26). He was a person full of schemes and plots, but he was broken, torn down, and dealt with by God again and again to the point that God changed his name and called him Israel (32:28), meaning "prince of God." Jacob became a prince of God. This means that after passing through God's breaking, Jacob was filled with the element of God.

According to the record of the Bible, we can see a wonderful thing about Jacob in his old age; he was entirely different from what he was as a young man. In his youth Jacob had plans, views, ideas, and tricks. He was full of schemes; he knew how to deal with his mother, father, uncle, wives, children, and God; he even wrestled with God. This speaks of Jacob's natural capabilities. When he wrestled with God, it was not God who would not let him go but Jacob who would not let go of God. Consequently, God had to touch the socket of his hip, which caused Jacob to limp (vv. 22-32). Jacob knew how to deal with people, but in his old age, his entire being was changed; he became a man without any plans. In his old age Jacob did not have any tricks, plans, or schemes, but he was filled with God. There were no schemes or craftiness in him; there was only God. There were no opinions or views; there was only God. He was truly Israel.

In his youth and middle age he was a typical Jacob with tricks, capabilities, ways, and rules. But in his old age he was an Israel with no methods, views, or opinions. His every step was God. Although Jacob seemed to be nothing more than an ordinary person, he was not under Pharaoh when he came before him; he even stretched forth his hand to bless Pharaoh (47:1-10). This shows that he had a position before God and that he was great.

If a beggar comes before us, we may not be able to stretch forth our hands to bless him because God does not have much ground in us nor is there a sufficient element of God in us. If this is our case, when we stand before a beggar, we will not think that we are greater than he is or have more than he has. Consequently, we will not stretch forth our hands to bless him. When Jacob stood before Pharaoh, however, he stretched forth his hands to bless Pharaoh. This indicates that he had weight and position, that he was great, and that he was Israel, the prince of God, because he had been broken. We need to see that what we call blessing, happiness, and peace were but refuse in Paul's eyes (Phil. 3:8). Often blessings, happiness, and peace hinder us from gaining God. Hence, in order for us to gain Him, God must strip us of all blessings, happiness, and peace.

## GOD'S BREAKING BEING FOR GOD'S BUILDING

God needs to break us because what hinders God from being constituted into us is our person. This tearing down in the negative sense is really a building up—whatever is related to our tearing down is also related to God's being built into us. The more we are torn down, the more God will be built into us. We will gain God not only objectively but also subjectively. The result of God's being built into us is that we become Israel, the prince of God.

God's breaking is not a matter of being cruel to us but of being gracious to us. What God takes away is but refuse; it is something physical. What He tears down is our worthless self. However, what God builds into us is Himself, the peerless and infinite One. The end of the Bible shows the New Jerusalem with the tree of life. However, the tree of life is shown not only at the end of the Bible but also at the very beginning of the Bible. The New Jerusalem at the end of the Bible is not a structure built with refuse, clay, wood, and brick. No! The New Jerusalem is a structure built with pure gold, pearl, and precious stones, all of which refer to God Himself. The New Jerusalem is just God Himself in essence, appearance, nature, and glory.

God's work throughout the generations is to eliminate all the refuse, clay, wood, grass, and stubble in order to bring in the pure gold, pearl, and precious stones needed for His building. What kind of persons are we? Are we men of gold? Or are we men of clay, men of wood, and men of stubble? It is correct to say that we are men of clay because man was made with clay. However, we are not merely men of clay but also men of grass, for all flesh is like grass (1 Pet. 1:24). Hence, we are men of grass, men of the flesh. In terms of being created, we are men of clay; in terms of being fallen, we are men of grass and wood; that is, we are men of the flesh. First Corinthians 3:12 says that those who work for God should not build with wood, grass, and stubble but with gold, silver, and precious stones. God's breaking work in us is not His evil treatment of us but rather his kind treatment and special care for us. He wants to remove the clay and tear down the wood, grass, and stubble in us, and then build Himself into us. If we consider this carefully before the Lord, we will be joyful even when facing great afflictions, because our sufferings will bring us pure gold, pearl, and precious stones.

## GOD'S GENUINE WORK IN MAN BEING BREAKING

Everyone who is led by God must experience the Lord's breaking work in him continuously. Problems will occur in our homes, in our careers, in our service in the church life, or even in our work for the Lord so that God can build more of Himself into us. Hence, we should not have the mistaken concept that by fearing God and living before Him, we will have a smooth way in everything we do and obtain people's praise, glory, and respect. The one who respects us today may

deride and trample us under his feet tomorrow. When someone admires us, we should put his admiration under our feet,
because he may admire us for half a year or a year, but he
may also look down on us and slander us one day.

God will not allow someone in His hand to be the object of
constant attention and flattery like a pretty flower in a vase.
Sooner or later, God will destroy the vase and remove our
beauty so that people will look down on us. We should not
think that all the saints will admire and respect us because
we have been sent by God, called by God, and entrusted with
His work. This is not the case. One day all the brothers and
sisters may reject and despise us. Even though they may not
oppose us or say anything against us outwardly, they will
despise and criticize us inwardly.

The leading brothers in the churches have all drunk from
this cup of suffering. Please remember that the ultimate benefit that the Lord of resurrection wants us to gain comes from
the judgment and criticism of men. Those who have been
instructed, taught, helped, and supplied by us for many years
eventually may reward us with nothing but judgment and
criticism. This is the way of one who serves the Lord; no other
way is better or higher than this.

Those who agree with us and admire us today may be
those who fiercely persecute us in the future. God will never
allow any of His servants to be praised or exalted by man.
Sooner or later, God will tear down what is praiseworthy in
us and cause us to be base and reproachable in man's eyes.
This is God's breaking. The genuine work of God's hand is to
break us. The anointing and the discipline of the Holy Spirit
are good works of God, but the harshest work of God is the
breaking. May the Lord have mercy on us, and may we, who
are learning to serve Him, hear this word so that we will not
be shaken when we encounter these things in the future.
Instead, may we know God's breaking work deep within.

## THE DEEPER THE MAGNANIMITY, THE STRONGER THE SELF

Moreover, we must bear in mind that when we encounter
God's breaking, we should not respond magnanimously. When

we encounter God's breaking and it is difficult to accept, we should accept it rather than bear it. What does this mean? Chinese philosophers teach people to be magnanimous. However, magnanimity is incompatible with the teaching in the Bible. The teaching in the Bible requires that we be broken. To be magnanimous means that we have the ability to swallow difficulties. However, the more we swallow difficulties, the more we are full of the self without any of God's element. This is not the teaching in the Bible. The teaching in the Bible requires that we be broken and torn down so that God may enter into us.

Suppose the Lord allows a certain brother who is serving the Lord in the church to be opposed by another brother. At such a time, he should not take the Chinese way of being magnanimous, which means that he should try to enlarge his capacity and deepen his sense of tolerance. Instead, the Bible says that our outer man needs to be consumed and that our inner man needs to be renewed. The opposition of a brother comes from God's breaking hand. Therefore, we need to ask God to shine on us and show us what He wants to break in us. This is not a matter of being magnanimous and forbearing; this is a matter of being broken. The greater our magnanimity, the stronger our self will be. The most magnanimous person has the strongest self.

The way of a Christian is not the way of being magnanimous but the way of being full of wounds and scars. Someone may say, "No matter how people treat me, I do not care. I can take it." This person may be magnanimous, but he is full of the self. Although he has a large capacity, there is no wound or opening in him, so life cannot flow out from within him. When a person who is according to the principle of magnanimity encounters circumstances, he will pray, "O Lord, enlarge my capacity." This is not the truth or teaching of the Bible. The Bible teaches that we need to be consumed, not enlarged. Our outer man needs to be consumed day by day instead of being enlarged. God causes us to be cast down in order to consume us. All the problems in our daily living are for consuming us. This is why Paul said, "Though our outer man is decaying, yet our inner man is being renewed day by day" (2 Cor. 4:16).

To be magnanimous is not the teaching in the Bible; to be consumed is the teaching in the Bible. Hence, we must remember that every time we encounter a difficult situation, we should not take the way of being magnanimous but the way of being broken. Our wife may trouble us, but we should not respond with magnanimity or tolerance, because this is not the way of a Christian. The way of a Christian is to prostrate ourselves before God when our wife troubles us and to ask, "O God, what needs to be broken in me?" We should have the light and the teaching of the anointing within; we need revelation within to see the area that God wants to break in us. We need to receive God's "axes" and "knives," that is, the troubles from our wife in the areas that God wants to break us. Sometimes even a wife is not enough; we may also need six children and even the saints in the church.

### RECEIVING GOD'S BREAKING IN THE LIGHT

We should prostrate ourselves before God and receive God's dealings. We should learn to be in the light to receive God's breaking. We should never pursue magnanimity, which is just a tool to cultivate, build up, and enlarge our self. Rather, we should learn to prostrate ourselves in God's light and receive his breaking and tearing down without trying to cover ourselves. When everyone praises a forbearing brother whose wife quarrels with him all day, we should not follow them to praise him. We should realize that his magnanimity is only preserving, enlarging, and building him up. We should not try to be magnanimous and forbearing; rather, we should learn to prostrate ourselves in God's light, receive His breaking, and allow the environment to break us and tear us down.

# CHAPTER TWENTY-ONE

# THE RESULT OF THE WORK BEING BASED ON THE WORKER

## FELLOWSHIP CONCERNING THE WORK IN THE CHURCHES

*Church A: In general, the saints here love the Lord but do not have a solid foundation and, therefore, greatly need guidance. Even the responsible ones for various services have not been perfected so that they can truly bear burdens in a practical way. Over the past year we have paid much attention to the gospel and have also done some edifying work, but the results have not been apparent. Overall, our problems can be grouped into three categories. First, because the spiritual weight of the leading brothers and sisters is inadequate, our impact is low, and we have little supply. The number of elders is insufficient—one lives far away, and another is busy with many affairs. Second, there are not enough deacons; some of the deacons do not even come to the meetings. This puts us in a difficult position. Moreover, most of the responsible ones in the small groups have been saved for only a short time; their foundation is shallow, and their pursuit in life is inadequate. Third, there are financial difficulties. The ceiling of the meeting hall is in need of constant repair this year, and the financial burden on the brothers and sisters has been very heavy.*

*Church B: Last year we focused on the aspect of service, but since the beginning of this year, we have turned our attention to the gospel. After preaching the gospel for a period of time, we will go back to the edification of the saints. Our problem is mainly related to an inadequate number of serving ones. In comparison to the brothers, the sisters are doing better.*

*They go out to visit and take care of the sisters. Among the brothers, however, few are involved in the shepherding work. Hence, the condition of the service is relatively weak. This is a great problem. Furthermore, the shepherding in the schools is very difficult and weak. In short, the problems in this church may be put into three categories: an inadequate number of serving ones, insufficient learning on the part of the brothers, and not being clear concerning the way to go on. I also have many problems. My main problem is that I do not have sufficient knowledge of the truth. I feel that my motives are pure, but my knowledge is lacking, my faith is small, and my patience is short. For instance, I arranged for the brothers to take care of certain matters. When I saw that they were unable to carry out these matters properly, even after doing them over and over again, I could not bear it and did them myself.*

*Church C: The number of people is slowly increasing in the church here, and problems are also increasing. I have consecrated myself before the Lord and committed myself to the Lord so that I am in God's hand. However, when God's hand comes through the environment, I cannot bear it, and I reject it. In the past two years the Lord has used many things to tear me down. In the conference in Manila, one of Brother Lee's messages regarding purity in motives touched me very much. I feel that in the matter of learning to serve the Lord, I am full of ambition, but I thank the Lord for showing me that being torn down is related to having pure motives.*

*The church here is actually quite immature. There are problems in the service because many of the brothers and sisters have been saved for only a short time. When saints from overseas come to visit us, it is easy for them to find the "altar" but not the "Ark." In our service meetings, many opinions were expressed, and there was no mutual understanding; therefore, we had to stop. There was no way to go on. In terms of the outward service, we have gospel preaching, and we respect the leading of the apostles. Besides the various services in the church, every Lord's Day afternoon we also go to prisons or to places where people gather, such as factories or hospitals, and do some gospel work to lead people to the Lord.*

*In terms of numbers, we have more than five hundred*

*saints and as many as two hundred attending the Lord's Day meeting. According to the human perspective, the outward taber-nacle of the church looks good, but the spiritual weight within is lacking. In terms of spiritual pursuit, it is very difficult to bring the brothers and sisters into the reality of pursuing.*

*The church here also has a particularly large number of young people. We sympathize with their heavy load of school-work and thus have not led them properly. Recently, we spent four mornings in the young people's meeting to speak to them about loving the Lord, consecration, the anointing, and the discipline of the Holy Spirit. We hope that they will exercise in these basic lessons. In addition, there are a number of saints serving in the military, and it is difficult to lead them because, even though they are zealous and love the Lord, their free time is limited.*

*Although we have four responsible brothers, in reality there are only three; one brother encountered some difficulties and has virtually stopped serving. Concerning the deacons, the number is relatively low, and concerning the responsible ones for the small groups, it is difficult to help them to rise up. The sisters are stronger than the brothers; regardless of wind, rain, or scorching sun, they carry out their visitation work steadily, persistently, and diligently. Most of the problems among our young people are related to making friends and to marriage. Unless we give them proper attention and shepherding, these matters will become great problems. Furthermore, if we are care-less, some of our fellowship related to service will turn into mere friendships, which is a kind of leaven. These are our problems.*

*Church D: We have the same problems that the previous churches have. We emphasize the leading of the saints and edification in life and truth. We are from a small locality, but we have big problems. We feel deeply that our learning in the service does not carry much weight because we do not have any real exercise and experience. This is our lack. We are unable to render the saints any practical help in their prob-lems because our learning is limited. Although we very much want the brothers and sisters to take the practical way, we are unable to achieve what is desired due to our own inadequacy.*

*Furthermore, our leading of the saints has no order, and we are short of the love of nursing mothers. A sanatorium with a total of three thousand beds in five different locations is nearby, and a few sisters work there. Some saints also are relatives of the patients, and there is a total of about two hundred saints meeting there. They normally take the bus to get there, and each way takes an average of one hour. Because the saints are very seeking, we go every week and give them some fellowship and leading. A nearby town with ten brothers and sisters has begun to have meetings. Another town has two Taiwanese brothers and sisters who are very seeking. They have invited us to preach the gospel. There are many opium addicts who are suffering very much and need our care. The more we go on, the more we feel a great need; however, inwardly we are worn down and cannot meet the need.*

*Regarding my personal problems, I am one who rarely admits defeat. Hence, I am full of ambition and hope that the church I am in will not be behind others. When many situations come up, I suffer within. The meetings are low, and I want to use some human methods to enable the meetings to have an atmosphere of God's presence. This is my natural man. In terms of coordination, I feel somewhat pressured. I lose my temper easily, and I do not have any true learning. In terms of the truth, it seems that I have some understanding, but it is not deep, and in terms of my service, I also do not have a foundation. Concerning our service, we have a few who always serve, but we have been unable to perfect more saints to coordinate with us. Concerning edification, the saints have not grown much in life, and the spirit of the gospel is very weak. This is our true condition.*

## NOT BEING DISCOURAGED
## BUT NEEDING TO LEARN IN SERVING

The fellowship from these churches shows that there are a few important points that truly need our attention. First, in all of the brothers' fellowship we should all see the common principle that our work is always based on our person. What we are in our being determines the work that we can do. What we gain in the work does not depend on how much we hope and expect; it depends on what we are in our being.

Please do not be discouraged. We should never be discouraged in our work only because we have not done enough or not done things well. Many things cannot be carried out or done well simply by our endeavoring, nor can they be successfully accomplished by our striving. Rather, what we accomplish is based upon what we are. Hence, even if we have not done so well or done so much, we do not need to be discouraged, because discouragement serves no purpose.

On the other hand, we must devote a great deal of effort to work on ourselves, including the way we conduct ourselves and the way we do things. We need a deep knowledge of the Lord, we need the experiences of life, we need to be skillful in handling matters, and we need to know people in an adequate way. We must devote some effort to learn in all these aspects. For example, a brother, who was full of ambition after finishing the training last year, recently decided to go back to his locality and do better than others. This kind of ambition is not only useless but also should be rejected. Genuine work is not determined by our ambition but by our genuine condition before the Lord. The outcome of our work will be determined by the effort we put into the truth, into prayer, into the pursuit of spiritual life, and into our dealings with every matter. Hence, we must continually pursue to know the Lord, to know life, and to know people.

## THE RESULT OF THE WORK
## BEING BASED ON THE WORKER

The young brothers and sisters tend to focus on pursuing the work. However, more than ninety percent of the work, when it is actually carried out, depends upon our diligence to be in the spirit, our conduct in the spirit, our skillfulness in doing things in the spirit, and our learning to know the Lord and know people. This kind of diligence may not seem like it is doing a work, but it truly enables us to do our work properly. If we disregard these things and do not devote any effort to them but, instead, only want to do a work, we will not accomplish anything, and our work will not yield any result. The result of our work is based absolutely on the weight of our work, and the weight of our work is based absolutely on what we are. In other words, God cares more for what we are than for what we do. What we are is more important than what we do.

## MAKING A REAL EFFORT BEFORE THE LORD—WORKING WITH ALL-OUT EFFORT

The young brothers and sisters must devote a great deal of effort before the Lord. In our living and in our conduct, we do not need to have lofty ambitions, expecting to do some great work. If this is what we care for, we should be prepared to wake up to an empty dream. We do not need to be ambitious in the work, nor do we need to determine anything. Instead, we simply should cultivate what we are in a diligent manner. We should not expect to do so much in Taiwan to accomplish something in the churches nor expect to reach a certain stage in the work among the churches to become the most accomplished and capable worker. All of these expectations are futile and should be condemned because they all come from man's natural concept and vain imagination.

Each of us should pray earnestly to the Lord daily, asking Him to enable us to devote our effort to learn how to conduct ourselves, pursue the experience of life, and pursue the knowledge of the truth. We should also ask the Lord to make us skillful in doing things and insightful in knowing people. We must devote more of our effort in these points. As a result, we will produce a work even though we have not done very much. Conversely, if we ignore these points and concentrate all our efforts on working, our work will fail and amount to nothing.

Actually, we need to devote a great amount of effort just on learning how to conduct ourselves. As a fellow brother, I frequently go to the workers' homes. According to my observation, the way co-workers conduct themselves is lacking in many aspects. Forgive me for saying this: they not only lack proficiency in studying the Bible but also are short in the knowledge of the truth. Furthermore, they are poor in the way they conduct themselves. They are not well-trained in knowing and evaluating people and in conducting themselves and doing things. May the Lord be merciful to us so that we could receive this word humbly.

May the Lord cover me as I say something concerning my personal testimony in this matter. Before I was saved, when I was nine years old, the Lord put me in a situation in which I needed to work in order to sustain my livelihood. While working, I learned some skills concerning how to handle matters, and I also learned how to know people. I cannot boast about this, but it truly was a help, even a great help, to me.

The Lord can testify for me that a work was produced when I was saved because I had this kind of preparation in my character. In July 1932 I was called to do the Lord's work. At that time I had just turned twenty-seven. Before then, I never had the heart to do some kind of work; I never had such a heart inwardly. By the Lord's mercy, however, I have been fully occupied with the work from the day I was called by the Lord. I have been occupied with an all-out effort in pursuing the truth, in reading the Bible, in studying spiritual matters, and in finding the secret of contacting others. If we do this, we will be equipped practically to know the truth and be well-trained in conducting ourselves and in doing things.

## THE EFFECT OF THE WORK NOT DEPENDING ON HOW MUCH WE DO BUT ON HOW MUCH WE LEARN

We should never put the fruit, the result, of our work as the goal. Only the Lord knows how many people will be saved through us; we do not know. Only the Lord knows how many churches will be helped through us; we do not know. We do not know how many churches will be established through us and how many saints will be edified through us; this is up to the Lord. Moreover, only the Lord knows how much truth and how many messages will be released through us; we do not know. The only thing we know is that we should devote effort to these matters. Our effort should be used mainly for learning, not for working.

The work does not depend on how much effort we exert; rather, it depends on how much we learn. Learning is the real work; the real work of serving the Lord is ninety-five percent learning, and five percent doing. The more we learn, the more effective our work will be. However, we should not estimate the effect; we should let God do the estimating, and God's estimation will be determined at the judgment seat in the future. Our sight should never be set on results but on how we conduct ourselves, deal with God's life, and handle matters. Ultimately, we must pay attention to these points and devote more of our effort to learn them.

## MAKING AN EFFORT TO PRODUCE SERVING ONES

Recently, I dealt severely with a certain brother who was quite peculiar. Regardless of what was put in his hands, he would work without common sense, consideration, and discernment. Consequently, the result was always a mess. One day I saw him and asked what he was doing. He said that he was reading a spiritual book. I said, "You should learn to do something practical." I told him that if he did not learn how to do things, he would not be able to leave Taipei. He replied, "But there are not enough serving ones, elders, and responsible ones for the homes." This exposes our true condition. There are not enough responsible ones and serving ones because we give messages ninety percent of the time while learning to conduct ourselves and do things only ten percent of the time. In other words, we put in less effort related to our conduct and to doing things than we do in giving messages. Our work is unable to produce serving ones because we are inadequate in the way we conduct ourselves and do things.

The inability of our work to produce useful people is a serious problem that we should not ignore. If we serve in a certain place for two or three years without producing an elder and some serving ones, it is because of what we are. If someone else were in our position, he would probably produce some useful elders in a year or less. In other words, those who can only give messages, but who are not skillful and experienced in the way they conduct themselves and do things, cannot produce useful people. For example, a bricklayer easily can produce a few workers in less than a year by simply training some apprentices. This is not achieved by speaking but by leading others to work. This is the case with the Lord's work even more. If our personal dealings are insufficient, if our knowledge of the truth is deficient, if our handling of matters is not skillful and experienced, and if our knowledge of people is shallow, we will not be able to produce useful people even if we know doctrines from books and can tell them to others. Producing useful people requires effort. Only those who make an effort can produce useful people in the work.

## BEING DILIGENT IN KNOWING THE TRUTH AND LABORING TO LEARN HOW TO CONDUCT OURSELVES AND DO THINGS

I hope that we can look at these two things together. We must be diligent to know the truth, and we must labor to learn to be skillful in the way we conduct ourselves and do things. Giving messages can stir up people's emotions to love the Lord but cannot enable those who have been stirred up to be perfected and useful. In order to perfect them and make them useful, we need to labor before the Lord. After our labor, we should spend another year and a half to work; as we work, we should bring the saints with us in order to perfect them, like a bricklayer brings his apprentices along with him for training. We do not need to open a school to teach the saints or have any kind of special training; rather, we can simply be faithful to bring the saints with us. After a year or less of working with us, they will be perfected to become useful ones.

On the one hand, the saints cannot rise up to serve the Lord after only hearing a message and being touched; they still need to pass through the stage of edification. Indeed, we have been lacking in this aspect. On the other hand, we have not been doing a proper perfecting work on some of the saints who have a heart for the Lord. These two aspects reveal our lack, and the main reason for our lack is that we have not learned enough. If we were more positive in these two points, the majority of our problems would pass away.

## THE WORKERS NEEDING TO LEARN WITH GREAT EFFORT

Because the workers and serving ones in various places have not made much effort, many saints have not been perfected, and the number of useful people is close to zero. A shortage of useful people is a great problem in the churches. The way to solve this problem is for all the workers to make a greater effort to learn.

Recently, as I was fellowshipping with the brothers about these matters, we all felt sorrowful inwardly. There are at least one to two hundred people in most of the churches in Taiwan. However, we face the most difficulty in the matter of leading the responsible ones. According to our present situation, nearly every major city has a full-time worker. However, if there is a need for these ones to go to another area of the work, their locality immediately will have a shortage of useful ones. This is a serious problem. If our work cannot produce useful ones, the workers will be entangled and unable to cooperate with the move of the Holy Spirit.

The number of deacons is even a greater problem. There is a significant lack in the number of deacons in every place because we have not taken the time and effort to perfect the saints through practical training in order to see who has the capacity to be a deacon. Such people are not only lacking but non-existent in certain places. As a result, churches have been established in various places, but there are no coworkers who can be sent to help the churches produce useful saints. This is a very heavy burden within us, yet no one can go out to do this work.

If we trace these problems back to their source, we will see that the definite, unique reason for these problems is that we have not put forth an adequate effort. For example, if one goes somewhere to establish a school, it is easy to recruit students; he needs only to post a few advertisements and posters on the streets, and people will come and enroll. However, after the students enroll, the real problem involves how to teach the students and how to arrange the classes, dormitories, and teachers. Recruiting students is easy; instructing them is not. Giving messages and preaching the gospel are somewhat equivalent to advertising and recruiting for students. After people hear the gospel, they are saved and stirred up in their heart to love the Lord, and after they hear a message, they become burning and are willing to serve the Lord. But how shall we lead and instruct them? How shall we bring them, little by little, onto the right track? What we do depends on how much we have learned and what we are.

I have been weighing a great matter continually before the Lord. Should the co-workers from all over the island stay in Taipei, learn together, and then return to their respective localities to work at the end of the year, or should they go back now? There are things that need to be done in the various localities, but I am afraid that if we do not put forth enough effort to learn, we will not be able to reach our goal even though we may want to be fast. Hence, there are two basic principles: first, we must learn, and second, learning requires that we make a sufficient effort.

### A FINANCIAL PRINCIPLE—
### EACH CHURCH NEEDING TO BE SELF-SUFFICIENT

A brother from a certain locality spoke regarding the matter of finances, saying that the saints have been exhausted in taking care of the church's finances and offerings, and it seems that they have no strength to go on. This seems understandable, but in principle it may not be right. In terms of the work, the financial means may reach a point of exhaustion, but in terms of the church, the financial means should not reach a point of exhaustion. If those in a local church do not have the heart to serve, this should not create a financial problem, and if they do have the heart to serve, their service should be according to the saints' capacity, in other words, according to the saints' financial capacity. In the matter of service, no local church should look to other localities for its finances; in the Bible we cannot find the principle of one church relying on another church financially. A church in a locality is like a family. After being established, no family should expect help from other families. We should not have such an attitude. Otherwise, we will not be a family but some other entity. If there is no financial capacity, a church should not be established. If a church is established, it should serve according to its financial capacity. This is a great principle.

A few years ago we did something very risky in the work in order to care for the needs of all the churches on the island of Taiwan. At that time the overall environment forced us to care for the financial needs of the churches in Taiwan and even for the financial needs of their meeting halls. When we did this, we were taking a great risk, and we were afraid that the churches would misunderstand and think that they could obtain financial support from the work as long as they had some serving ones. This practice is not according to the principle in the Bible, and it will result in "missions." Christianity in China had this kind of concept. There was a thought that as long as the saints loved the Lord and served God zealously, money would pour in from other countries. Hence, people in every place built meeting halls, hired evangelists, and so on. This negative thing was produced by Western missionaries working in China.

There is a very important principle related to finances. Wherever saints rise up to serve God as a local church, the local saints should bear the responsibility for the service and expenses. If the saints in a locality do not have that much material offering, the locality should not have much service. In the Old Testament all the furnishings in God's tabernacle came from the Israelites; they did not come down from heaven. If a locality cannot provide its own money, we should not expect money to be given from other places. This is a basic principle.

Henceforth, the expenses for the work can be used only for places in dire need; we have no way to accommodate the localities that have meeting halls. Responsible brothers in various places should note that when there is more financial capacity, they can do more service, but when they do not have the capacity, they do not need to have so much service. For instance, a brother serving in a certain place should be very simple. If he is financially able, he can build two small rooms to serve as the church business office; if not, he does not need to do anything.

As long as we have money and capacity, we can do more; if we do not have the capacity, we should do less. For example, some brothers from a certain locality once fellowshipped with us about their desire to care for the meeting places of two other churches. We said that it would be better not to do this. If the places could not afford rent, it would be better simply to meet in the saints' homes, and if this is not possible, they should find a cheaper location. I am not joking; this is a matter of principle. When the first group of saints began breaking bread in Tsinan, they broke bread in a cemetery on a remote hill. They gathered around a table used for sacrifices and put the bread and cup on it. This was the beginning of the meetings in Tsinan. At that time they were only poor students; later some of them sold their clothing and gradually saved up some money for a meeting place. This is the proper way.

The saints in Taiwan at the present time cannot possibly be poorer than those students. One brother wrote to me, saying that he went to a certain place where there was no meeting hall, and he asked me to help. At that time I was in Southeast Asia. When I sensed the tone of the request, I immediately refused. Thank and praise the Lord that when people refuse us, God cares for us. They finally have a meeting hall in that place. We must learn to look to God and not rely on man. These decisions rest with the local saints. We must let the brothers and sisters see that a church must be self-sufficient financially in order to rise up to function.

## THE CHURCH NEEDING TO CARE FOR THE LORD'S WORK AND THE LORD'S WORKERS

Now only a few of those who serve God full time in various places are being supported by the churches. This is wrong. The churches must return to supporting the Lord's work. At the beginning the work sympathized with the financial shortage of the saints, and we did not want to put the burden of the work on the workers themselves. Up until now, the needs of the workers have been taken care of almost entirely by the work; more than ninety percent of their needs are being borne by the work. However, in terms of the saints in each locality, it is abnormal for the work to support the churches. As a whole, the churches in Taiwan have been quite blessed and are quite good. In the past, however, the churches in Taiwan received the service of the workers while overlooking the needs of the workers and of the work, not having the slightest concern for the workers' living. This is extremely abnormal; this should not be the case. Bringing up this shortage is not for the purpose of soliciting contributions from the localities for the work and the workers but for us to be clear concerning the real situation and to have the proper giving.

By the Lord's grace we can say one thing boldly. All the churches in Taiwan have the ability to care for the needs of the work and the workers, and our heart to serve is unquestionable. However, there must be a change from the abnormal situation of the churches asking for support to one in which offerings are given for the work and the workers. May the brothers in all the churches look to the Lord's leading and speak about this to the saints clearly. However, we should not give the saints the impression that we are asking for their money; rather, we must help them to see that they have a responsibility toward the Lord's work and the Lord's workers. At the same time, we should ask what effect there will be on the Lord's work if all the churches and the saints on the whole earth are like those in Taiwan. How will the Lord's workers live? We must help the brothers and sisters see this matter clearly.

What the Lord has given the churches in Taiwan is rich, abounding, and overflowing. However, when there is a conference, the work has a great number of expenses; we even take care of the transportation of the participants. Nevertheless, few saints care for the work. All the churches should have a normal fellowship regarding finances unless we believe that the work is not of God. As long as the work is of God, we should have fellowship. I hope that the brothers in all the churches will have more fellowship on this matter. May we practice this together in every place so that the Lord's work and workers can receive the proper care.

# CHAPTER TWENTY-TWO

# NEEDING TO BE EARNEST AND NOT LOOSE IN WORKING FOR THE LORD

## FELLOWSHIP CONCERNING THE WORK IN THE CHURCHES

*Church A: Our situation is somewhat desolate. There is no focus in the work. Because of our special geographic location and the great mobility of people, there is a great need for the preaching of the gospel. However, the gospel is greatly hindered because of our immaturity. Moreover, those who have been added to the coordination in the church service are lacking in both quality and quantity. There are problems in other areas as well. For example, we are limited by the size of the meeting hall, and it is not so convenient for the saints to meet because most are poor. The whole church has been praying and fellowshipping, hoping to strengthen the meetings in the homes, but in the end, it is difficult to spread. However, we must confess that the main hindrance is that there is too much of the human element and too little of the element of Christ. Among us there is too much room for the self; it is not easy to deal with the flesh, and it is difficult to see our self in our fellowship with the Lord. We repent before the Lord and hope that in the fellowship we may be able to see the naturalness and complexity of our self.*

*Church B: Our work is divided into two aspects. On one hand, many saints have just begun meeting with us and cannot function properly, so our meeting is not like meeting and our singing is not like singing. The focus of our work, therefore, is on edification. On the other hand, we mainly focus on the elderly ones and the young ones in regard to shepherding the saints. Although our locality is small, there are four high schools, a teachers' college, and three elementary schools; we have young brothers and sisters in all of them. Thus, we have a young people's meeting once a week.*

*Our lack is in the inadequate number of serving ones and the high mobility of people. This makes the work extremely difficult. Moreover, since we are in the eastern part of the island, which is a relatively poor region, it is difficult for the saints to be trained because they have to take care of their livelihood. Sometimes it is difficult even to arrange the chairs. Moreover, we are very immature spiritually because the church carried some flavor of Christianity when it first began. Concerning myself, I am a person with a little soul and a small capacity; I truly fall short before the Lord.*

*Church C: Overall, we pay much attention to ministering the word, but we do not have much action because the saints are not able to keep up. The focus of the work is on the preaching of the gospel, but the saints do not have much of a heart for the gospel. Among the saints, most are military personnel, and a few are students and teachers. We do not have meetings in Taiwanese for the saints who are in their forties and fifties. There are few experienced brothers, and there are fewer experienced sisters. Hence, the work of visitation is very poor, and I personally have not touched the key to visitation. As far as service is concerned, it is difficult to bring in serving ones. There are a few who come to the meetings, and it is even more difficult to bring them into service. This is our big problem. I personally feel that the most difficult thing is that our capacity is insufficient and that we often act in our flesh. There have even been quarrels in the responsible brothers' meetings.*

*Church D: The focus of our work in the past was on preaching the gospel, but the gospel has not yet been widely spread. At the beginning we gained several Taiwanese saints, but because we do not have a Taiwanese brother to lead them, they were all lost. In the aspect of life, we hoped to have a living of morning watch, but eventually, it did not succeed. There is a great lack of useful people; there are a little over forty saints meeting here. There also is a lack of leading on the sisters' side. Because the location of the meeting hall is not so accessible, it is not easy for people to gather together.*

*Furthermore, the four responsible brothers of the church are not open to one another.*

*Church E: At present there are about twenty brothers and sisters having prayer meetings in three homes, but the church has not yet been established.*

*Church F: The condition of the church here is rather weak and poor. As far as meetings are concerned, there are fifty to sixty who meet during the week and over a hundred who meet on the Lord's Day. The total number of saints is two hundred and sixty-six. The sisters' meetings are comparatively strong. There are meetings at four different places per week, but the work is rather fragmentary. We pay attention to the reading of spiritual publications, and there are brothers specifically responsible for leading the saints in this study; consequently, there has been some result. We have been hoping to lead the saints into the aspect of life, but no one dares because no one has been manifested to be more advanced and able to take the lead. Most of the time we lead the brothers and sisters in groups and work with them through the fellowship meeting.*

*Church G: There are about thirty saints here. Two months ago the Holy Spirit was working so strongly that some brothers and sisters, upon receiving the outpouring of the Holy Spirit, went out to preach the gospel and visit people, regardless of rain or shine. Some people, however, attacked us, especially the sisters, by saying that it was the work of Satan. This misunderstanding caused much damage. Although the church has been recovered, we are still in a battle. We rent our meeting hall, but because the landlord is quite unreasonable, the saints find it difficult to bear. At the same time, few saints have the feeling that the church is their home.*

*Church H: There are thirty-two brothers and sisters in our locality. The condition of the church is good, and we can afford the rent of our meeting hall by ourselves. There are seven to eight saints who specifically give themselves to the Lord, so the Lord has some spread here. During the past two conferences, several brothers from a surrounding locality came to perfect us. There are seven to eight brothers in that church who are able to minister the word. Thank the Lord, all the brothers and sisters are able to serve God faithfully. My biggest shortcoming is my looseness. Yesterday when I was fellowshipping with my roommate, he also said that I am a loose person. This kind of looseness causes the church to suffer. Although my heart is eager, I have truly missed much grace. Looseness is my greatest shortcoming, and next is my habit of accommodating; hence, my demands on myself and on the brothers and sisters are not so strict and absolute.*

### THE SECRET TO WORKING FOR THE LORD—
### BEING EARNEST AND NOT LOOSE

Recently, we planted two small trees at the workers' home. Because of the interior remodeling, we moved the plants again and again. Once the remodeling was complete, we thought of two brothers who majored in agriculture. One of them is the brother who said that he is loose. At that time I said to him, "Concerning the matter of transplanting trees, because you are the agricultural specialist, I will leave it to you." He said that he is loose and accommodating; it is really true. I was very bothered by his looseness and accommodation. I am absolutely a novice in gardening, but when I saw the way he moved the plants, I knew that it would not work. I did not know whether to cry or to laugh.

About this time last year we asked the brothers to move the trees. However, some trees died after being moved; even now the trees are in a state of desolation. Consequently, I thought that it might not be a good time to move the trees this year. Then a brother brought someone from a nearby city who assured me that if I let him move the trees, they would live. Thus, the transplanting began. As I observed him, I learned the secret. The brothers who moved the trees last year uprooted the trees without leaving very much soil attached to the roots. In the end, the transplanting was not very successful, because few trees survived. The person who moved the trees this year not only kept the trees alive but even kept their leaves from falling. The wax apple tree, for example, not only is living, but its leaves are still green. The two loquat trees are not only alive but also exceptionally fruitful.

From this I learned that it is actually not a matter of who is an "expert" but of the transplanting method. The trees transplanted by the "expert" brother withered; however, the trees transplanted by the other man not only are alive but also are bearing significant amounts of fruit. Of course, the discipline of the Holy Spirit also may have played a part in the results. Whether we succeed in a certain matter does not depend on whether we know how to do it. Rather, it depends on our ability to grasp the secret of doing everything in a practical and thorough way without being loose. I was troubled and bothered inwardly when I saw the looseness and carelessness of the "expert" brother, because he was supposed to be an expert. He should have known the secret of transplanting trees, but because he was not earnest and thorough and did things in an accommodating way, there was no result. The success of every matter does not depend on whether a person knows how to do it; this is secondary. The primary point is that he must be earnest and not loose. This is especially true when we go out to work; we must not be loose. If we are loose, we will not be able to accomplish anything.

The brothers who shared earlier are all full-time serving ones, but they all said that their work is not good. Some spoke of a lack of financial cooperation from the church, and while this may be a reason, it is not the main reason. The main reason lies in the fact that the person himself is incapable of meeting the need. A person who specializes in a certain profession should be able to do his job successfully, but if he is loose, his work will be ineffective even though he has spent much money and time to be trained. If the brothers are this way in the church year after year, how can they produce people?

All our problems relate to the fact that our being is inadequate. When a matter is considered, the time and effort are utilized and money is expended, but there is no result. This is the situation related to the brothers' work. They "plant trees" and spend much time and effort, but nothing avails. The only good point may be that they experience the discipline of the Holy Spirit. From the fellowship of these few brothers, the Lord has shown us that our problems are related to nothing other than our looseness. What should we do? This simple time of fellowship has pointed out many loopholes and shows that we do not know how to work. If we truly knew how to work, our localities would surely take on an entirely new look. These words have exposed many loopholes, proving that we do not know how to work.

The fellowship of the responsible brothers in various places concerning their actual situation shows that their looseness, sloppiness, and accommodation has ruined the Lord's work even though they make an effort and pay a price. I hope that all the young brothers and sisters will learn a serious lesson in this matter.

For example, I once asked a brother to sweep the room. He was very obedient, and he took the broom and began sweeping. If this brother was earnest in doing things, regardless of his skills, he should have started sweeping from the corners. However, he took the broom and swept only the middle part of the room. When I pointed to a corner, he swept the corner; when I pointed to another corner, he swept that corner. How can a person do a good work with this kind of attitude? From just this matter of sweeping, we can see whether or not he knows how to work. In the end, I had to show him how to thoroughly sweep the floor myself. This kind of person cannot work, and even if he does work, it will be useless because he does not know how to start and where to focus his effort. Cleaning the floor is a simple matter. When we clean the floor, for example, we need to consider whether we should use a broom or a mop. If we do not even know how to do a simple task, how can we handle the practical matters of the church and the work when they are placed in our hands?

The fellowship and reports of the various churches show that the problems they have are not the real problem. The greatest problem is that the serving ones do not know how to work. If we know how to work, our financial difficulties will not keep us from being able to "dig" out money when it is needed. Money does not fall down from heaven; it must be "dug" out by the workers. When some brothers go to a certain place to labor, there is no material supply; however, when others go to the same place to labor, there is an abundant supply. This shows that some do not know how to work. We should never believe that the place where we are laboring is short of financial capacity. There is much gold buried in the ground. If we know how to work, we will be able to "dig" out the gold. When we dig away all the problems, gold will appear spontaneously. We must see that our person is the problem. All the problems are related to our being.

## LEARNING HOW TO CONDUCT OURSELVES AND DO THINGS

Several full-time serving brothers have moved to a certain place. It has been said that this particular locality "wastes" the most number of people in Taiwan, meaning that many people are not actually being used in God's work. It seems as if they are squandering their time day after day even though there are at least three and a half full-timers. I have often considered how to reduce the expenses there. I have been there a few times, and I have seen that the living of the saints is quite comfortable. It will be difficult to accomplish some kind of work there. We must let the saints see that many things are upon us and that we are not able to cope; rather, we need their help. When the saints are busy cleaning the meeting hall, we should not be standing around and doing nothing. If we do this, it will prove that we do not know how to work and that we do not know the brothers and sisters.

We should not think that giving our time means that we are able to work. We must have much more learning before we are able to work. In particular, young brothers must learn. If a young brother who is serving full time lives in the meeting hall, he should take care of cleaning the meeting hall so that he can boldly tell the saints, "Dear brothers and sisters, I have been doing the cleaning, but I am not able to take care of many other things, so please come and help me." If this is the case, no one in the church will say, "Why do the young serving ones not do anything but live on the church's support?" When all the saints are doing something, but we are standing around and doing nothing, what kind of feeling will they have? When they come to the Lord's Day meeting and see that we are reading Genesis 28, inwardly they may say, "Why does he not find a job? Why is he simply receiving financial support from the church?" This shows that we are immature and do not know how to conduct ourselves in the church. One time I was truly bothered. In the meeting hall some saints were cleaning, some were preparing the meeting area, and some were preparing meals. Even though everyone was busy, a full-time serving brother was sitting and playing the piano. Everyone was busy and sweating, but he was sitting comfortably and playing the piano for amusement. Can such a person truly work for the Lord? We should never think that we can serve God as long as we do not watch movies, play mah-jongg, or quarrel with people. This is not the case. If the sweat of the saints cannot affect us, how can we serve God?

Neither doctrine nor theology counts; only our actual living before the Lord counts. We must have some basic knowledge regarding how to conduct ourselves. When the sisters are busy serving a meal, should we be enjoying some leisurely activity? When the brothers are laboring and sweating during the cleaning, do we not have a proper sense of things? This shows that we lack a feeling concerning how to work, how to take care of matters, and how to conduct ourselves. I mention these situations so that we can have a feeling in regard to these matters. We need a daily exercise. I am sharing so much because I hope that we will not only hear some doctrine but will truly learn something. In this way we will be useful.

### CONCERNING THE SERVICE TRAINING

We will have a regular training for the responsible brothers and sisters from various churches and district meetings. We will not have an open registration; therefore, we ask the responsible brothers in all the churches to recommend and register the saints from their localities. As far as qualifications are concerned, elders who want to join the training from all the churches will be accepted in principle. I hope that the churches will recommend those who are willing to learn and have a great ability to learn. University students or those who have just graduated from universities are the most suitable. We expect that such ones would have a desire to serve the Lord for their whole life; therefore, we would encourage them to first receive some training and then decide whether or not they should get a job in the future. We also will accept the stronger ones among the deacons. If other saints want to participate, they can audit the classes, but we will not correct their mistakes or give them the opportunity to exercise. It is best if we have only sixty to eighty people at the most. We will lead them to minister the word, to visit people, to take care of practical matters, and to read the Bible. We will also give them homework and require them to practice and exercise in a strict way. Then we will evaluate and adjust them.

In addition, I need to make a statement concerning three matters. First, the fact that we accept the saints to the training does not mean that they will become workers. This is merely a training for serving the Lord. Accepting someone to be trained does not mean that we acknowledge him as a co-worker. When the training is over, some may still need to find a job, and some who quit their jobs for the training may need to go back to their careers after the training. Second, we are not responsible for the living of the trainees after the training. Third, I hope the halls in Taipei will arrange accommodations for those who live in Taipei. For those who are from other places, I hope that the work will make arrangements for them. The auditors must make arrangements for themselves.

CHAPTER TWENTY-THREE

# CONCERNING THE CHURCH AND SERVICE

## OUR ATTITUDE TOWARD
## OTHER CHRISTIAN INDIVIDUALS AND GROUPS

In the state of confusion concerning the church today, we should have a proper attitude toward other Christian groups. First, we must acknowledge that all those who believe in the redemption of the Lord's precious blood and who have received the life of God are our brothers and sisters in the Lord, regardless of where they meet or the way that they take. We should never think that Christians who do not meet with us do not have the Lord's life, nor can we say that Christians who do not meet with us do not love the Lord. Neither of these concepts is correct. Apart from us, there are thousands upon thousands of saved ones, and among them there are many who genuinely love the Lord.

Second, we should have personal fellowship and contact with these brothers and sisters, but we should try to avoid having any relationship with their organizations. We associate with individuals because they are our brothers and sisters, not with the groups or organizations. However, our fellowship should have a twofold purpose. On one hand, we may receive some spiritual help from them; on the other hand, we may grant them some spiritual help. Except for these two reasons, fellowship would be unnecessary. We must learn to be upright and honest before the Lord. If others render us help, we should be humble to receive the help, and we must be willing to render help to others according to their needs. This is the greatest, even the unique, reason to contact other believers. If not for mutual supply, there is no need for fellowship. This should be our attitude toward other Christians.

We do not agree that our brothers and sisters should have a part in any Christian group or organization, because Christian organizations today have many problems. Even with those who preach the pure gospel, so to speak, their group, organization, and understanding of God are mostly not according to the truth. The Lord can testify for us that we have no intention to criticize them, but their organizations absolutely hinder people from following the Lord.

On one hand, we acknowledge that there are brothers and sisters in Christian organizations and that we should have fellowship with them. On the other hand, we do not agree that the organizations themselves should exist, nor do we endorse any contact with these organizations, because they hinder people from knowing the Lord. Although we do not endorse this, there is no regulation among us about it, and this is not an item of our faith. In other words, whether a brother or sister who breaks bread and worships the Lord among us contacts or participates in any Christian organization is a matter for him or her before the Lord. We do not exercise any control in this matter. However, for the sake of serving the saints, we must speak an honest word before the Lord. We do not agree that the brothers and sisters participate in any Christian group or organization. If some think that it is profitable for them to go, this is a matter of their own before the Lord. Perhaps some may not have an adequate understanding regarding this matter, but one day, if they are shown mercy, they will realize that these organizations cannot help them to gain more of Christ. However, we are not here to control the brothers and sisters. This matter should be public and open because in our responsibility in the service, we must speak honestly of this to the brothers and sisters.

In 1947 when we were laboring in Shanghai and Nanking, a Western brother from the China Inland Mission came to see me after a conference and said, "Thank the Lord for opening the door of the gospel at various universities; the Lord is blessing this work." Then he added a humble request that we join them in their move for the gospel at these universities. At that time there were many Christian youth fellowships preaching the gospel at various campuses, but we had a different attitude. We paid no attention to what others did but focused only on doing the Lord's work faithfully. We were entrusted by the Lord, and our brothers were at several universities in Shanghai. Hence, the gospel work at the National Chiao Tung University was very effective, and many brothers and sisters were pursuing the Lord. Moreover, many brothers at the Medical College of National Defense and even at the National Central University in Nanking were saved. Since our gospel work at various universities was very much blessed by the Lord, the Western brothers from the China Inland Mission hoped that we would cooperate with them.

At that time I replied, saying, "Regarding this matter, we feel that this may be good. However, there is a need for us to clarify a few matters. First, what we believe is also what you believe; our faith is the same as yours. In the matter of fervently preaching the gospel, we are the same, and there is no problem. Second, in the matter of leading the saved ones to be edified and to know the Lord's life, we believe that you are the same as we. However, we have encountered a problem in China for over twenty years." At this point he began to become nervous. I continued, "Brother, regarding the gospel that we preach, you absolutely say Amen, and regarding the truth of edification we speak, you also agree. However, since we were raised up by the Lord in China some twenty years ago, we have been opposed and troubled by Christianity. We have been opposed and troubled, not because of the gospel we preach or the truth of edification we speak but because we absolutely negate today's organized Christianity. Brother, we agree with one another in terms of the gospel and spiritual edification. I simply hope that when you go to the campuses, you will present only the gospel to people and nothing else." He nodded, and I believe he understood my answer and our position. From that time on, he never corresponded or met with us. We absolutely repudiate any organization of Christianity, but they cannot drop their organization. In this matter we can never be one.

This Western brother was quite understanding. He knew that because we could never abandon our standing, we could not agree to his request. In terms of the gospel and spiritual edification, he did not need to make any request of us. In terms of practice, however, he belonged to an organization that we could not be a part of and have rejected for over twenty years. He was clear that we rejected their form of organized Christianity, not the gospel or the truth that they preached. This is the reason I told him that it would be good if they brought only the gospel rather than organizational things to the young people at the universities. This is our attitude.

We acknowledge that many of God's children preach the gospel and speak the word of life; we do not deny this. However, before the Lord and by His grace, we repudiate the organizations of Christianity. We do not endorse the saints' contact with these organizations, but this is not a matter of exercising control over the saints. Whether or not the saints contact them is up to them.

Some brothers and sisters have asked why we do not invite brothers from Christianity to minister the Word to us and why we do not minister the Word to other Christian groups since some of the brothers among us minister the word quite well. Our answer remains the same; we cannot have a part in an organization. Some brothers among them truly may be gifted, knowing how to speak the truth and rendering help to people. We also confess that they need the blessing we have received and the light we have seen. Nevertheless, in order to avoid confusion and trouble, we should not have contact with their organizations. Christianity is full of confusion, and this hinders people from knowing the Lord.

For example, a certain Christian group that teaches orthodox doctrines sometimes invites a modernist to preach modernistic doctrines, including an overseas preacher who is quite popular in Taiwan. He is a modernist who does not even believe in the incarnation of the Lord Jesus, the conception of the Lord Jesus through the Holy Spirit, the virgin birth, the power of the Lord's blood to wash away sins, the Lord's resurrection, the Lord's ascension to the third heaven, or the Lord's coming again in the future. He does not believe in these seven matters. However, these matters are crucial points of the gospel. If they are taken away, our gospel is not really the gospel. This shows how confusion in Christianity hinders believers from knowing the truth and God's salvation. When people listen to him, they may be touched by his eloquence, but in fact, they unknowingly have been damaged.

We have no intention to exercise control over the brothers and sisters by preventing them from receiving help from others. Based on our experience over the years, however, we see that the benefits we receive from the preaching of outsiders or from our preaching to other groups cannot offset the loss we suffer. It is not worth the effort, so it is better not to do it.

Based on our experience of over twenty years, we have come to the conclusion that we should not be concerned about what others are doing; we simply should live before the Lord. Toward others, we do not need to interfere, and toward ourselves, we should faithfully follow the light we have received from the Lord. A certain person's preaching may be edifying, but we will not invite him to speak because of the confusion in his background and environment, nor will we go to his group. On the positive side, we are not being idle or wandering around. We have a specific commission and things that we want to accomplish. There is no need for us to invite others to carry out our commission. This is not being proud; it is simply the fact.

The Lord has commissioned us with a work in Taiwan that we will have a difficult time finishing even if we doubled our manpower and time. We truly have no time to do anything apart from our responsibility. Neither should we expect people from the outside to render greater help. If the Lord shows us that there is a group of people apart from us who can render us genuine help because of the blessing they have received, we would willingly invite them to share their blessing with us. This fellowship concerning our attitude toward other Christians and Christian groups is necessary because the saints are at different levels and in different conditions; that is, some know how to discern, and others do not. Please remember that this is our attitude; it is not a creed or a by-law among us. The saints have their own liberty. As long as they have not committed any obvious sin against the Lord, they can have fellowship at the Lord's table.

## THERE BEING A CENTER OF WORK
## AMONG THE CHURCHES,
## BUT NOT AN ORGANIZATIONAL CENTER

Do the churches have a center of organization? When we read the New Testament, it is easy to think that Jerusalem was an organizational center. I studied in a Christian school when I was young, and I read a footnote in the Bible they published which said that Jerusalem was the headquarters of the churches. Because I was not clear about the truth, I thought it was true. As I read the Lord's word more, I gradually became clear that the churches do not have an organizational center on the earth. Jerusalem was not the headquarters of a centralized organization. Jerusalem was a center, but it was a center not in organization but in the work. According to the Scriptures the churches do not have a center as far as organization is concerned. The churches in Jerusalem, Samaria, and Antioch were all equal. There was no center in organization, no headquarters or branches, no higher branch controlling a lower branch.

In terms of the appearance of the churches locally, there is no center; no church can control another church. However, in terms of the work and spiritual supply, there is a center. At that time Jerusalem was the center of the work in all the places. When the churches encountered spiritual problems and needed spiritual supply, Jerusalem was the center of the supply, but it was not a center in terms of organization. Jerusalem was the center of the work and of the spiritual supply. This is a basic principle in the Bible.

## A WORD OF FELLOWSHIP REGARDING FOUR MATTERS

### The Church Having No Financial Center

We need to explain four matters to the brothers and sisters. First, we do not have a financial center. We do not have a center for our money and finances. All the missions and denominations have a centralized place for their finances, and then from the center, money is distributed. This is called a financial center. According to the light and principle of the Bible, however, we do not want and dare not have a financial center, because once there is a financial center, there is an organization automatically.

We all know that money is a very strong thing. Money is related to power, and money unconsciously brings in human relationships. It is difficult for someone to receive money from another person without being under his control. Whoever has money has authority. It is precisely for this reason that we do not want a financial center. Throughout the years we have not had a financial center among us. Even today, if a brother serves the Lord full time, only he knows how much support he receives.

Sometimes a brother who is taking the lead has a good reputation and receives a greater commission. The saints may entrust him with a large sum of money and ask him to use it in the Lord. At this point, he may be led to give some to a certain brother. Only he and the Lord know of this transaction; a third person is not involved. No one should control a brother through money. If there is control, it should come from the Lord. One who serves the Lord should not consider the money he receives as a salary that he deserves. If this is the case, there is an organization, and he is under man's control. I hope that this matter is made clear to us once and for all. There is no financial center among us.

We should never think that the church in Taipei is the headquarters and the financial center of the churches in Taiwan. If we have such a concept, we should drop it quickly because it is erroneous. It is wrong for brothers and sisters who have some financial capacity to think that their money should be sent to Taipei when they are led by the Lord to give. If they are led to send money to Taipei, that is all right; however, the saints should not have the concept that there is a financial center, because this violates the authority of the Holy Spirit. This is a great matter. If finances come to one place, an organization will emerge, and man's control certainly will be present.

## Serving Ones Exercising Faith
## to Meet Their Daily Needs

Second, many who have been shown mercy want to rise up to serve the Lord. These ones should rise up to serve the Lord, but they also should be clear that those who serve the Lord must take care of their daily needs. No one is responsible for us; neither is a church or the center of the work responsible for us. If we are shown mercy and have a desire to serve the Lord, we must deal with this matter before the Lord thoroughly and directly. If we are stricken by poverty or hunger, we should not approach people for help, because no one is responsible for us. This matter should be clearly fellowshipped at the very beginning. We have received mercy and have risen up to serve God because of His calling. Hence, the Lord is our Helper. We should receive supply from Him and not ask anyone to bear this responsibility.

If a school hires someone to be a teacher, the school is responsible for him; if the school does not pay him his salary, he can appeal to the court. However, when we rise up to serve God, we must realize that a person, center, or organization has not hired us; rather, the Lord Himself has called us. Therefore, we need to look to the Lord about the responsibility for meeting our needs.

Although there are brothers and sisters in many places who feel that they should serve the Lord full time, this does not mean that they have been hired or employed by us or that we should be responsible for their living. This is not the case. The responsible brothers in all the churches must have an accurate understanding of this matter. There is no financial center or governing center among us. I can honestly say that I do not know how much money the church in Taipei spends, because I do not control the finances of the church in Taipei.

The finances of all the churches are independent of one another. They are set before the Lord and not controlled by man. I hope that the brothers and sisters who love the Lord and that the saints who love the churches will try their best to care for the needs in the churches, including the needs of the full-time serving ones. I hope that among us no one will control or govern the matter of finances but that we will have sweet fellowship with all the churches in mutuality.

When we first rose up to serve the Lord in Taiwan, most of the brothers and sisters did not have the understanding concerning this matter; therefore, the needs of many serving ones were not taken care of in a proper way. However, the Lord has had mercy on us in this matter, and the supply is beginning to come. From now on, the churches and the saints should learn to take care of the needs of the full-time serving ones; at the same time, the serving ones should learn not to rely on man but instead to look to the Lord and live before Him. In these matters we must learn the lessons well. We need to deal with the Lord, exercising our spirit to draw near to Him and exercising our faith to trust in Him. Moreover, we need to learn to cooperate with Him in faith and to be dealt with by Him.

### Learning to Give for the Needs of the Work and the Workers

Third, the Lord has truly been gracious to us and has kept us so that we do not have an organizational center, and we do not have someone who controls our finances. If there is one, it is the Holy Spirit, the Lord Himself. I hope that all the full-time serving ones will learn to look to the Lord, and all those who love the Lord in the churches will learn to be led to give for the needs of the work and the workers. If a worker receives more offerings, he should not save them for his personal use but should care for the needs of other co-workers. It should be that he who gathers much has no excess, and he who gathers little has no lack. Some co-workers, who have a more prominent standing, may receive more offerings. Such ones should care for the co-workers with lesser standing. Since all the co-workers labor together for the Lord's work, we should not think that the Lord's abundant support is only for our personal use. We need to take care of the other co-workers.

Those who have not learned to live before the Lord like to spend on themselves rather than caring for others; they are willing to watch others suffer. Under normal circumstances, if a co-worker has received more, he should take care of others. The Lord wants us to be strong in this matter so that we will not fall under man's control or into a sense of inferiority. This, however, does not mean that there is no center in the work or in spiritual matters. Paul was the leading one among the Gentile believers, and Peter and John were the leading ones among the Jewish believers. This was not an organization but a center as the base of the spiritual work. The Lord entrusted the work to these leading ones, and they were entrusted to do the Lord's work.

## Learning to Walk in the Proper Way of the Lord without Any Deviation

Fourth, we must learn to walk in the proper way of the Lord without any deviation. We should not say that we can be loose because the churches are financially independent and because we do not have a center of work. This is wrong. We must take care of both aspects. In this way we will learn to have proper fellowship and spiritual supply without involving human control or methods. On the physical side, we do not rely on man, we are not under man's control, and we do not have a center. However, on the spiritual side, regarding the work, we have a center, and none of us can act independently.

### A WORD OF FELLOWSHIP REGARDING JOINING THE TRAINING

There are several principles which I hope the responsible brothers from all the churches can be clear about. First, as we fellowshipped earlier, all those who join the training must be those who have the capacity to be co-workers. Second, we need to take care of the needs of the churches in our localities and the needs of the trainees in a balanced way. We need to decide, based on the needs, who should stay in the churches and who should come and join the training. Third, those who join the training must come for the whole time. If some could come only at the beginning but cannot stay until the completion of the training, we should not consider them. Fourth, we should never push someone to leave his job to come to the training. A person should be clear whether or not he should leave his job permanently; we cannot replace the function of his conscience. It is best for the working ones to stay in their jobs, unless they themselves feel to do so and have a clear confirmation from the leading ones to leave. We need to find out if those who want to leave their jobs for the training have been persuaded by others or whether they want to do so themselves. Fifth, we need to consider people's financial capacity. According to our budget, those who come to the training must take care of their own expenses; we have no way to take care of them. We must let them know this clearly.

# ABOUT THE AUTHOR

Witness Lee was born in 1905 in northern China and raised in a Christian family. At age 19 he was fully captured for Christ and immediately consecrated himself to preach the gospel for the rest of his life. Early in his service, he met Watchman Nee, a renowned preacher, teacher, and writer. Witness Lee labored together with Watchman Nee under his direction. In 1934 Watchman Nee entrusted Witness Lee with the responsibility for his publication operation, called the Shanghai Gospel Bookroom.

Prior to the Communist takeover in 1949, Witness Lee was sent by Watchman Nee and his other co-workers to Taiwan to ensure that the things delivered to them by the Lord would not be lost. Watchman Nee instructed Witness Lee to continue the former's publishing operation abroad as the Taiwan Gospel Bookroom, which has been publicly recognized as the publisher of Watchman Nee's works outside China. Witness Lee's work in Taiwan manifested the Lord's abundant blessing. From a mere 350 believers, newly fled from the mainland, the churches in Taiwan grew to 20,000 in five years.

In 1962 Witness Lee felt led of the Lord to come to the United States, and he began to minister in Los Angeles. During his 35 years of service in the U.S., he ministered in weekly meetings and weekend conferences, delivering several thousand spoken messages. Much of his speaking has since been published as over 400 titles. Many of these have been translated into over fourteen languages. He gave his last public conference in February 1997 at the age of 91.

He leaves behind a prolific presentation of the truth in the Bible. His major work, *Life-study of the Bible,* comprises over 25,000 pages of commentary on every book of the Bible from the perspective of the believers' enjoyment and experience of God's divine life in Christ through the Holy Spirit. Witness Lee was the chief editor of a new translation of the New Testament into Chinese called the Recovery Version and directed the translation of the same into English. The Recovery Version also appears in a number of other languages. He provided an extensive body of footnotes, outlines, and spiritual cross references. A radio broadcast of his messages can be heard on Christian radio stations in the United States. In 1965 Witness Lee founded Living Stream Ministry, a non-profit corporation, located in Anaheim, California, which officially presents his and Watchman Nee's ministry.

Witness Lee's ministry emphasizes the experience of Christ as life and the practical oneness of the believers as the Body of Christ. Stressing the importance of attending to both these matters, he led the churches under his care to grow in Christian life and function. He was unbending in his conviction that God's goal is not narrow sectarianism but the Body of Christ. In time, believers began to meet simply as the church in their localities in response to this conviction. In recent years a number of new churches have been raised up in Russia and in many European countries.

OTHER BOOKS PUBLISHED BY
## *Living Stream Ministry*

### Titles by *Witness Lee:*

| | |
|---|---|
| Abraham—Called by God | 978-0-7363-0359-0 |
| The Experience of Life | 978-0-87083-417-2 |
| The Knowledge of Life | 978-0-87083-419-6 |
| The Tree of Life | 978-0-87083-300-7 |
| The Economy of God | 978-0-87083-415-8 |
| The Divine Economy | 978-0-87083-268-0 |
| God's New Testament Economy | 978-0-87083-199-7 |
| The World Situation and God's Move | 978-0-87083-092-1 |
| Christ vs. Religion | 978-0-87083-010-5 |
| The All-inclusive Christ | 978-0-87083-020-4 |
| Gospel Outlines | 978-0-87083-039-6 |
| Character | 978-0-87083-322-9 |
| The Secret of Experiencing Christ | 978-0-87083-227-7 |
| The Life and Way for the Practice of the Church Life | 978-0-87083-785-2 |
| The Basic Revelation in the Holy Scriptures | 978-0-87083-105-8 |
| The Crucial Revelation of Life in the Scriptures | 978-0-87083-372-4 |
| The Spirit with Our Spirit | 978-0-87083-798-2 |
| Christ as the Reality | 978-0-87083-047-1 |
| The Central Line of the Divine Revelation | 978-0-87083-960-3 |
| The Full Knowledge of the Word of God | 978-0-87083-289-5 |
| Watchman Nee—A Seer of the Divine Revelation ... | 978-0-87083-625-1 |

### Titles by *Watchman Nee:*

| | |
|---|---|
| How to Study the Bible | 978-0-7363-0407-8 |
| God's Overcomers | 978-0-7363-0433-7 |
| The New Covenant | 978-0-7363-0088-9 |
| The Spiritual Man • 3 volumes | 978-0-7363-0269-2 |
| Authority and Submission | 978-0-7363-0185-5 |
| The Overcoming Life | 978-1-57593-817-2 |
| The Glorious Church | 978-0-87083-745-6 |
| The Prayer Ministry of the Church | 978-0-87083-860-6 |
| The Breaking of the Outer Man and the Release ... | 978-1-57593-955-1 |
| The Mystery of Christ | 978-1-57593-954-4 |
| The God of Abraham, Isaac, and Jacob | 978-0-87083-932-0 |
| The Song of Songs | 978-0-87083-872-9 |
| The Gospel of God • 2 volumes | 978-1-57593-953-7 |
| The Normal Christian Church Life | 978-0-87083-027-3 |
| The Character of the Lord's Worker | 978-1-57593-322-1 |
| The Normal Christian Faith | 978-0-87083-748-7 |
| Watchman Nee's Testimony | 978-0-87083-051-8 |

*Available at*
Christian bookstores, or contact Living Stream Ministry
2431 W. La Palma Ave. • Anaheim, CA 92801
1-800-549-5164 • www.livingstream.com